To Hugh Cecil,
with best wishes,

Warfare
in the
Twentieth Century

Also from Unwin Hyman

THE BIRTH OF INDEPENDENT AIRPOWER
British Air Policy in the First World War
Malcolm Cooper

BRITISH STRATEGY AND WAR AIMS, 1914–1916
David French

EUROPEAN ARMIES AND THE CONDUCT OF WAR
Hew Strachan

FIRE-POWER
British Army Weapons and Theories of War, 1904–1945
Shelford Bidwell and Dominick Graham

THE ORIGINS OF THE SECOND WORLD WAR
RECONSIDERED:
The A. J. P. Taylor Debate after Twenty-Five Years
edited by Gordon Martel

THE WAR PLANS OF THE GREAT POWERS, 1880–1914
edited by Paul Kennedy

Warfare in the Twentieth Century

THEORY AND PRACTICE

edited by

Colin McInnes
University College of Wales, Aberystwyth

G. D. Sheffield
Royal Military Academy, Sandhurst

London
UNWIN HYMAN
Boston   Sydney   Wellington

Published by the Academic Division of
Unwin Hyman, Ltd
15/17 Broadwick Street, London W1V 1FP

Unwin Hyman, Inc.
8 Winchester Place, Winchester, Mass. 01890, USA

Allen & Unwin (Australia) Ltd,
8 Napier Street, North Sydney, NSW 2060, Australia

Allen & Unwin (New Zealand) Ltd in association with
the Port Nicholson Press Ltd,
60 Cambridge Terrace, Wellington, New Zealand

First published in 1988

British Library Cataloguing in Publication Data

Warfare in the Twentieth century: theory and practice.
1. Warfare 1900–1978
I. McInnes, Colin, 1960–   II. Sheffield, G. D., 1901–
355'.02'0904
ISBN 0-04-355034-7
ISBN 0-04-355035-5 Pbk

Library of Congress Cataloging-in-Publication Data

Warfare in the twentieth century: theory and
practice/edited by Colin McInnes, G. D. Sheffield
     p.   cm.
Includes index.
ISBN 0-04-355034-7 (alk. paper).
ISBN 0-04-355035-5 (pbk.: alk. paper)
1. Military art and science – History – 20th century.
2. Military history, Modern – 20th century.
I. McInnes, Colin. II. Sheffield, G. D.
U42.W38 1988   88–5615
355'.009'04–dc19   CIP

Typeset in 10 on 12 point Sabon
and printed in Great Britain by
Billing and Sons Ltd, London and Worcester

Contents

Editors' Introduction   *page* ix

Contributors   xiii

1 Total War   *Ian F. W. Beckett*   1

2 Colonial Warfare 1900–39   *Keith Jeffery*   24

3 *Blitzkrieg* and Attrition: Land Operations
   in Europe 1914–45   *G. D. Sheffield*   51

4 Naval Power   *Geoffrey Till*   80

5 The Theory and Practice of Strategic Bombing
   John Pimlott   113

6 Nuclear Strategy   *Colin McInnes*   140

7 Limited War   *Robin Brown*   164

8 Guerrilla Warfare: Insurgency and Counter-insurgency
   Since 1945   *Ian F. W. Beckett*   194

9 The Battlefield Since 1945   *D. J. Pay*   213

Further Reading   236

Index   237

Editors' Introduction

The twentieth century has been dominated by war, or by preparations for war, in a way that is unparalleled in history. The first forty-five years of the century saw the scope of warfare vastly expanded; battle became larger, involving increasing numbers of personnel and machines, and covering ever greater areas. Entire economies and societies were organized for war, bringing social change in its wake, so the reality of conflict was, for the first time, brought home to every single member of states such as Britain and the USSR. Furthermore, the evolution of air power thrust civilians into the line of fire as manned aircraft rained high explosive down on to vulnerable cities with the aim of killing ordinary people and destroying their dwellings. The second half of the century in one sense has brought a shift in emphasis away from the 'total' wars of the first. Although Europe since 1945 has been free of old style wars, the world of the nuclear age has not been noticeably more peaceful. Under the 'nuclear umbrella', subconventional, or guerrilla wars have proliferated. Many conventional 'limited' wars have been fought since 1945 as a reminder that the era of the armoured fighting vehicle, artillery piece, tactical aircraft and infantryman is not yet over. In another sense, of course, there is the ominous possibility that any future war would be even more 'total' than those of 1914–18 and 1939–45. A whole theory – almost a science – of deterrence has evolved since 1945, aiming to prevent wars by threatening potential enemies with mass destruction. The possibility of deterrence failing and nuclear weapons being used has ensured that war has remained as much a reality to men in the second half of the century as it was to those in the first half.

The enormous impact of war on the twentieth century has been marked by a gradual recognition of the importance of the study of the subject. Until recent years, the field of 'military history' tended to be narrowly defined as the study of generalship, battles and campaigns – what has been described rather unkindly as 'drum-and-bugle' history.* However, the realization of the importance of war has led to non-military historians being drawn to the study of warfare and taking paths rather different from the traditional one. Historians of social change, literature and science, to name but a few, as well as scholars who would not necessarily describe themselves as historians at all have made important contributions to the study of conflict. The term 'military history' is no longer adequate to describe such a vast area of study. Thus terms such as war studies or strategic studies have been applied to the new discipline.

The change from military history to war studies has broadened the appeal of the subject. Whereas in previous years teachers of history at all levels tended to deal merely with 'causes and consequences' of wars, now increasing numbers of schools, colleges and universities are running courses that involve the study of conflict. Much important work has been undertaken in this field, but the editors, who are both professional teachers of the subject, became aware that a gap existed between academic monographs and 'popular' works, and that a single volume work that would present some of the major themes of warfare in the current century in an easily accessible manner would be useful. It is hoped that this present volume will help to plug that gap, and that it will be of use and interest not only to students and teachers of the subject but also to that nebulous class, the 'intelligent general reader'.

Warfare in the Twentieth Century: Theory and Practice is not intended to be a comprehensive survey of every facet of conflict since 1900. Instead, a group of scholars was invited to contribute chapters on certain key themes that the editors felt were vital to the development of warfare in the present century. These themes are as wide-ranging as warfare itself. Subjects such as the impact of war upon society, theories of insurgency and counter-insurgency and nuclear strategy are considered, as well as rather more 'traditional' topics such as tactics and strategy on land, the role of sea power and the evolution of strategic bombing. No attempt has been made to dictate the pattern of the individual chapters, so each contributor has taken a slightly different approach to his own subject. One theme runs throughout, however – the dichotomy between the theory of war and its practice, for it is as true in the penultimate decade of the century as it was in

*   Paret, Peter, 'Introduction', in *Makers of Modern Strategy from Machiavelli to the Nuclear Age* (Oxford: Clarendon Press 1986), p. 5.

the first that, in war, things rarely go according to plan. The editors' hope is, that by providing a clear and up-to-date collection of essays on various aspects of warfare in the twentieth century, something will have been done to bridge the gulf between the academic student of conflict and the rest of the population – for one thing is clear, no one in the twentieth century can afford to ignore war.

CJ McI and GDS
UCW, Aberystwyth and
Old College, RMA, Sandhurst
October 1987

Contributors

Dr Colin McInnes is Defence Lecturer in the Department of International Politics, University College of Wales, Aberystwyth. He has written a number of articles on defence and strategic studies and is author of *Trident: The Only Option?*

G. D. Sheffield MA, is Senior Lecturer in the Department of War Studies, The Royal Military Academy, Sandhurst. He is editor of *Vimy Ridge to the Rhine: the War Letters of Christopher Stone 1914–1918* and is currently writing the official history of the Royal Military Police.

Dr Ian Beckett FRHistS, is Senior Lecturer in the Department of War Studies, RMA, Sandhurst, and has written extensively on a wide range of military topics. He is author of *The Army and the Curragh Incident 1914*, *Rifleman Form*, joint editor of *A Nation in Arms*, *Politicians and Defence* and *Armed Forces and Modern Counter-Insurgency*. He is also general editor of the Manchester University Press 'War, Armed Forces and Society' series and UK editor of the forthcoming *Journal of Small Wars and Insurgencies*.

Dr Keith Jeffery is Senior Lecturer in History at the University of Ulster at Jordanstown. He is author of *States of Emergency: British Governments and Strikebreaking since 1919* (with Peter Hennessy), *The British Army and the Crisis of Empire 1918–1922*, and editor of *The Military Correspondence of Sir Henry Wilson 1918–1922*.

Dr Geoffrey Till is Principal Lecturer at the Royal Naval College, Greenwich, and also lectures in the Department of War Studies, King's College, London. He is author of *Air Power and the Royal Navy*, *Maritime Strategy in the Nuclear Age*, *The Sea in Soviet Strategy*, *Modern Seapower* and editor of *The Future of British Sea Power* and *Britain and the Northern Flank*.

Dr John Pimlott is Deputy Head of the Department of War Studies, RMA, Sandhurst, and has written widely on many aspects of modern warfare. He is co-author of *Middle East Conflicts*, *Vietnam: the History and the Tactics*, and joint editor with Ian Beckett of *Armed Forces and Modern Counter-Insurgency*.

Robin Brown MScEcon, was formerly lecturer in the Department of Politics, University of Aberdeen, and is currently lecturer in the Department of Politics, University of Lancaster. He is author of *Arms Control: Has the West Lost Its Way?*

Dr John Pay was formerly lecturer in the Department of International Relations, University of Keele, and is currently Senior Lecturer at the Royal Naval College, Greenwich and visiting lecturer in Department of Systems Science, The City University, London. He has contributed to a number of studies of modern warfare.

NOTE   The views expressed in this book are those of the individual authors concerned, and should not be taken to represent the views of any official body or organization.

Warfare
in the
Twentieth Century

1

Total War

IAN F. W. BECKETT

The historiography of total war

In the last twenty years, historians have come increasingly to recognize the often pivotal role played by war and conflict in historical developments. In the process, the interpretation and understanding of the impact of war upon states, societies and individuals have been transformed. In particular, the concept of 'total war', as applied to the two world wars of the twentieth century, has become a familiar one and a matter for modern historiographical debate. Generally, the term 'total war' is used by historians not only to describe the nature of the world wars but also to differentiate such wars from other conflicts. The study of total war within the context of war studies or studies of war and society is largely a product of the 1960s, but the term itself is older. Ludendorff appears to have used the term first in his memoirs, published in 1919, but it was also employed in a ritualistic fashion during the Second World War. Josef Goebbels, for example, threatened the Western Allies with 'total war' in a celebrated speech in February 1943 and was himself appointed Reich Plenipotentiary for the Mobilization of Total War in July 1944; Winston Churchill also used the phrase in an address to the United States Congress in May 1943. Now, the term has become almost synonymous with the concept of war as a catalyst of far-reaching social change, and it is in precisely that sense that total war is a subject of continuing historical debate.

The American scholar, J. U. Nef, whose *War and Human Progress* was published in 1950,[1] may stand perhaps as representative of an earlier period of historiography, when war was regarded as having a purely negative impact, in so far as it was at all relevant to historical development. However, there were other scholars in the 1950s whose

1

work was suggestive of the future approach to the question of war
and social change. Richard Titmuss made a connection in 1950
between the two in his volume, *Problems of Social Policy*, for the
British official history of the Second World War[2] while Stanislas
Andrzejewski offered the 'military participation ratio' in 1954,[3]
which postulated a firm correlation between the extent of wartime
participation by society in the war effort and the amount of subsequent
levelling of social inequalities. The English historian, G. N. Clark, also
produced during the 1950s a pioneering study of war and society
in the seventeenth century,[4] but the real broadening of historical
perspectives with regard to what became known as war studies came
in the following decade. A comparison of Michael Howard's classic
military history of the Franco-Prussian War, published in 1961,[5] with
his *War in European History*[6] fifteen years later may serve to indicate
the profound historiographical change that occurred.

In the forefront of that change was Arthur Marwick, whose study of
British society in the First World War, *The Deluge*,[7] published in 1965,
was followed by *Britain in the Century of Total War* in 1968 and *War
and Social Change in the Twentieth Century* in 1974.[8] Marwick was
not the only historian in the field and the titles of Gordon Wright's
The Ordeal of Total War in 1968 and Peter Calvocoressi's and Guy
Wint's *Total War* in 1972 were also indicative of the new approach.[9]
However, it was largely Marwick who established the framework for
the study of total war. Four 'modes' put forward in *Britain in the
Century of Total War* had become a 'four-tier model' in *War and
Social Change in the Twentieth Century*, by which the changes effected
by total war might be gauged and compared between different states.
Thus, for Marwick, total war implied disruption and destruction on
a vast and unprecedented scale; the testing of the existing social
and political structures of states and societies; the participation,
in the context of the total mobilization of a state's resources, of
previously disadvantaged groups in the war effort; and, lastly, a
'colossal psychological experience'. The cumulative effect would be
real and enduring social change. The model became familiar to a
wide readership through the 'War and Society' course introduced by
Marwick and his colleagues at the Open University in the 1970s.[10]

To be fair to Marwick, the model was only offered as a 'rough tool',
but it is undeniable that the idea of war as a determinant of major
change has had a profound impact during the past decade. Indeed,
this concept has been described recently by Michael Bentley as one

of the most common 'misapprehensions' in the perception of modern British social history.[11] From the beginning, too, some historians were far more cautious than Marwick in their appraisal of the impact of total war upon society. Examples are Angus Calder's *The People's War*[12] – a title itself derived from a British propaganda slogan in the Second World War and echoed in a 1986 television series and accompanying book on Britain at war[13] – which was published in 1969, and Henry Pelling's *Britain in the Second World War*, published two years later.[14] More recently, Brian Bond has described total war as being as great a myth as the idea of total victory or total defeat[15] and, while the debate has continued to be waged within the context of parameters laid down by Marwick, recent and current research has done much to suggest that the social impact of total war in the twentieth century should not be overstated.

The emergence of total war

A preliminary consideration is that the acceptance of the periods between 1914 and 1918 and between 1939 and 1945 as those of total war implies that conflicts prior to the twentieth century were more limited. Traditionally, historians have described the late eighteenth century as a classic era of 'limited war', in which armies were relatively small in size and would manoeuvre with the intention of avoiding rather than engaging in battle. Campaigns would be designed to exhaust an opponent's economy by occupation in search of strictly limited political and dynastic aims. Societies as a whole would hardly be touched by the impact of war and, indeed, a prevailing bourgeois assumption that military activity was not the destiny of mankind ensured that trade flourished between states at war. Examples usually cited of the normality of social intercourse include Laurence Sterne's visit to Paris during the Seven Years War (1756–63) and the continuance of the Dover to Calais packet service for a year after France in 1778 had joined the United States in the American War of Independence (1774–83). Closer analysis, however, reveals that war between 1648 and 1789 was limited, in the words of John Childs, 'only when it was compared with the holocaust that had gone before and the new totality of the Napoleonic wars'.[16] As surely as the Thirty Years War (1618–48) had devastated Germany, reducing its urban population by 33 per cent and its rural population by 45 per cent, so incipient warfare during the next 120 years laid waste much of central Europe and the Low Countries at regular intervals. Conventions applied by armies in relation to each other did not extend to civilian populations, as the French army's ravages in the Palatinate in 1688 and 1689 or both the Russian and Swedish armies' depredations in the Great Northern War (1700–21) well illustrate. In any case, for all their balletic appearance, battles were murderous affairs, the 'butcher's bill' at Malplaquet in 1709 of an estimated 36,000 casualties not being surpassed until the battle of Borodino in 1812. Borodino itself was then exceeded by the 127,000 casualties at the four day 'Battle of the Nations' at Leipzig in 1813. The cumulative effect of such conflict upon areas that were fought over was considerable. Equally, participation in five major wars between 1689 and 1783 was a major stimulus for English industry and trade at a crucial early stage in the world's first industrial revolution.

None the less, warfare was to become increasingly more total in its impact during the course of the nineteenth century, which can be taken as representing an extended transitional period. During the French Revolutionary and Napoleonic wars (1792–1815), the motive forces of nationalism and democracy combined to create a mass French citizen army through the introduction of universal male conscription. The success of this 'nation in arms' or 'armed horde' resulted in the example being emulated elsewhere, notably in Prussia. Although the concept of the nation in arms came under sustained attack after 1815 from monarchs and restored monarchs, who distrusted its social and political implications, the actual system of short-service conscription survived in Prussia. The military victories then won by Prussia in the German wars of unification of 1864, 1866 and 1870 and the ability of short-service conscription to produce large numbers of trained reserves upon mobilization encouraged European states – with the exception of Britain – to reintroduce Prussian-style conscription. Although the forms of universal service adopted were necessarily selective in practice, states were rapidly accepting the national birthrate as an index of military power. Moreover, the transformation wrought by the technological innovations of the industrial age, particularly the development of the railway, ensured that ever larger armies could be mobilized theoretically more quickly than hitherto and sustained in the field for far longer.

At the same time, industrialization dramatically increased the destructive capacity of armies by providing them with weapons of enhanced range, accuracy and rate of fire. By 1870, a firefight between opposing infantry, which might have been conducted at 60 yards range seventy years before, had now stretched to a possible 1,600 yards and a breechloading rifle such as the Prussian Dreyse now fired seven rounds for every one from a smoothbore musket of the Napoleonic era. By the 1880s and 1890s magazine rifles, quick-firing artillery and machine guns had all entered service with major European armies. Just before the First World War, most armies were also experimenting with aircraft, even if it appeared to require a considerable feat of imagination to conceive that airmen could offer any valuable intelligence while flying over the ground at speeds approaching 30 mph. At sea, too, wood, sail and round shot had given way to iron and steel, steam and screw propellor, and shell, while mines, submarines and torpedoes all threatened the traditional supremacy of the capital ship.

Through the innate conservatism of European military and naval officer corps, the significance of much of the change that had taken place during the nineteenth century was misinterpreted. Contrary to popular belief, soldiers did recognize the problems inherent in crossing the so-called 'empty battlefield' in the face of modern firepower, but they believed mistakenly that they could solve the difficulty simply by closing with an enemy more rapidly. Moreover, the use of bayonet, lance and sabre implicit in this 'offensive spirit' ideally complemented traditional military ideals of honour and glory, which some feared devalued by the unwelcome intrusion of technology and professionalism into an overwhelmingly aristocratic occupation. While soldiers conspired to discount the more uncomfortable evidence of such conflicts as the American Civil War (1861–65), Franco-Prussian War (1870–71) and Russo-Japanese War (1904–5), civilians were equally seduced by the general trend in the later nineteenth century towards popular nationalism, imperialism, militarism and crude social Darwinism into a more ready acceptance of war and conflict as an appropriate test of nationhood and national virility. There were pacifists but, in 1914, it was nationalism and not inter-nationalism that triumphed across Europe. Similarly, a succession of international conferences, such as those at St Petersburg in 1868 or at the Hague in 1899 and 1907, failed to find a universal readiness among nation states to compromise their future freedom of manoeuvre by accepting meaningful limitations on the actual conduct of war.

Wars between 1789 and 1914, while such developments were occurring, were hardly devoid of impact upon those societies that waged them. In the case of Britain, for example, the manpower problems experienced during the Crimean War (1854–56) were very similar to those encountered in the First World War, and losses sustained in the twenty years of almost continuous warfare between 1793 and 1815 were almost certainly proportionately higher in terms of men under arms than in the First World War.[17] Military participation in Britain was also probably greater in proportion to the male population between 1793 and 1815, and it is at least arguable that the resulting social, economic and political upheaval in the immediate postwar period was of more significance for the future pattern of British society and democracy than developments in the aftermath of either of the world wars. Of course, the wars of German and Italian unification were of very limited duration, but they still had profound political consequences for Europe.

There was once a tendency to view the American Civil War largely in terms of its military developments and to focus upon such innovations as armoured trains, the first clash of armoured warships, the first loss of ships to mines and submarine torpedoes, the first extensive use of the telegraph, and so on. In fact, the largely amateur armies fought the war on the battlefield as if it were the last Napoleonic encounter rather than the 'first modern war' but it is now recognized widely that the war was truly modern in terms of its impact upon society. Both the northern states of the Union and the southern states of the Confederacy deployed large numbers of men in the field but, for the predominantly agricultural Confederacy, war also demanded efforts to create an industrial economy to challenge the far greater manufacturing potential of the North. It had become essential to outproduce as well as to outfight an opponent. Despite its efforts at industrialization, the mobilization of 75 per cent of its white male population, and unprecedented participation by white women and blacks in industry and agriculture, the Confederacy was doomed to defeat by the superiority of the North's numbers and resources. The inescapable logic of the attempt to create a war economy was the recognition that a society that sustained a war became as much a legitimate target for military action as an army that waged war on its behalf. Thus, in the autumn of 1864, Sheridan's Union forces swept down the southern 'bread basket' of the Shenandoah valley while Sherman's armies wrought equal destruction in cutting a swathe from Atlanta to the sea in November and December 1864 and through the Carolinas in the following months in a determination to expose the Confederacy to the 'hard hand of war'.[18]

The world wars

Thus, there are sufficient examples of the way in which the impact of war upon society was increasing through the nineteenth century to suggest that the world wars should be regarded as a natural progression from earlier conflicts rather than as unique. But, of course, this is not to suggest that the impact of world war was not greater than that of earlier wars through the sheer scale of conflict enhancing the effect. Quite obviously, both world wars were global in scope, although both began as European conflicts. In the First World War, the Central Powers comprised Imperial Germany, Austria-Hungary, Ottoman Turkey (from October 1914) and Bulgaria (from October 1915), but the Allies eventually embraced twenty-two states including the major European powers of Britain, France, Imperial Russia and Italy (from May 1915) and their colonies and dependencies, and also Japan, the United States (from March 1917), Liberia (from August 1917) and Brazil (from October 1917). Similarly, the Second World War widened with the aggression of Germany, Italy (from June 1940 to September 1943) and Japan (from December 1941) bringing in the Soviet Union (from June 1941) and the United States (from December 1941), although the Soviet Union did not join in the war against Japan until August 1945. Successive German and Soviet occupation contributed to a bewildering proliferation of contradictory declarations of war by many eastern European states during the war, while, between February and March 1945, no less than ten states ranging from Peru to Saudi Arabia declared war on both Germany and Japan and a further two on Japan alone.

Total war therefore implies a far wider global conflict than previous wars and, while limited war suggests a degree of constraint, self-imposed or otherwise, total war implies a lack of constraint. In practice, total war was still a relative concept in both world wars since, as an absolute, it was unrealizable through a lack of instantaneously destructive weapons. Nevertheless, belligerents could not be accused of failing to attempt the absolute even if they were unable to mobilize all their resources at the same time and at the same point. In effect, they employed all the weapons they felt appropriate rather than all the weapons available in every case. The array and potential of weapons increased dramatically over previous wars. For example, in eight days before the opening of the British offensive on the Somme on the Western Front on 1 July 1916, British artillery fired 1.7 million shells at German positions. In fourteen days preceding the opening of the Passchendaele offensive on 31 July 1917, the British fired 4.2 million shells. In addition to the weight of shell, horrendous new weapons were introduced in search of an elusive breakthrough. Gas was first used on the Western Front at Langemarck near Ypres on 22 April 1915, although it had previously been used by the Germans at Bolimov on the Eastern Front, and, in July 1915, flamethrowers were used effectively for the first time by the Germans at Hooge near Ypres. In all, over 150,000 tons of varying gases were produced during the First World War and caused an estimated 1.2 million casualties, of which more than 91,000 proved fatal. Tanks were also introduced for the first time by the British on the Somme on 15 September 1916.

Although gas was not used in the Second World War other than in the context of Nazi genocide, its military use was pressed by a powerful military–industrial lobby in Germany. There were also considerable technological advances that further enhanced the destructive power of the belligerents. Paradoxically, the speed of the early German *Blitzkriegs* actually made these operations less costly in terms of casualties than trench warfare during the First World War but, equally, there was the development in the capacity to bring aerial destruction to civilian populations. Ultimately, Germany utilized its V1 and V2 rockets and the Allies, of course, dropped the first atomic weapons on Japan.

The conscious abandonment of most if not all restraints was paralleled by the wider war aims adopted by belligerents in total war. Limited dynastic aims had given way to sweeping territorial aggrandisement and the total destruction of states and of peoples. It could be argued in this respect that the necessary manipulation of the population of democratic states through propaganda and other means, in so far as this proved possible, in order to sustain the war effort introduced as great a push towards total war aims as the attempt by authoritarian or totalitarian states to impose their ideologies on others. Thus, on the one hand, the Germans pursued total domination in the Second World War, while Britain and the United States adopted a declaration of the need for the unconditional surrender of Germany at the Casablanca conference in January 1943. At Cairo in November and December 1943 Britain, the United States and nationalist China also agreed to strip Japan of all those overseas possessions taken by her forces since 1894.

Quite clearly, the participation of many states and their willingness to use extreme means to achieve wide aims resulted in destruction of life and property on an unprecedented scale compared with previous wars. In all, the First World War is thought to have resulted in 10 million dead and 20 million maimed or seriously wounded, leaving 5 million women widows and 9 million children orphans. The Second World War may have cost 30 million dead in Europe, although other estimates put Soviet losses alone at well over 20 million dead. Although figures for the First World War usually exclude an estimated 1.5 million Armenians exterminated by the Turks in 1915, those for the Second World War do include an estimated 5.9 million Jewish victims of Nazi genocide. Moreover, as many as 26 million people may have become displaced from their country of origin during the Second World War through forced transportation or other reasons: in Britain alone, which did not suffer such displacement, there were still 60 million changes of address during the Second World War. Compared with previous wars, also, civilians had become subject to sustained and deliberate attack to an unprecedented degree. During the First World War, some 1413 British civilians were killed by aerial attack, but, between 1939 and 1945, German bombers and rockets accounted for 51,509 civilian deaths in Britain. Hamburg suffered approximately 50,000 dead in a week in July and August 1943, and calculations of the loss of life at Dresden on a single night in February 1945 range from 35,000 to 135,000. In all, total German civilian losses to aerial bombardment may have been 593,000 during the Second World War. USAAF 'fire raids' on Japan caused an estimated 100,000 deaths in Tokyo on one night in March 1945, or approximately the same number of immediate deaths at both Hiroshima and Nagasaki combined in August 1945.

The loss of life in individual states could be grave, but total war was not necessarily a cause of demographic loss overall. In France, the loss of life during the First World War did cast a long shadow, at least in political terms, and draconian laws were introduced against birth control and abortion in the interwar period. Yet, it would appear that more men and women married than might otherwise have been the case. In Britain, as Jay Winter has pointed out, the war was dysgenic in that some sectors of society volunteered for war service in larger

numbers than others and many of the working class were physically
unfit for service through prewar deprivation. Hence, the idea of a 'lost
generation' current in Britain in the 1920s and 1930s had some basis
in fact. But, as Jay Winter has also demonstrated, infant mortality
declined through the improvement in the nutrition of mothers and
children with the redistribution of food and increased family income
consequent upon wartime changes in public health policy. These,
paradoxically healthier, standards of living were not eroded by
the depression years.[19] Similarly, J. J. Becker has concluded that
standards of living were not materially diminished in France during the
First World War.[20] Unexpectedly, too, there was a close correlation
during the Second World War between Britain, which suffered little
real violence and deprivation, and most other European countries in
terms of more and earlier marriages, increased fertility, and decreased
infant and maternal mortality. Such demographic gains were achieved
despite the estimated 27 million deaths worldwide from the Spanish
influenza pandemic of 1918 and 1919. The latter in itself was once
attributed to war-related conditions of less resistance to infection and
easier transmission of disease through armies but, in fact, it hit neutrals
as hard if not worse than belligerents and the highest mortality rates
were recorded in the United States and India. Advances in medicine
were of considerable account in preventing disease during and after
the Second World War. It must also be borne in mind that total war is
a stimulus to medical development and, even in the First World War,
soldiers were far more likely to survive serious wounds than any of
their predecessors on countless battlefields in the past.

The reduction of suffering and much else to statistics is unfortunate
but unavoidable in conveying the totality of the world wars. Similar
repetitive statistics are available to compute the undoubted losses of
property and of manufacturing and agricultural production as a result
either of direct attack or of occupation. Certainly, the cost of waging
war had increased spectacularly. In 1870, for example, it has been
suggested that the Franco–Prussian War cost Prussia and the other
German states some 7 million marks a day, whereas the First World
War cost Imperial Germany an estimated 146 million marks a day
in 1918. Just 18 months' participation in the First World War cost
the United States $112 billion, but the Second World War cost the
United States some $664 billion. In fact, such exact calculations of
the direct and indirect costs of war are notoriously difficult to make
and quantitative evaluations may not in themselves be particularly

helpful in suggesting the impact of war upon the economy. Structural changes are far more significant and, in this regard, both world wars were of unquestionable importance as economic events. As a result of the First World War, there was not only a global depreciation in the value of currencies, which had repercussions in terms of currency instability in the interwar years, but also a decentralization of the international economy. Europe's share of world production and trade fell through the stimulus afforded non-European competitors. Much the same effect was reproduced during and after the Second World War with the growth of manufacturing capacity outside Europe and a legacy of post-war economic planning very different to the policies followed prior to the war.[21]

The primary beneficiary of the stimulus to non-European economies in both world wars was the United States, which moved from being an international debtor before 1914 to an international creditor on a large scale. In the process, the United States also emerged as a global power, even if subsequently choosing isolation for another twenty years. The First World War also destroyed four empires – those of Imperial Germany, Austria-Hungary, Tsarist Russia and Ottoman Turkey. It left a legacy of new states in eastern Europe, such as Poland, Czechoslovakia, Hungary and Yugoslavia, with significant racial minorities. It directly fostered the growth of nationalism among subject peoples in those empires that did survive. The British, whose empire reached its greatest extent in 1919 with the acquisition of former German colonies and custody of new Middle Eastern territories, encountered nationalism in such areas as Palestine, India and Ireland. Later, the Second World War made a significant contribution to the further decline of western Europe vis-à-vis the United States and the Soviet Union. Moreover, the occupation of much of South-East Asia by the Japanese struck severely at the hold of the remaining European colonial powers. Nationalism was fostered both through the establishment by the Japanese of puppet governments and quasi-nationalist organizations and also through the emergence of anti-Japanese opposition movements, such as the Viet Minh in French Indo-china and the Malayan Peoples' Anti-Japanese Army (MPAJA) in Malaya, which proved equally opposed to the return of former colonial administrations once the Japanese had been defeated. It would be difficult to argue that such global changes in the balance of power would not have occurred but for the world wars. Both wars also saw some attempt at a new internationalism in the shape of institutional mechanisms for world order – the League of Nations and the United Nations – although such ideals were not entirely novel.

The growth of state control

The collapse of some states and the post-war political challenges to others suggests that Marwick is perfectly correct in postulating total war as a testing experience for the institutions of state. Certainly, the world wars did promote far greater state control in its broadest sense as a response to wartime challenges. In 1914 a spate of emergency legislation, such as the revived Prussian Law of Siege of 1851 in Imperial Germany and the Defence of the Realm Act (DORA) in Britain, enabled the state to assume wide powers. In all cases the railways were swiftly nationalized and, in Britain and France, this was followed by state control of mines and the shipbuilding industry. Precisely the same pattern occurred in the United States in 1917 and key areas such as munitions, food and manpower policies were submitted to intervention and control by new governmental agencies. In Britain, the Ministry of Munitions was created in May 1915 with an accompanying Munitions of War Act extending state control to munitions factories to prevent strikes, suspend trade union activities and to prevent free movement of labour. More new creations followed Lloyd George's appointment as prime minister in December 1916 (such as the Ministry of Labour and Ministry of Food), although often with ill-defined responsibilities. Canada created an Imperial Munitions Board; Austria-Hungary, a Joint Food Committee; the United States, a War Industries Board and a Fuel and Food Administration; Imperial Germany's new agencies included the War Wheat Corporation, the War Food Office and the splendidly named Imperial Potato Office. In the Second World War, Britain established new ministries of supply, home security, economic warfare, information, food and shipping, and aircraft production. New executive agencies wielding wide powers in areas previously untouched by the state appeared in the United States as well, the number of government employees there increasing from 1 million in 1940 to 3.8 million by 1946. Even the Vichy regime in France experienced the growth of organization committees in the supervision of the wartime economy.

In essence, it is this control of the economy that lies at the heart of the concept of total war, because it is assumed that a state is required to mobilize all its resources in order to survive. However, it has become increasingly apparent that many of the wartime creations did not necessarily alter the prewar structure. Much of the dramatic change once attributed to Lloyd George's premiership in Britain during the latter stages of the First World War is now seen more in terms of administrative continuities with that of his predecessor, Asquith.[22] The new centralized War Cabinet was not the administrative revolution Lloyd George claimed, many of its functions being hived off to ad hoc sub-committees in the manner of the War Committee it replaced. In terms of manpower policy at least, co-ordinated manipulation and distribution of mobilized resources was not effected until late 1917[23] and, in many respects, similar effective control of food production and distribution was only achieved in July 1918. Businessmen were introduced to government by Lloyd George and they also featured in the United States, where Wall Street broker Bernard Baruch headed the War Industries Board, and even in Imperial Germany, where Moellendorf and Rathenau of the electrical giant, AEG, were early appointees to the raw materials section of the war ministry. However, businessmen in government and the failure of the British Treasury to secure wartime control of the new ministerial creations were but temporary phenomena, with wartime controls speedily divested in Britain after the armistice.

In the case of Nazi Germany, there has been a lively debate on the extent to which Germany was already or became a total war economy during the Second World War. An earlier interpretation associated with Alan Milward postulated an economy designed for swift and lightning *Blitzkrieg*, which was then required to be converted into a total war economy from 1942 onwards under the guiding hand of Albert Speer. By contrast, Richard Overy has argued that fewer changes were required early in the war because the logic of Goering's Four Year Plan Office of 1936 was the creation of a total war economy, and that what Milward has seen as rhetoric prior to 1942 was rhetoric applied. This should be seen within the context of competing agencies and interests that promoted gross inefficiency rather than effective preparation for war, and also in the context of German miscalculations as to the likely starting date for that war. Thus, Speer's efforts should be regarded as an attempt to improve the performance of an economy already geared for total war rather than to initiate the process in the first place.[24]

Undoubtedly, however, total war did result in increased state control over the individual. Some state systems already involved a degree of coercion, citizens of Nazi Germany and Soviet Russia having relatively little choice as to the degree of their participation in the war effort. But increased state control was equally a feature of democracies. During the First World War, both British and United States citizens were exposed to military conscription for the first time in many generations. The restrictions of DORA in 1914 were easily exceeded by the theoretical powers of the British government under the Emergency Powers (Defence) Act of 1939 and its revised version in May 1940. However, there were few compulsory labour directions in Britain and, although Britain also went further than any other belligerent in taking powers for the conscription of women, the legislation was again used sparingly. But there was compulsory direction of men to serve in the mining industry – the so-called Bevin Boys – in 1943 and, following a spate of unofficial strikes, it became an indictable offence in April 1944 to instigate or incite industrial stoppages in essential war.work. Canada compulsorily transferred 127,000 workers from low to high priority employment under its National Service Civilian Regulations of January 1943 and, in the United States, the War Labor Disputes Act of the same year enabled governments to conscript strikers. In the First World War, both British and American governments had contemplated conscripting striking Midlands engineering employees and copper miners respectively. At a lower level, too, government impinged on everyday life in new ways, although in the United States the population tended to fight the wars, to use J. M. Blum's words, 'in imagination only'.[25] Bread was rationed in Imperial Germany in the First World War as early as January 1915, and meat rationing was introduced in Britain in February 1918. In the Second World War commodities such as butter, bacon, sugar, meat, tea, cooking fats and margarine were all rationed in Britain before July 1940. Both wars saw the imposition of a blackout in Britain and the licensing laws and summer time of modern Britain remain legacies of the First World War.

War and social change

Military and industrial conscription also reflected the greater demands made upon manpower in total war. Just as prewar soldiers in 1914 had not anticipated the kind of warfare that was to be waged on the Western Front, few politicians or soldiers had estimated correctly the extent of the demands which would be made upon industry. Britain, France and Imperial Russia all suffered 'shell shortages' in 1915, as did Germany in the following year. Part of the problem derived from the way in which skilled workers had been either conscripted or allowed to volunteer for war service in 1914 but, in any case, industries such as munitions expanded to such an extent that there was a massive growth in the labour force. In Italy, for example, those involved in war industries increased from 20 to 64 per cent of the industrial working force during the First World War, and in Imperial Russia there was a staggering increase from 24 to 76 per cent of the working force. Precisely the same happened in the Second World War. The shipbuilding industry in Canada, for example, alone increased its work force from 4000 in 1939 to 126,000 in 1943 and the United States labour force as a whole increased from 54 million to 64 million. Such increased demands provided new opportunities, not only for unskilled male labour, but for groups previously under-represented in the industrial labour force. In Imperial Germany, the number of women employed in industry increased from 1.4 million in 1914 to 2.1 million by 1918, and there were 800,000 more women in British industry in 1918 than in 1914 and two and a half times the number of women in United States industry in 1918 than a year previously. In the Second World War, there were 3 million more women in full or part-time employment in Britain in 1943 than in 1939 and 4.5 million more in the United States in 1945 than in 1940. In the United States, a parallel can be drawn with Negro employment in both world wars, the number employed in industry increasing from 2.9 million in 1940 to 3.2 million in 1944, for instance.

Particular attention has been devoted by historians to the condition of labour and to the question of the employment of women in total war. Total war invariably effected a stimulus for those sectors of the economy considered especially vital to war production: heavy industries such as coal, shipping and heavy metals, but also newer lighter industries such as chemicals, electrical goods and motors. In the United States, there was a boom in synthetic rubber manufacture during the Second World War owing to the loss of South-East Asian sources. As a result of such trends, unemployment declined rapidly and the position of labour generally was liable to be improved. One manifestation was the increase in trade union membership. In the

United States this rose from 2 million in 1917 to 3.25 million in 1918 and from 10.5 million in 1941 to 14.75 million in 1945. In Britain, the increase was from 4 million to 8 million between 1914 and 1918 and by one-third – to 8 million – during the Second World War. Through enhanced union strength, continued militancy on the shopfloor and the need of government to ensure a better relationship with labour, total war would then generally result in lower working hours and higher wages in real terms. In Britain, it is estimated that average working hours fell from 50 hours to 48 hours a week between 1914 and 1918 and, although they increased from 48 hours in 1939 to 54.1 hours for men and between 44.2 and 46.9 hours for women by 1943, they declined to an average 44–45 hours in 1945.

However, average figures do not always reflect reality. In British industry during the First World War, for example, much of the earlier interpretation of the effect of dilution of trade and the narrowing of differentials within and between differing sectors of industry was based on the experience of engineering. Further research has indicated that the experience of labour employed in other sectors such as shipbuilding was very different. Calculations were also made in terms of differences between wage rates and earnings, a presumption being made that skilled men paid by the hour would not benefit to the same extent as unskilled men paid by piecework rates, but this ignored the widespread official and unofficial bonuses and incentives provided for skilled labour during the First World War. In any case, there was no substantial reorganization of British industry in either of the world wars, prewar differentials being restored in 1918 so that, if labour could be said to have gained generally, most groups moved up together in broadly the same relationship as previously. In Britain, too, trade union membership declined rapidly in the 1920s and 1930s. In the Second World War, industrial wage differentials in Britain widened to such an extent that there was official concern at the level of wages in Midlands engineering and aircraft factories.

Another factor to be taken into account is wartime inflation: while, on average, wages in real terms kept ahead of inflation in Britain in both world wars, this was far from true in other states such as Imperial Germany. There, real wages fell and, although it can be said that the working class did relatively well, with unions forging a new partnership with employers in 1918, it did so only in the context of losing less than other social groups, which were affected even more in a society impoverished by wartime inflation. Similarly,

ERRATUM

The editors regret that the following references were inadvertantly deleted from Chapter 2, 'Colonial Warfare 1900–1939' by Keith Jeffery:

R. J. Gavin, *Aden under British Rule 1839–1967* (London: C. Hurst, 1975).

John Morgan Gates, *Schoolbooks and Krogo: the United States Army in The Philippines 1898–1902* (Westport, Conn. and London: Greenwood Press, 1973).

David Killingray, '"A swift agent of government": air power in British colonial Africa, 1916–1939', *Journal of African History*, vol. 25 (1984).

Walter Laqueur, *Guerrilla: a Historical and Critical Study* (London: Weidenfeld & Nicolson, 1977).

Joyce Laverty Miller, 'The Syrian revolt of 1925', *International Journal of Middle East Studies*, vol. 8 (1977).

Ronald Shaffer, 'The 1940 Small Wars Manual and the "lessons of history"', *Military Affairs*, vol. 36 (1972).

Edward M. Spiers, 'Gas and the North-West Frontier', *Journal of Strategic Studies*, vol. 6 (1983).

Brian R. Sullivan, 'A thirst for glory: Mussolini, the Italian military and the Fascist regime, 1922–36', PhD thesis, Columbia University (1984).

A. J. P. Taylor (ed), *Lloyd George: A Diary by Frances Stevenson* (New York: Harper & Row, 1971).

Charles Townshend, *The British Campaign in Ireland 1919–21* (London: Oxford University Press, 1975), and *Britain's Civil Wars: Counterinsurgency in the Twentieth Century* (London: Faber, 1986).

Richard E. Welch, Jr., 'American atrocities in the Philippines: the indictment and the response', *Pacific Historical Review*, vol. 43 (1974).

The editors regret any embarrassment this may cause.

although wages kept ahead of inflation in the United States in the Second World War, this was not the case in France. Generalization, therefore, is exceptionally hazardous and wide differences must be expected between and within varying social groups, not all of which might be in the position to benefit from the opportunities afforded by wartime participation in the labour market. Much remains to be done on the experience of social and occupational groups other than the working class and the unskilled – to give but one example, some of the most profound social changes in Britain in both wars took place not in industry but in the agricultural sector.

The judgement of the impact of total war upon the position of women is equally beset with difficulties of interpretation. As already indicated, there were measurable increases in female employment in most belligerents in both wars, Nazi Germany being the most notable exception. In many cases, however, it is the increase of women in areas such as transport or white-collar employment that is more significant than increases in the numbers in manufacturing industry, because the former employment was more likely to endure after the end of hostilities. The degree of female dilution in the munitions industry in both Britain and France in the First World War has been exaggerated, because most women were employed for specific functions and did not supplant skilled male labour. Equally, during the Second World War, British trade unions negotiated dilution agreements that protected male jobs. In many cases, many women may not have perceived wartime employment either as permanent or as an expression of long-term emancipation, and it can be argued that there was a significant revival of domesticity in Britain in 1945. Some trends can be perceived in Britain in terms of the increase in part-time female employment during the Second World War and the greater employment of married women and older women, although the proportion of married women within the female labour force as a whole was still relatively small. Clearly, however, wartime employment neither implied equality of pay nor an erosion of the sexual divisions of labour. It is also arguable how far the extension of the suffrage in Britain after the First World War reflected an appreciation of female participation in the war effort. The enfranchisement of women aged over 30 in 1918 compensated for that of the 40 per cent of the adult male population, mostly working class, who had not been able to vote prior to the war. Moreover, in France, although the Chamber of Deputies voted for female suffrage in 1919, the Senate repeatedly rejected it. It has been argued that the final conceding of the principle of female suffrage in France in 1944 reflected the role of women in the resistance movement, but, in fact, the leftward turn in the indirectly elected Senate – especially among radicals, who had previously opposed the vote for women – guaranteed such an outcome anyway. Yet, if the world wars did not improve the status of women, they did perhaps offer some women wider opportunities and freedoms. Again, generalization about the perceptions or expectations of women is no easy task.[26]

It is also largely in terms of perception that social change as a result of total war must be gauged. Of course, the tendency of the modern state to collect statistics ensures that there are some measurable social trends. In both world wars, there were likely to be more marriages, more divorces and more illegitimate births. In Britain, attendance at the cinema rose in both world wars and, in the Second World War, 'eating out' increased with the 79 million meals per week of May 1941 increasing to 170 million meals a week by December 1944. Crime rose also in both world wars, although this included offences against wartime regulations. In the United States and Britain, for example, juvenile delinquency increased in both wars. There was also enhanced urbanization. In Imperial Russia, the urban proletariat grew from 22 million in 1914 to 28 million by 1916, one-third of the increase taking place in St Petersburg, with particular repercussions when the widespread failure of the transportation system contributed to the hunger and unrest in the cities in 1917. In the United States, the First World War saw the beginnings of a large-scale migration of the Negro population from the rural south to the industrial north, and this continued both through the interwar period and the Second World War. The Willow Run township in Detroit increased its population by 32,000 during the Second World War owing to the location of production of B-24 bombers there, and Detroit as a whole increased by 500,000 inhabitants, of whom 12 per cent were blacks. Changes in occupation can also be measured, such as the permanent decline in the number of domestic servants in Britain during and after the First World War and, in Britain, it is also possible to measure the changes in the numbers paying income tax. In the First World War, this increased from 1.5 million in 1914 to 7.75 million in 1918 and from 1 million to 7 million among manual workers between 1939 and 1944.

The measurement of quantifiable trends contributes to some extent to an understanding of those that cannot be so calculated, such as the degree to which total war resulted in greater social homogeneity and the breakdown of class distinctions through participation. Two commonly expressed vestiges of this are the concepts of a 'war generation', emerging from the shared experiences of the trenches in the First World War, and the idea of a 'people's war' during the Second World War. In terms of the former, it appears doubtful that shared experience between officers and men in the front line brought a greater understanding between different classes in the postwar period, not least because of the considerable distinctions that were preserved in the relationship of officer and man. Richard Bessel and David Englander have concluded from a survey of the literature in this field that the war generation lasted 'only as long as it remained under fire'.[27]

The identification of a 'people's war' by contemporary socialist, and invariably middle-class, intellectuals in Britain during the Second World War has tended to disguise the persistence of class differences. A significant change was the postwar bargaining power of labour through trade unions, but this occurred within the existing structure of social consciousness and the structure of the trade union movement itself was also unchanged. The image of the happy communion of the London underground shelters during the Blitz and much else in popular mythology does not bear close investigation.[28] Much was made by Titmuss, for example, of the wartime reformist consensus that was said to have emerged as a result of the compulsory wartime evacuation of 1.75 million persons, mainly women and children, from inner cities and coastal towns in Britain in 1939. In fact, it would appear that most hosts were as working class as the evacuees themselves and the experience merely reinforced existing prewar analyses among middle-class observers of the nature of the working class. In any case, the great majority of the evacuees had returned to the cities by 1940.[29] In general, therefore, although there may have been some changes in social stratification during wartime, a temporary equalizing effect upon income had little impact upon class differences or the ownership of property. Nevertheless, total war does imply at least a temporary throwing together of different social groups, and it would be hazardous to deny altogether the impact of evacuation upon individuals or, for example, the presence in Britain during the Second World War of some 1.5 million foreign servicemen.

At the same time, although states did not go to war to transform their societies, total war did produce the ideals if not the reality of postwar social change and guided reconstruction. In the United States, the housing shortages resulting from the growth in urban population during the First World War and the attendant social problems did establish a precedent for federal intervention, which foreshadowed the programmes of the 1930s. Britain also experienced the intention for reconstruction through such measures as the Ministry of Health Act and the Housing and Town Planning Act of 1919. Economic depression left such promise unfulfilled but, during and after the Second World War, an apparent wartime consensus on guided change bore fruit in such measures as the Town and Country Planning Act, the Education Act, Keynesian declarations of full employment and the establishment of a welfare state along the lines of the Beveridge report of December 1942. Again, however, care must be exercised in interpreting postwar changes as novel. A broad consensus on such matters as family allowance provision and the principle of a National Health Service had existed before the war, and the 1944 Education Act did not materially affect the prewar status quo. Full employment rested upon the assumption that a condition already arrived at in wartime would be maintained, and the war generally created a false impression that emergency apparatus would also be maintained to ensure the preservation of social solidarity and the unchallenged consensus on a welfare state. Some changes resulted from the electoral success of the Labour party in 1945, itself arguably a result of the unguided change in popular expectation through enforced egalitarianism and creeping collectivization. But the Labour party had moderated during the war through participation in coalition government; in the United States, there was actually a shift to the right rather than the political left despite equal measures of guided social change. Though not rivalling the far-reaching provisions of Canada's Marsh report of March 1943, both Negroes and ex-servicemen were the theoretical beneficiaries of social measures in the United States. In reality, of course, discrimination against blacks continued, irrespective of presidential executive orders to the contrary, although the US Servicemen's Readjustment Act of 1944 – the 'GI Bill' – illustrated the ability of veterans' organizations to achieve far more through the power of pressure-group lobbies in the American system than through comparable veterans' organizations elsewhere.

In effect, wartime changes may not mean much in practical terms thereafter and the lack of success of British veterans' organizations merely illustrates how far change depended upon the political system of the state waging total war. Clearly, too, changes were potentially greater where a state collapsed under the strain of war, as in Imperial Russia in 1917, or suffered total defeat as in Germany and Japan in 1945. Generally, however, it would appear that institutional mechanisms are more liable to change than social structures, although here, too, the example of the British army as an institution in the First World War is instructive. In theory, it ought to provide clear evidence of the impact of total war, since a small prewar regular cadre of 250,000 officers and men expanded to almost 6 million in the course of the war, becoming theoretically more representative of society than ever before. In fact, the army remained unrepresentative of British society through the unequable distribution of war service and, in the long term, there was little or no change in its social structure or ethos owing to the survival of the prewar officer corps. Even the impact of service life may be challenged, since the popular image of men such as Robert Graves or Siegfried Sassoon as representative of the thousands who served in the army is hardly compatible with the reality.[30] In short, armies as institutions do not seem to change to the same extent as society is said to change as the result of total war.

Furthermore, it is also necessary to place wartime change and development within the context of long-term social trends, which often suggest evolutionary rather than revolutionary change during the course of the longer period. This would suggest, for example, that female suffrage would have come to Britain irrespective of the impact of the First World War, although that experience may have accelerated changes already taking place. Total war could not fail to generate some change through its sheer scale, but it is important to judge how far changes survived the immediate postwar situation that generated them and, indeed, how far such changes would have occurred in any case. In conclusion, therefore, it might be suggested that total war is an important and largely instructive concept, provided that its limitations are kept in mind.

Notes: Chapter 1

1   J. U. Nef, *War and Human Progress* (London: Routledge & Kegan Paul, 1950).
2   R. Titmuss, *Problems of Social Policy* (London: HMSO and Longman, 1950).
3   S. Andrzejewski, *Military Organisation and Society* (London: Routledge & Kegan Paul, 1954).

4 G. N. Clark, *War and Society in the Seventeenth Century* (London: Cambridge University Press, 1958).
5 M. E. Howard, *The Franco-Prussian War* (London: Hart-Davis, 1961).
6 M. E. Howard, *War in European History* (Oxford: Oxford University Press, 1976).
7 A. Marwick, *The Deluge* (London: The Bodley Head, 1965).
8 A. Marwick, *Britain in the Century of Total War* (London: The Bodley Head, 1968); ibid., *War and Social Change in the Twentieth Century* (London: Macmillan, 1974).
9 G. Wright, *The Ordeal of Total War* (New York: Harper Torchbooks, 1968); P. Calvocoressi and G. Wint, *Total War* (London: Allen Lane, 1972).
10 The Open University, A301 *War and Society* (Milton Keynes: The Open University Press, 1973).
11 M. Bentley, 'Social change: appearance and reality' in C. Haigh (ed.), *The Cambridge Historical Encyclopedia of Great Britain and Ireland* (Cambridge University Press, 1985), p. 327.
12 A. Calder, *The People's War* (London: Cape, 1969).
13 P. Lewis, *A People's War* (London: Thames Methuen, 1986).
14 H. Pelling, *Britain in the Second World War* (London: Collins/Fontana, 1971).
15 B. Bond, *War and Society in Europe, 1870–1970* (London: Fontana, 1984), p. 168.
16 J. Childs, *Armies and Warfare in Europe, 1648–1789* (Manchester: Manchester University Press 1982), p. 2.
17 C. Emsley, *British Society and the French Wars 1793–1815* (London: Macmillan, 1979), p. 169.
18 P. J. Parish, *The American Civil War* (London: Eyre Methuen, 1975).
19 J. M. Winter, *The Great War and the British People* (London: Macmillan, 1986).
20 J. J. Becker, *The Great War and the French People* (Leamington Spa: Berg, 1985).
21 G. Hardach, *The First World War, 1914–1918* (London: Allen Lane, 1977); A. S. Milward, *War, Economy and Society, 1939–1945* (London: Allen Lane, 1977); A. S. Milward, *The Economic Effects of the Two World Wars on Britain* (2nd edn. London: Macmillan, 1984).
22 K. Burk (ed.), *War and the State: The Transformation of British Government, 1914–1918* (London: Allen & Unwin, 1982).
23 K. R. Grieves, *The Politics of Manpower, 1914–1918* (Manchester: Manchester University Press, 1988).
24 A. S. Milward, *The German Economy at War* (London: Athlone Press, 1965); R. J. Overy, *The Air War, 1939–1945* (London: Europa, 1980); R. J. Overy, *Goering: The Iron Man* (London: Routledge & Kegan Paul, 1984).
25 J. M. Blum, *V was for Victory* (New York: Harcourt Brace Jovanovich, 1976).
26 P. Summerfield, *Women Workers in the Second World War* (London: Croom Helm, 1984); G. Braybon, *Women Workers in the First World*

War (London: Croom Helm, 1981); A. Marwick, *Women at War, 1914–1918* (London: Croom Helm, 1977).
27   R. Bessel and D. Englander, 'Up from the trenches: some recent writing on the soldiers of the Great War', *European Studies Review*, vol. 1, no. 3, 1981, pp. 387–95.
28   T. Harrisson, *Living through the Blitz* (London: Collins, 1976).
29   T. C. Crosby, *The Impact of Civilian Evacuation in the Second World War* (London: Croom Helm, 1986); B. S. Johnson, *The Evacuees* (London: Gollancz, 1968).
30   I. F. W. Beckett and K. Simpson (eds), *A Nation in Arms: A Social Study of the British Army in the First World War* (Manchester: Manchester University Press, 1985).

Further reading: Chapter 1

Bond, Brian, *War and Society in Europe, 1870–1970* (London: Fontana, 1984).
Calvocoressi, Peter, and Wint, Guy, *Total War* (London: Allen Lane, 1972).
Feldman, G. D., *Army, Industry and Labor in Germany, 1914–1918* (Princeton, NJ: Princeton University Press, 1966).
Gooch, John, *Armies in Europe* (London: Routledge & Kegan Paul, 1979).
Howard, Michael, *War in European History* (Oxford: Oxford University Press, 1976).
Marwick, Arthur, *War and Social Change in the Twentieth Century* (London: Macmillan, 1974).
Polenberg, Richard, *War and Society: The United States, 1941–1945* (Philadelphia: Lippincott, 1972).
Smith, Harold L. (ed.) *War and Social Change* (Manchester: Manchester University Press, 1986).
Thorne, Christopher, *The Far Eastern War: State and Societies, 1941–1945* (London: Allen & Unwin, 2nd edn, 1986).
Wright, Gordon, *The Ordeal of Total War* (New York: Harper, 1968).

2

Colonial Warfare
1900–39

KEITH JEFFERY

Colonial warfare, which may crudely be described as conflict between white forces (or at least forces commanded by white men) and non-white groups,[1] can be divided into three distinct modes during the period from the turn of the century to the beginning of the Second World War. In the first place there were wars of conquest fought by imperial powers against indigenous forces in order to secure territory. The second mode, while also involving conquest, comprised what might be termed wars of competition in which European – or 'Western' – armies fought each other for colonies. Thirdly, there were wars of pacification or 'peacekeeping' operations of various descriptions.

In general, straightforward wars of conquest were less common during the period in question than hitherto, because by 1900 most of the world had already been partitioned among the Great Powers (and a few others). Apart from in South America, only a handful of states enjoyed political independence in what is now called the 'third world', and the autonomy of such countries as Ethiopia, Siam and Afghanistan was often precarious indeed. Yet perhaps the two most important colonial wars of the period fall into this first category: the South African War of 1899–1902, which the British fought against the Boer republics of the Transvaal and Orange Free State, and the Italian conquest of Ethiopia in 1935–36.

With the division of the world among the Great Powers already largely completed, it might be supposed that as particular states grew more powerful and others declined, competition between these powers might be intensified and colonial wars of the second type become more common. In fact, despite sometimes quite intense imperial rivalries, the Great Powers demonstrated considerable dexterity in avoiding direct conflict. Crises, such as Penjdeh (1885) where British expansion

24

collided with Russian, and Fashoda (1898) where the British and French met, were defused before open hostilities developed. Indeed, relations between the Great Powers during the militant, so-called 'new' imperialism of the late nineteenth century were marked more by conferences and international agreements than by warfare. The response of the Great Powers to the Boxer Rising in China in 1900 illustrates this point. Rather than individual powers using the opportunity of internal chaos to indulge in a scramble for territory, Britain, France, Germany, Russia and the USA (among others) actually co-operated to protect their combined interests in the region.

The only exclusively colonial war between great powers in the twentieth century concerned two minor imperial states, Italy and Turkey, which fought over Libya in 1911–12. During the First World War, however, in a series of 'sideshows', distant from the Western Front, forces of the Triple Entente (mostly from the British empire) occupied German colonies in Africa and the Pacific, while in the Middle East British and some French troops pushed back the borders of the Ottoman Empire with assistance from Arabs keen to throw off the yoke of Turkish rule.

It is, however, the third type of warfare – 'pacification' – which is most characteristic of the early twentieth century. After 1900 the nature of colonial warfare in general changed from being concerned primarily with conquest and the imposition of imperial rule to a more defensive mode involving the maintenance of imperial control and ensuring the security of imperial possessions, influence and even spheres of interest. The British experience between the turn of the century and 1939 aptly illustrates this. In 1900 the British were still involved in their last great burst of purely colonial territorial expansion. In 1939, however, the chief colonial commitment was in Palestine, where the British administration was trying to hold the territory (allegedly of considerable strategic significance) against open rebellion on the part of the Arabs and grumbling discontent among the Jews.

During the twentieth century there has also been a qualitative change in the nature of colonial opposition to imperial rule with the emergence of ideologically based mass movements. Hitherto, mass opposition had generally stemmed from religious movements. This continued in a number of cases, such as the Islamic-based resistance in West Africa during the First World War and the range of risings throughout the Muslim world following the war in Somaliland (1919), the Celebes (1919), the Moplah rebellion in India (1921) and the Basmatchi revolt in the USSR during the early 1920s. But the mass challenge was now enhanced by two further factors: nationalism and communism. Nationalist conflict emerged most clearly in Ireland (1916–21), Egypt (1919), Syria (1925–7) and the Philippines (1935). The common feature of each of these examples – and of India, where the nationalist movement was strongly influenced by Gandhi's doctrine of non-violence – is that they were sufficiently developed to sustain an educated middle class, who helped to provide the leadership for a liberation struggle. Here, too, we find the emergence of an urban dimension, which was to become very significant in colonial warfare after 1945. There were specifically communist-led risings in Java (1926–7) and Indo-China (1930–1), but communists were also assumed to be behind many other colonial disturbances. It was widely believed in the French army, for example, that the interwar unrest in North Africa, the Middle East and Indo-China were all part of a 'revolutionary chain' that threatened France and the French Empire.[2] The Soviet leader Grigory Zinoviev gave this view credence when at the First Congress of the Peoples of the East in Baku during September 1920 he called for a 'holy war' against imperialism.[3] These ideological challenges – an aspect of the 'modernization' of colonial warfare – prompted an emphasis more on the political and civil/police aspects of warfare than on classical military operations.

The French experience of colonial warfare

The most wide-ranging analysis of colonial warfare before the Second World War was conducted by the French, who developed a body of doctrine based on the experience and reflections of three prominent colonial commanders: Bugeaud, Galliéni and Lyautey. Beginning with the occupation of Algeria in the 1830s, and powerfully boosted after 1871, especially in West Africa, the French empire had expanded largely through military conquest. Soldiers, rather than traders or missionaries, were the agents of territorial acquisition. This naturally, had an effect on the nature of French colonial warfare. Marshal Thomas-Robert Bugeaud, who became Commander-in-Chief and Governor-General of Algeria in 1840, when frustrated by the Arabs' understandable reluctance to stand and fight in a pitched battle, sought to adapt the traditional North African technique of the *razzia* (raid) in order to cut off the Arab tribesmen from their supplies and livelihoods. In Douglas Porch's words, 'Bugeaud elevated the *razzia* to the level of total war'.[4] He employed a stringent scorched-earth policy, destroying villages, burning crops and cutting down trees. 'In Africa', wrote one contemporary French general, considering a problem common to much twentieth-century colonial warfare, 'how do you act against a population whose only link with the land is the pegs of their tents? . . . The only way is to take the grain which feeds them, the flocks which clothe them. For this reason, we make war on silos, war on cattle, the *razzia*.'[5]

The use merely of military force to subdue a territory and its inhabitants did not, however, serve the particular purposes of colonial warfare as it came to be understood by a later generation of French soldiers. Unlike conventional warfare, which aims at the destruction of an enemy, colonial warfare, as one French commentator asserted, aims 'at the organization of the conquered peoples and territory under a particular control'.[6] Thus it involves political, social and even economic action as well as military operations, and a balance must be struck between decisively defeating the adversary and securing the territory concerned in as good a condition as possible. Joseph-Simon Galliéni, while serving in West Africa and later in the Sudan, became disenchanted with the costly and destructive methods usually employed by the French army. After his appointment to command a frontier province in northern Indo-China in 1892 he began to develop a more subtle approach involving the progressive occupation of territory, combined with the establishment of markets and civil public works, such as wells or roads. In the face of criticisms that this approach was not directed (as it should have been) towards the complete and emphatic destruction of local opposition – characterized by the colonial administration as 'bandits' – Galliéni's superior, General Duchemin, defended the method by observing that one rarely if ever had the chance to destroy a gang of bandits as a group. But, and here Galliéni's methods have a strikingly modern aspect, Duchemin argued that the bandit was 'a plant which could only survive in particular soil' and the most certain way of eradicating banditry was to alter the soil.[7] The local inhabitants, upon whom the bandits relied, should be persuaded of the material (and presumably also moral) benefits of French rule.

Galliéni himself was able to implement his methods not only in Indo-China but also in Madagascar, after he was appointed Governor there in 1896. He clearly laid down that the best way to pacify the new colony was through 'the combined action of force and politics. We should remember that in colonial struggles we should not destroy except as a last resort, and, even in that case, we should only destroy in order to build better.' Assessing the relative importance of military and political action, Galliéni unequivocally asserted that 'political action is much the more important'. The 'true role' of the colonial officer, he maintained, was that of an administrator. Following the period of conquest, all that the soldiers would have to do in a military sense was colonial policing, a task which might in any case be performed better by special forces and professional police themselves.

Galliéni had an able and articulate champion in Hubert Lyautey, who had joined him in Indo-China in 1894 and accompanied him (as chief of staff) to Madagascar. In 1900 Lyautey, who had a reputation as a challenging – and troublesome – military thinker, published a celebrated and influential article on the 'Colonial role of the army' in the *Revue des Deux Mondes*. Quoting Galliéni (and Duchemin) approvingly, Lyautey elegantly and persuasively set out the case for a broad perspective to be taken with regard to colonial warfare, which he argued was simply part of a seamless robe of 'conquest, occupation, pacification'. Soldiers, indeed, must act also as administrators, policemen, even as 'overseers, workshop managers, teachers, gardeners, farmers'.[8] In 1917, reflecting on armed conflict in general, he maintained his belief that war in the colonies was not the mindlessly destructive activity currently being pursued in Europe. 'The magnificence and beauty of colonial war', he affirmed, 'is that on the very next day following the conflict it is the creator of life.'[9]

What Lyautey describes, of course, is not just colonial warfare, but colonial *conquest* and the establishment of a stable and secure colonial regime. We are struck by the clear good sense of his repeated emphasis on the fact that the colonial role of the soldier is not exclusively military. Yet it is a myth – certainly in the twentieth century – that any high-ranking soldier's task is ever exclusively military, but it is one that has been keenly sustained by both soldiers and their political masters. Soldiers like to see themselves as simply skilled professional technicians who can provide a specialized expertise in the service of the state. Theirs is literally 'not to reason why'. This kind of attitude suits governments admirably, and they generally connive with their military employees to maintain the fiction that the political and military functions can be kept distinct.

Lyautey challenged this assumption, and his apparently benign conception of France's colonial mission found favour in some political circles. Since he held out the possibility of trouble-free conquest combined with the establishment of an efficient, productive and contented colony, he was given the opportunity (unusual for a theorist) of putting his ideas into practice. Between 1903 and 1910 Lyautey served in Morocco and Algeria, where he was able to develop his ideas on progressive occupation. The establishment of a French protectorate over all Morocco proceeded only very gradually. 'It will advance', he wrote to Galliéni in 1903, 'not by columns, nor by mighty blows, but as a patch of oil spreads, through a step by step progression, playing alternately on all the local elements, utilizing the divisions and rivalries between tribes and between their chiefs.'[10] Lyautey sometimes characterized this strategy of the oil slick or *tache d'huile*, as being like shrapnel bursting from a single centre. This latter simile is perhaps the more suitable, for what is largely missing from Lyautey's cheerful vision of French colonial warfare is that basically the process was about domination and violent conquest.

Lyautey himself, though undoubtedly a thoughtful and humane man, and by no means the worst colonial governor – the climax of his career was his time as the first French resident general and commander in chief in Morocco from May 1912 to October 1925 – created a myth concerning colonial warfare that is at once too systematic, too benign and too romantic to accord with reality. His job in Morocco – like that of any other man in a similar position – was to secure the imperial power's interests in the country as unequivocally as possible Lyautey believed that French lives would be saved (both in the short and long term) only by extending colonial control gradually and by working through the existing local aristocracy. Owing to his 'genius' writes one historian, the conquest of Morocco 'did not lead to the killing of the native leaders, but to their incorporation in a reorganised structure of government'.[11] Lyautey certainly had to rein in the martial enthusiasm evinced by some of his subordinates, which in any case could lead to military disaster. In November 1914 a Colonel Laverdure mounted a surprise attack on Zaian tribesmen near Kenifra in the Middle Atlas, which resulted in the worst defeat suffered by the French in Morocco with thirty-three French officers and more than six hundred men being killed – a surprise indeed.

Yet, despite all his considerable political deftness and persuasiveness, ultimately even Lyautey depended on the use of force. As he

persuaded tribal leaders to submit to French protection, military posts
were established in the interior. Sometimes this actually provoked
violence, as with the uprising in eastern Morocco in 1908. But, in
any case, apparently the only effective way to bring recalcitrant
tribesmen to heel was by punitive military action. Indeed, Douglas
Porch maintains that 'the "Lyautey method" in practice boiled down
to a series of reprisal raids for damage inflicted; the dreadful *razzia*
was institutionalized and perpetuated'.[12] Lyautey, moreover, did not
leave Morocco pacified. A shadow was cast over the end of his time
as resident general by the outbreak of Abd el-Krim's Riff Rebellion
in 1925. Although the rebellion was undoubtedly encouraged by the
incompetence of the European administration in Spanish Morocco,
the wholesale defection of tribes in the French sector to Abd el-Krim's
side demonstrated Lyautey's failure to persuade significant numbers
of Moroccans of the virtues of French rule.

The so-called Riff war of 1925–26 and the continued pacification
of Morocco to the mid-1930s involved both the French and the
Spanish in major military operations. Lyautey's celebrated emphasis
on political and social methods was put to one side. The French
mobilized 160,000 troops, few of whom, it seems, spent much time as
workshop managers or gardeners. The campaign against Abd el-Krim
and that of 1931–34, which was conducted by pupils of Lyautey,
Generals Huré (the commander), Catroux and Giraud, depended
less on political action than on purely military techniques. Although
Catroux stressed that the goal of pacification was 'to transform the
dissidents into associates', the only persuasion initially employed was
that of complete military dominance. Large bodies of troops were
supplied from carefully prepared bases. The initial advance into the
mountainous rebel-held territory was by mobile auxiliary troops,
supported by artillery and air bombardment, and followed by formal
occupation by regular troops. The only essential 'public works' which
the troops provided were roads to ensure effective supply lines and
the efficient movement of mobilized units.[13]

The experience of General Gouraud, another of Lyautey's pupils,
demonstrates the extent to which Lyautey's 'method', if it existed
at all, did so only in the person of the veteran Marshal himself.
Gouraud, who had been closely associated with Lyautey in Morocco
before the First World War, was appointed high commissioner of
the former Turkish province of Syria in October 1919. The Syrians
did not welcome French suzerainty, even under a League of Nations

mandate, and in March 1920 the Second General Syrian Congress in Damascus proclaimed the independence and integrity of Greater Syria (including the Lebanon), as a constitutional monarchy under the Sharifian King Faisal. Under strong pressure from Paris to remove this challenge, Gouraud, who had seventy thousand effective troops under his command, moved against the Sharifians in July 1920 and with overwhelming force, including the use of aeroplanes, occupied Damascus and forced the Arab government to flee. Gouraud's administration thereafter, like that of his two successors, Weygand and Sarrail, was based on strict martial law with few concessions made to Syrian opinion or specifically 'political' action on the Lyautey model. Indeed, the insensitivity of the French administration in Syria and Lebanon provoked a number of minor revolts after 1920 and a major one in 1925, when the whole French position in the mandate seemed threatened. General Sarrail's response was draconian. In October 1925, after insurgents had infiltrated Damascus, Sarrail ordered the rebel-held districts to be bombarded by artillery and air continuously for nearly twenty-four hours. An estimated 5,000 Arabs were killed or wounded, with 137 French people killed and 500 neutrals killed or wounded. In the face of domestic and international outrage, Sarrail was recalled. The following May, however, his civilian successor, Henri de Jouvenel, also bombarded residential areas of Damascus, although this time after a warning had been given. In contrast to the Lyautey method, it was only after the soldiers had failed and been replaced in Syria by a civilian governor that any sort of political accommodation – or 'pacification' – was achieved.

Imperial policing: Britain and the United States

There was no British theorist comparable to Lyautey. British soldiers, largely uncontaminated by rationalism, tended to adopt a robustly pragmatic approach to colonial warfare. The British, of course, could draw on a very substantial body of experience – greater than any other colonial power – and their rather ad hoc attitude towards fighting colonial campaigns reflected its length and diversity. It also stemmed from the fact that most of the British experience was ultimately successful. There were, however, two Irish officers who addressed the problem of colonial warfare in general with a measure of official sanction: Major (later Major-General Sir) Charles Callwell and Major-General Sir Charles W. Gwynn. Callwell's volume *Small Wars*, which went through three editions between 1896 and 1906, was published by HM Stationery Office for the War Office General Staff. The Chief of the General Staff specifically recommended the third edition to army officers 'as a valuable contribution on the subject of the conduct of small wars', but he noted that the volume should not be regarded 'as an expression of official opinion'.[14] The lack of any official study of colonial warfare, indeed, was one of the reasons behind Gwynn's volume, *Imperial Policing*, published in 1934. Gwynn, who was Commandant of the Staff College from 1926 to 1930, found that there was no satisfactory publication which dealt with 'a subject which is of increasing importance'[15] and he devoted his time in retirement to writing the book, which was quickly adopted as a standard text in the Staff College.

Callwell's book is primarily a manual of tactics and good advice, which draws principally on Britain's nineteenth-century experience. Small wars are divided into three main classes: 'campaigns of conquest or annexation, campaigns for the suppression of insurrections or lawlessness or for the settlement of conquered or annexed territory, and campaigns undertaken to avenge a wrong, or to overthrow a dangerous enemy'. By the time Callwell wrote his study, however, only the second category was really of relevance for Britain. It was a type of conflict about which the author had few romantic illusions. 'As a general rule', he wrote, 'the quelling of rebellion in distant colonies means protracted, thankless, invertebrate war.' Callwell stressed the importance, in every type of small war, of commencing with an absolutely clear objective. In case of 'expeditions to put down revolt', he observed that these were 'not put in motion merely to bring about a temporary cessation of hostility. Their purpose is to ensure a lasting peace. Therefore, in choosing the objective, the overawing and not the exasperation of the enemy is the end to keep in view.' Later, Callwell adds that in pacification operations, 'the enemy must be chastised up to a point but should not be driven to desperation . . . Wholesale destruction of the property of the enemy may sometimes do more harm than good.'[16] Thus far Callwell and Lyautey are in agreement, for the establishment of a lasting peace clearly implies political as well as military action. But Callwell absolutely excludes any consideration of the political side of colonial warfare from his study.

Small Wars deals in considerable detail with tactical matters, but Callwell's most interesting observations concern guerrilla warfare and the general problem of bringing the enemy to battle. He warns special-ly against letting any campaign degenerate into 'desultory warfare', since for regular troops this is 'the most tedious and harassing form which hostilities can assume'. Yet the enemy will mostly try to avoid 'engagement in the open field' and commanders may have to tempt him to fight or draw him on 'by skilful dispositions'. But these options may not obtain and a colonial general will often have to cope as best he can with a variety of guerrilla warfare. Callwell proposed a combination of defensive posts and mobile columns in order to deal with a guerrilla warfare challenge. 'If possible', he wrote, 'the whole area of operations should be sub-divided into sections', which should each have defensive posts, supply depots and columns. 'The sections must be further parcelled out into convenient and well-defined areas for the purpose of clearing the country of the supplies which may be useful to the enemy.' While the fortified posts and depots could secure territory, Callwell maintained that 'the essence of operations against guerrillas is to be found in utilising the troops available as far as possible for mobile columns'. These units must be able to travel light and should be 'as small as possible consistent with safety'.

In the third edition, lessons from the recent South African War were drawn about guerrilla warfare. The initial British response to the guerrilla phase of the war – from the summer of 1900 onwards – was an elaborate system of flying columns. But Callwell dismissed these as 'only flying columns in the sense that they were self-contained as regards supplies'. They were in fact not very mobile at all, consisting mostly of infantry, heavy ox-waggons, and frequently also having artillery. 'Their movements were lethargic', commented Callwell. Their only virtue was the thoroughness with which they could clear the country of livestock and supplies, but they scarcely constituted any direct threat to the Boer guerrillas. Only when fully mounted – 'genuinely mobile' – columns were organized were the British able successfully to take on the Boer commandos.

Callwell also addressed himself to the difficult problem of reprisals. 'The adoption of guerrilla methods by the enemy', he realistically observed, 'almost necessarily forces the regular troops to resort to punitive measures directed against the possessions of their antago-nists.' But there was an objection in principle to carrying off cattle, destroying dwellings and so on. 'To filch the property of irregulars when they are absent', wrote Callwell sanctimoniously, 'is not the true spirit of waging war against such opponents; the proper way to deal with them is to kill them, or at least to hunt them from their homes and then to destroy or carry off their belongings.' British troops, however, maintained Callwell, 'have had practically no experience of such conditions'.[17] But here he ignored the guerrilla phase of the South African War, where Kitchener had systematically divided up the Boer land with lines of blockhouses and applied a scorched-earth policy, gathering the population into concentration camps, where twenty thousand Boer women and children died.

One of the things that clearly dates Callwell's book is his rather dismissive attitude towards guerrilla action, which, he observed, 'in fact, means almost of necessity petty annoyance rather than operations of a dramatic kind'.[18] In such circumstances, too, the regular forces could afford to adopt the kind of high-minded and humane approach favoured by Callwell. There is, moreover, no real suggestion that a colonial power might actually lose a guerrilla struggle, yet this possibility is precisely one of the chief differences between nineteenth- and twentieth-century colonial warfare. For the most part, Gwynn also glossed over some of the more distasteful aspects of colonial warfare, even though by 1934 the British had had considerable experience of guerrilla action. Gwynn himself 'thought it inadvisable to draw on experiences in Ireland, instructive from a military point of view as many of them are'.[19] While the case-studies he selected for the volume – including Amritsar and Egypt in 1919, the Moplah rebellion (1921), Palestine and the Burma Rebellion (1930–32) – illustrate the extent to which colonial warfare had effectively become 'imperial policing', he barely discusses the more punitive side of anti-guerrilla (or counter-insurgency) campaigning.

Gwynn provides a much more recognizably modern analysis of colonial warfare than Callwell and his opinions echo some of those propounded by the French school of thought, although he by no means waxes quite so lyrical about the need for soldiers themselves to take on civil functions. Four general principles of imperial policing were laid down by Gwynn. The first was 'that questions of policy remain vested in the civil Government and, even when the military authorities are in full executive control, the policy of the Government must be loyally carried out'.[20] This principle clearly expresses the traditional British constitutional position whereby the civil power is ultimately supreme. Yet in the colonial context, with scattered forces deployed in distant territories, such civil control was difficult to assert. Individual commanders often virtually had a free hand to conduct operations just as they chose. Twentieth-century improvements in communications, however, tended to restrict their freedom of action, by enabling both the colonial and the metropolitan civil administration to keep in closer touch than hitherto.

Both newspaper and, later, newsreel, reporters were also able to capitalize on technological advances. Press despatches from South Africa stimulated public demands at home to mitigate Kitchener's anti-guerrilla campaign, and newspaper coverage of the Anglo-Irish War of 1919–21, which particularly criticized the British reprisals policy, did much to undermine public support for a 'military' solution. Other colonial forces enjoyed a similar experience. Anti-imperialist sections of the American press keenly examined every allegation of atrocities in the Philippines in 1901–2, while Mussolini so acutely felt the international condemnation of the use of gas in Ethiopia in 1936 that he ordered Marshal Badoglio to execute any Europeans who had witnessed it.

Gwynn's second principle, 'that the amount of military force employed must be the minimum the situation demands', reflected both the political constraints under which colonial campaigning increasingly fell and the domestic British stance regarding military aid to the civil power. In 1911, after a series of fatalities during industrial disputes, the government law officers had laid down that troops called in to assist the police should only use 'such force as is reasonably necessary'.[21] In keeping with the climate of legality that characterized all of Britain's twentieth-century counter-insurgency campaigns, this guideline, which was never precisely defined, or tested in the courts, applied in all aspects of imperial policing. The dangers of breaching this principle were sharply and bloodily illustrated in the Amritsar massacre on 13 April 1919. After an outbreak of anti-British agitation in the Punjab, during which four Europeans died, the local commander, Brigadier-General Dyer, broke up a prohibited meeting of between ten and twenty thousand people by firing 1650 rounds of ammunition during a period of ten minutes. An estimated 379 Indians were killed and more than 1200 wounded. The political impact was tremendous and Anglo-Indian relations were soured as never before. Dyer was censured by an official enquiry and required to retire early. The affair and its aftermath left Britain's colonial military commanders in no doubt that their actions would be scrutinized closely and that exemplary force was to be applied very sparingly indeed.

Allied to the employment of minimum force was Gywnn's next principle, 'that of firm and timely action'. Although something of a platitude, this injunction inferred the need for good intelligence – another essential for all military operations. In the particular circumstances envisaged by Gwynn the acquisition of that intelligence was not just the army's responsibility, and it is clear from his last principle – 'co-operation' – that the army should work very closely indeed with the machinery and forces of the civil power. The ideal, perhaps, as under martial law, was unity of control, although this was something largely eschewed by the British. Most of Britain's colonial campaigns during the period in question, and since, have in fact been marked by incoherence and a frequently damaging confusion of civil and military responsibilities. In Ireland (1919–21), where in the end the war was lost, the division of responsibilities between the civil administration, the police and the military command was never properly sorted out. British practice, nevertheless, was generally to keep the civil and military leaderships separate. This contrasted with that of other colonial powers, where the appointment of a supremo or a military pro-consul, such as Marshal Lyautey, was favoured.

That Gwynn's book represented the army's collective wisdom regarding imperial peacekeeping is confirmed by a forty-one page War Office tactical manual, *Notes on Imperial Policing*, issued in the same year as Gwynn's volume. The main threat was perceived as a guerrilla challenge: 'The enemy, although possibly well armed, has usually no open and recognized military organization, and acts largely by subterranean methods, offering no opportunity of locating and defeating his forces by the ordinary methods of war.' What methods, then, might be employed? Disturbed areas could be controlled with cordons, particular areas in towns or villages might be raided, 'or isolated and searched', and 'terrorism may be countered by a policy of collective punishment, or in extreme cases reprisals may be undertaken'. Reprisals, however, should only be used sparingly and, since the general military object 'is to restore civil government, . . . no measures should be taken which would inflict needless indignities on the civil population, or lead to subsequent bitterness'. Due warning, moreover, should be given of reprisals, which 'must be regarded as a method of coercion, and not as a means of punishment or arbitrary vengeance, and their nature must not be excessive'.[22]

This policy, as outlined in *Notes on Imperial Policing*, almost seems civilized. But, by its very nature, any system of reprisals or 'collective punishments' could never be more than a crude response to the often incoherent (or 'invertebrate' as Callwell put it) challenge posed by colonial enemies. Beyond the simple need to conquer or subdue a territory as quickly and forcefully as possible, reprisals often stem from frustration, inadequate intelligence and an underlying sense on the part of the forces employing them even of the rightness and justice of their own cause. Operating in a very poor intelligence environment, the Crown forces in Ireland resorted to both official and unofficial reprisals.

Other colonial powers had similar experiences. The French used massive aerial bombardments in Morocco in reprisal for surprise attacks or ambushes. Frustration seems to have been the main factor behind US Marine abuses of combatants and civilians in the Dominican Republic between 1917 and 1922. A contemporary enquiry concluded that part of the problem lay in the troops' duties extending beyond a purely military role. 'The Marine Corps', it concluded, 'is intended to be a fighting body and we should not ask it to assume all sorts of civil and political responsibilities unless we develop within it a group of specially trained men.'[23] Air-borne reprisals were covered in the US Marines' *Small Wars Manual*, which, although warning that drastic punitive measures could 'create sympathy for the revolutionists . . . destroy lives and property of innocent people, and . . . have adverse effect on the discipline of our own troops', realistically allowed for the possibility of a commanding officer using some 'mild' form of reprisal to keep his troops from resorting to stronger methods. Marine pilots were advised to drop warning messages on the towns or villages concerned, allowing civilians time to get away.

The worry about frustrated soldiers overreacting in guerrilla warfare conditions was understandable, considering the problems encountered in the pacification of the Philippines in the early 1900s. Although parts of the pacification campaign, especially that conducted by General J. Franklin Bell in southern Luxon, were handled comparatively sensitively, terror tactics were also widely employed. They were 'usually the work of junior officers and enlisted men inspired by anger, boredom, and racial animosity, and freed by the nature of the war from close supervision by their superiors'. The nature of the war, too, apparently freed troops from adhering closely to the normal laws of war. In December 1900 General Arthur MacArthur proclaimed that, since guerrilla warfare was against 'the customs and usages of war', those participating in it 'divest themselves of the character of soldiers, and if captured are not entitled to the privileges of prisoners of war'. On 28 September 1901, in the town of Balangiga on Samar Island, a breakfast mess line of unarmed American infantrymen was attacked without warning by Philippine *insurrectos*. Forty-five Americans were killed and eleven wounded. Their commander, General Jacob ('Hell-Roaring Jake') Smith responded by ordering his troops to 'kill and burn' and turn Samar into 'a howling wilderness', which they went some way towards doing.

The Marine Corps' *Small Wars Manual*, first issued in 1935, drew on experience in the Philippines, the Caribbean and Central America. The revised edition of 1940 provides a guide to the subject that combines aspects of French and British doctrine. Compiled by Major Harold H. Utley, who had commanded Marines in Eastern Nicaragua, the *Manual* noted that from an American point of view small wars were 'conceived in uncertainty . . . conducted often with precarious responsibility and doubtful authority, under indeterminate orders lacking specific instructions'. This meant that considerable responsibility fell upon individual commanders, who had the duty of maintaining the essentially 'friendly' (*sic*) nature of American involvement. Five phases of intervention were envisaged. The first two phases comprised the arrival of American forces and their deployment in field operations. In this second stage, while the Marines were securing their control over the host country, it was essential to establish a native army or constabulary, which, in the third phase of intervention, would co-operate with the American forces in pacifying the country and which would eventually take over responsibility for peacekeeping. In the fourth stage, the American forces would play an overtly political role by ensuring that 'free and fair' elections could take place, supervised by an American Electoral Mission, which, if necessary, might provide 'emphatic instruction' to guide candidates, voters and the electoral process as a whole. The final phase was marked by the withdrawal of the Marines.

The *Manual* emphasized the difference between colonial conflict of this sort and conventional war. Like Lyautey, the authors noted that military and political action continued simultaneously and they recommended that the culture and history of the host country should be thoroughly studied. Special care, too, should be taken to handle the civilian population sensitively. Like Gwynn, the writers of the *Manual* accepted that maximum force was to be avoided, since violence alone might alienate the host population. In addition, domestic American political opinion – which was usually opposed to overseas interventions – had to be taken into account. The 428-page 1940 *Small Wars Manual*, an admirable guide to 'state of the art' counter-insurgency doctrines, had no impact at all on practice. American concern with 'small wars' was swept away after Pearl Harbor and the successor in 1949 to the 1940 *Manual* was only a ten-page pamphlet.

Variations on a theme:
the Soviet Union, Spain, Portugal and Germany

In the early part of the twentieth century armies did not devote much time to reflecting about colonial warfare. The syllabuses of military academies and staff colleges were understandably dominated by the study of conventional war. As in the American case, such work as was done on colonial conflict frequently came as a response to actual campaigns. In Soviet Russia, for example, Marshal Tukhachevsky published a series of articles in 1926 that drew on experience both during the civil war and in the establishment of Soviet control in Central Asia, especially against Muslim Basmatchi partisans. Tukhachevsky argued that military operations had to be co-ordinated with political and economic action. He also noted that the suppression of insurgency often took quite a long time. This was certainly so with the Basmatchis. Although the main force of the Bashmatchi rebellion had been broken by 1923, sporadic fighting continued until 1928 in the mountains of southern Bukhara and until the mid-1930s in the Turkmen steppes.[24]

Despite (or perhaps because of) their dismal military record in Latin America and the Philippines, the Spanish were slow to develop any colonial warfare doctrine. Although it became increasingly likely that Spanish troops (who from 1907 were securing the protectorate in Morocco) would clash with the local tribes, there was apparently no planning for this contingency. After stiff fighting in 1910–11, the general staff prepared 'a sort of manual dealing with the techniques of irregular warfare', but this and other staff work was widely ignored by combat officers who preferred to rely simply on *cojones* ('guts' – literally testicles).

Even when a soldier who had thought about the problem was put in charge, it proved difficult to reconcile theory and practice. In 1919

Major-General Dámaso Berenguer was appointed High Commissioner in Morocco, with instructions to bring the whole protectorate under full Spanish control. The general had served in previous North African campaigns and had actually published a short book on military tactics in Morocco, in which he advocated proceeding through short, well-planned advances and emphasized the importance of political and diplomatic action. Berenguer, however, was continually pressed by Madrid to act with boldness and vigour. He also had problems with the military governor of Melilla, Major-General Fernández Silvestre, who was theoretically his subordinate but had seniority as a general and had once been Berenguer's own commanding officer. Berenguer, therefore, did not interfere when, in May 1921, Silvestre launched a push into the Riff mountains in the west of the territory in order to subdue the Berber leader, Abd el-Krim. But Silvestre over-extended himself and in July his demoralized and ill-equipped troops were forced to withdraw from the advanced Spanish bases at Igueriben and Annual in the Riff. The retreat quickly turned into a panic-stricken rout, which Abd el-Krim fully exploited. The disaster cost the Spanish more them 8000 dead (including Silvestre, who apparently committed suicide) and it brought down the government in Madrid. But Abd el-Krim's growing ambitions in Morocco brought the French and Spanish together against him, and he was obliged to surrender in May 1926. The pacification of Morocco, however, dragged on into the 1930s.

Theory also diverged from practice in the Portuguese empire. Henrique de Paiva Couceiro, who has been compared to Galliéni, Lyautey and Lugard, had a carefully worked out pacification strategy for the Dembos and Kongo regions of northern Angola during his time as governor of the colony from June 1907 to June 1909. By his own account, his campaign had five main objectives: the establishment of military garrisons, road building, the building up of political contacts with local leaders, missionary work and agricultural development. But in practice, like Lyautey, his actual method boiled down to not much more than a series of raiding expeditions which he called 'flying police columns'. As they penetrated into the interior, however, they tended to provoke resistance. By 1913 there was widespread revolt in the Kongo, which was not put down until January 1916. The typical style of Portuguese colonial warfare differed little from that of other European powers. In the north of Angola, for example, Captain Eugenio Ribeiro de Almeida with sixty troops subdued the Dembos region in 1918 at a cost of only six soldiers wounded. In four weeks, however, his small force used up thirty-four thousand cartridges.[25]

The German general staff, as might be expected, systematically analysed their overseas military experiences. In particular they studied those of the troops sent to China in 1900–01 as part of the international force formed to suppress the Boxer Rebellion. These soldiers had loyally followed the Kaiser's exhortation as they left Hamburg to behave 'like the Huns under King Attila'. The general staff's studies of colonial warfare were modelled on the punitive style set in China. In the words of one historian, these studies were 'singularly crude. Extreme violence, gruesome reprisals and racialist arrogance were the *leitmotivs* of the general staff's orders and regulations on the subject.'[26]

The evidence, however, provided by German involvement in colonial warfare is mixed and not, on the whole, much worse than that of other European powers. German soldiers certainly acted with extreme severity during the Hereros and Hottentot revolts in South West Africa (1904–7) and the Maji-Maji rebellion in Tanganyika (1905–7). During the latter an estimated 75,000 Africans died (from a community of one million), while in South West Africa more than 60,000 Hereros (out of a total of 80,000) perished, and half of the 20,000 Hottentots. In each of these cases most of the victims suffered from famine and disease and only a small proportion died in battle.

Even during the Hereros revolt German policy was not uniformly brutal. The Governor at the start of the revolt, Major Theodor Leutwein, having been ordered by Berlin that he enforce unconditional surrender on the rebels, argued that the longer-term needs of colonial development demanded that the Hereros be treated with some subtlety. 'The rebels must know that a line of retreat is open to them which does not in every case lead to death', he wrote. 'Otherwise we will drive them to desperation and the war will end in a fashion which will be to our disadvantage.' He felt that if the rebels had nothing to lose, they would fight to the bitter end. The annihilation of the tribesmen, he added, would be 'an economic error. We need the Hereros as herdsmen and workers.' The government in Berlin, however, continued to take a very strong line, urging particularly that Leutwein seek to bring the Hereros to open battle, where the superior German firepower would be decisive. But in March and April 1904 the Hereros, fighting on their own ground and guided by the tactical acumen of their leader, Samuel Maherero, avoided pitched battle and inflicted a number of defeats on the Germans. Berlin responded by appointing a new military commander, General Lothar von Trotha, who announced that his policy would be 'to use force with terrorism and even brutality'. Maherero, overconfident, perhaps, after his early successes, allowed himself to be drawn into battle, and be defeated, at Waterberg on 11 August. German artillery took a terrible toll of the fifty thousand massed Herero followers and their cattle, and the survivors were driven off into the Kalahari desert. Trotha followed this victory up with his famous *Schrecklichkeit* ('frightfulness') order of 2 October 1904 in which he vowed to kill every Herero male in the colony and expel all Herero women and children. This was a little strong even for Berlin, and Trotha was obliged to modify the policy. Those Hereros who surrendered would not be shot but branded with the letters GH – *gefangene* (captive) *Herero* – and put to forced labour.

Trotha's policy of extermination, the *Vernichtungsstrategie*, had an unanticipated result in that it appears actually to have provoked the Hottentot rising, which erupted in October 1904. The Hottentots proved more difficult to pacify. Although fewer in number, unlike the Hereros they declined to stand and fight and the Germans at first had difficulty in coping with the guerrilla challenge. Despite proclaiming that the Hottentots would suffer the same fate as the Hereros, Trotha and his 15,000 German regulars proved unable to cope with an elusive enemy who never numbered more than 1500. Only after Trotha had been sacked did the new commander, Colonel von Diemling, bring the rebels to heel by systematically cutting off their supplies and establishing a series of 'flying squads' at fortified posts in the south of the colony, who harried Hottentot bands driven to the offensive in search of food.[27]

In many ways the Germans' most successful involvement with colonial warfare occurred during the First World War in East Africa. Despite the legacy of repression that followed the Maji-Maji rising, the local German commander, Paul von Lettow-Vorbeck, with a predominantly African force, held out against a vastly larger British army throughout the war. Von Lettow-Vorbeck developed a classic guerrilla campaign based on small units, high mobility and good local intelligence, which, perhaps, demonstrated ways in which weaker powers could fight stronger ones. The lesson was certainly learnt by Arabs in the guerrilla campaign sponsored by the British against the Turks in Arabia from 1916 onwards. The irony of these wartime campaigns was that imperial powers themselves – or their agents such as Lettow-Vorbeck or T. E. Lawrence – developed techniques that would later be used against them by anti-colonical forces.

The impact of technology

The tremendous boost given to military technology by the First World War was inevitably felt in the colonial sphere. Before 1914, colonial military engagements broadly fell into two categories. In the first place, massed indigenous armies took on generally smaller units of colonial troops in set-piece battles. The second category comprised formally organized colonial forces trying to deal with more mobile and elusive bands of warriors, whose familiarity with the terrain and superior ability to live off the land made them very difficult to pin down. This kind of guerrilla, or insurgency, warfare (although in the nineteenth century it was rarely sufficiently coherent to be fully described thus) became increasingly characteristic of colonial campaigns, so that in the twentieth century 'colonial warfare' has become almost synonymous with guerrilla warfare or insurgency. The move away from pitched battle was principally due to technological advances in weaponry, which shifted what might be described as the 'terms of firepower' decisively in favour of colonial forces. Breech-loading rifles, improved explosives – the British-developed cordite, for example, was a particularly stable compound suited for use in tropical extremes of climate – and, above all, machine guns were especially decisive from the late nineteenth century onwards. At Omdurman in September 1898, for example, Maxim guns, high velocity artillery shells and dum-dum bullets (another British advance for use in the empire) sustained Kitchener's famous victory in which he lost forty-eight men dead as against between ten and twelve thousand dervishes. As Hilaire Belloc's Captain Blood wisely remarked: 'Whatever happens we have got / The Maxim Gun, and they have not'.

By the First World War, the imperial powers had even more than the Maxim gun. In terms of colonial warfare the single most significant technological development was that of air power. The enhancement of speed and mobility provided by aeroplanes gave colonial administrations an edge in punitive power that could scarcely be matched by indigenous peoples. Anti-colonial fighters might be able to acquire modern rifles and even machine guns, but aeroplanes were out of the question: they were expensive, difficult to purchase and required considerable technical support to keep them flying. Constraints such as these proved too great even for Abd el-Krim, the first guerrilla leader in history to possess aircraft of his own, whose 'Air Force of the Riff' was still-born. The first actual employment of war-planes, indeed, occurred in a colonial conflict, during the Italian-Turkish war of 1911–12, when planes were used for reconnaissance and bombing raids. Before 1914 both the Spanish and the French also used planes during operations in Morocco. During the First World War, aircraft were employed both in Egypt and during the campaigns for the German colonies, but it was not until after 1918 that they really came into their own in colonial warfare and imperial policing.

The British made substantial use of air power, in frontier war, internal rebellion and smaller-scale police operations. In many quarters the aeroplane was seen as the panacea for Britain's postwar imperial security problems: cheap, efficient, modern. Using planes, too, made the whole unpleasant procedure more surgical and scientific. Here colonial warfare reflected wider developments in that technicians, usually at some distance from the killing, became increasingly important. In March 1919 'aeroplanes performed very useful service' in quelling nationalist unrest in Egypt, and after the Afghan War of 1919 it was reported that the bombing of Kabul had been an important factor 'in producing a desire for peace at the headquarters of the Afghan Government'. The most important early use of aircraft, however, was in Somaliland in operations against the so-called 'Mad Mullah', Sayyid Mohamed Abdile Hasan, who had been a thorn in the side of the colonial administration for two decades. In the late autumn of 1919 a mixed force comprising the Somaliland Camel Corps, a battalion of African infantry and light bombers of the Royal Air Force's 'Z' Unit commenced operations and in a matter of weeks had dispersed the Somali dervishes.

The most extensive British use of air power between the wars was in the Middle East, where the RAF assumed primary responsibility for security in Iraq, Trans-Jordan and Aden. In the Middle East a technique of 'air blockade' was developed, which depended for its effectiveness on excluding recalcitrant groups from their settlements. A 1936 RAF memorandum on air policing argued that, if rebellious tribes could be prevented from occupying their homes, they would 'have no option but to submit'. This technique appears to have had some success, and certainly allowed the government to save money by reducing regular army garrisons in the territories concerned. The RAF, however, could not wholly dispense with ground forces and found it necessary to recruit gendarmerie units. In Aden, for example, the Aden Protectorate Levies were raised in 1928 to replace the last resident battalion of British troops. The use of air policing also required the establishment and maintenance of ground installations, especially in the early days when the range of aircraft was limited. In Aden this obliged the British to build a multiplicity of landing grounds throughout the Protectorate, which, although primitive, in turn constituted a static defence commitment. The flexibility and mobility of air power, therefore, was not quite total. This fact was remarked on by General Niessel in an account of air power in French Morocco in the 1920s. The utility of aircraft in remote districts where they were most needed, he said, was limited by the difficulty of establishing and maintaining ground installations such as repair shops. Yet the French used aircraft as extensively as the British. They assisted ground forces during the Druze rising in Syria in 1925 and were employed to bomb communist-held villages in northern Vietnam in 1930.

Air bombardment raised criticism on the humanitarian grounds that innocent civilians might suffer. British politicians and officials often worried about the political impact of unrestricted air bombardment. In Peshawar (India) in 1930 the Royal Air Force was restricted in effectiveness by the government's insistence that it only attack identified bands of Afridi tribesmen 'instead of bombing villages which might have made the tribesmen see reason at an early stage'. In Palestine in 1936 aircraft were not allowed to bomb 'within five hundred yards of a dwelling or village' and no bombs heavier than twenty-five pounds were permitted 'without special and prior permission'. In 1929–30 US planes operating against Sandinisto insurgents in Nicaragua were instructed not to risk civilian casualties. They could not, therefore, bomb the guerrillas out of the villages. It was 'an enormous frustration for the pilots'. On the other hand, there are reports of United States Marine pilots in the Caribbean refusing to bomb for fear of hitting civilians. But, however frightful air bombardment might seem to be, there was reluctance to prohibit its use. When the question came up at the 1932 Geneva Disarmament Conference, Britain refused to give up 'the use of such machines as are necessary for police purposes in outlying places'. Other countries, Lloyd George told Frances Stevenson, 'would have agreed not to use aeroplanes for bombing purposes, but we insisted on reserving the right to bomb niggers!'[28]

The greatest humanitarian concern was stimulated by the combination of air power with another First World War advance, gas, during the Italo-Ethiopian War of 1935–6. The Italian invasion, launched in October 1935, was held up by unexpectedly stout resistance and, in order to repulse an Ethiopian counter-offensive in December, the Italian commander Marshal Badoglio ordered the use of poison gas. Eventually, at the beginning of January, the Ethiopian advance was halted at the river Takaze where small groups of Italian aircraft saturated the river crossings with mustard gas. Throughout the war gas was widely used. In early March 1936 the Italians' perfected gas tactics were employed to destroy the army of Ras Imru, the most able Ethiopian general. The enemy's line of retreat was channelled by the action of Italian bombers, which saturated the countryside with persistent mustard gas. Forage was sprayed to poison pack animals. Fords across rivers were particularly singled out for treatment, and as the Ethiopians crossed at one point they were saturated in a great cloud of phosgene, chlorine and mustard gas, through which the Italians shelled them with high explosive. The immediate surroundings were set on fire with incendiaries and the defeated Africans were forced to flee under continuous bombardment. Such were the benefits of scientific warfare. Badoglio's tactic of massive bombardment followed by infantry attacks echoed that employed in the trench warfare of 1914–18; indeed, earlier in the campaign the War Under-Secretary, Baistrocchi, had criticized the Marshal for relying on outdated methods, rather than exploiting the mobility and manoeuvrability of his mechanized and airborne forces.

The Italians were not the only imperial power to use gas. Ironically, the humanitarian argument had been employed by Winston Churchill in 1919 in order to support its use. Addressing himself to 'the use of gas against natives', he asserted that it was 'a more merciful weapon than high explosive shell, and compels an enemy to accept a decision with less loss of life than any other agency of war. The moral effect', he added, 'is also very great.' Despite Churchill's powerful advocacy, the government refused to allow the army to use gas on the North-West Frontier. The argument of the Secretary for India, that such an action would have 'very serious political and moral consequences', seems to have convinced the Cabinet against the proposal. The British army, nevertheless, did use a considerable quantity of SK gas shells against Arab insurgents during the Mesopotamian rebellion in 1920. In Morocco, both the Spanish and the French were alleged to have used gas during the Riff War in 1925.[29]

The scientific and technological developments of warfare, especially during the First World War, contributed substantially to the destructive power that European – and American – armies could bring to bear in colonial conflicts. These developments, of course, were not confined just to aircraft and gas. Mechanization in general enhanced the mobility of units, and it is difficult to underestimate the importance of wireless in improving military communications. But technological developments on their own did not always guarantee success. This lesson should have been learnt in the nineteenth century – Little Bighorn, Isandhlwana, Adowa – yet the twentieth century also saw its share of such disasters. Apart from the greatest of these, the French defeat at Kenifra in 1914 and the Spanish rout at Annual in 1921, the Portuguese in southern Angola suffered what has been extravagantly described as 'a second Adowa' in 1904 when Ovambo tribesmen killed 137 European troops and 168 African.[30] The Portuguese also suffered a serious rising in Mozambique in 1917, which was not finally subdued for three years. The newly-occupied Italian colony of Libya rose in revolt in 1914 and the Italians were driven back to the coast at a cost of five thousand casualties. The colony was not finally reconquered until 1931. And in the initial stages of the Hereros Rising, the Germans found that technological superiority actually acted as a constraint: their army's dependence on railways for reinforcements and supplies seriously compromised its mobility.

Conclusion

On the whole, colonial warfare during the first four decades of the twentieth century developed in line with conventional conflict, in that it became more technologically based, more 'total' and less 'winnable'. Even though technological superiority carried the Italians through in Ethiopia, in general purely military strategies no longer seemed sufficient. There were signs in the years before the outbreak of the Second World War that imperial armies might find colonial warfare increasingly tough going. The emergence of guerrilla warfare – especially of the urban variety, first in Ireland and subsequently in

Palestine in the 1930s – was a harbinger of future colonial conflict. The growing coherence of colonial resistance movements and their ideological underpinning, be it nationalist or communist (or both), also posed a greater challenge than hitherto. Once the new methods and the new ideologies became fused, moreover, western armies might never again be able to depend on winning a colonial war.

Notes: Chapter 2

1   There are only two exceptions to this rule during the period in question: the Anglo-Irish War (1919–21) and the Japanese aggression in east Asia in the 1930s.
2   Paul-Marie de la Gorce, *The French Army, a Military-Political History* (London: Weidenfeld & Nicolson, 1963), p. 215.
3   E. H. Carr, *The Bolshevik Revolution 1917–23*, Vol. 3 (Harmondsworth: Penguin, 1966) pp. 262–3.
4   Douglas Porch, 'Bugeaud, Galliéni, Lyautey: the development of French colonial warfare', in Peter Paret (ed.), *Makers of Modern Strategy, from Machiavelli to the Nuclear Age* (Oxford: Clarendon Press, 1986), p. 380. This essay by Porch (pp. 376–407 in the Paret volume) and Jean Gottman, 'Bugeaud, Galliéni, Lyautey: the development of French colonial warfare', in E. M. Earle (ed.), *Makers of Modern Strategy* (Princeton, NJ: Princeton University Press, 1943), pp. 234–59, are the two main analyses of French colonial warfare doctrine.
5   Porch, 'Bugeaud, Galliéni, Lyautey', p. 380.
6   Gottman, 'Bugeaud, Galliéni, Lyautey', p. 234.
7   Report (1895) from Général Duchemin to Général Rousseau, governor-general of Indo-China, quoted in Lieutenant-Colonel [Hubert] Lyautey, 'Du rôle colonial de l'armée', *Revue des Deux Mondes*, January 1900, p. 313.
8   'Fundamental instructions of General Galliéni' 22 May 1898, quoted in *Revue des Deux Mondes*, January 1900, pp. 316, 318.
9   Quoted in Robin Bidwell, *Morocco under Colonial Rule: French Administration of Tribal Areas 1912–1956* (London: Frank Cass, 1973) p. 13.
10 Gottman, 'Bugeaud, Galliéni, Lyautey', p. 248.
11 Bidwell, *Morocco under Colonial Rule*, p. 1.
12 Porch, 'Bugeaud, Galliéni, Lyautey,' p. 393.
13 Gottman, 'Bugeaud, Galliéni, Lyautey,' pp. 253–4. See also G. Ward Price, *In Morocco with the Legion* (London: Jarrolds, 1934).
14 Col. C. E. Callwell, *Small Wars. Their Principles and Practice* (London: HMSO, 3rd edn, 1906), p. 4.
15 Major-General Sir Charles W. Gwynn, *Imperial Policing* (London: Macmillan, 2nd edn, 1939), p. 1.
16 Callwell, *Small Wars*, pp. 27, 41–2, 147, 149.
17 ibid., pp. 97, 106, 130–1, 134, 136, 139–40, 145–6.

18 ibid., p. 127.
19 Gwynn, *Imperial Policing*, p. 8. As a grandson of the Irish Nationalist leader William Smith O'Brien, Gwynn was well aware of the passions that could be aroused by discussing Irish affairs.
20 ibid., p. 13.
21 Keith Jeffrey, 'Military Aid to the civil power in the United Kingdom – an historical perspective', in Peter J. Rowe and Christopher J. Whelan (eds) *Military Intervention in Democratic Societies* (London: Croom Helm, 1985), p. 53.
22 *Notes on Imperial Policing, 1934* (London: War Office, 1934) pp. 10–12, 40.
23 Bruce J. Calder, 'Caudillos and *Gavilleros* versus the United States Marines: guerrilla insurgency during the Dominican Intervention, 1916–24', *Hispanic American Historical Review*, vol. 58, no. 4 (1978), pp. 662–9; and Allan R. Millett, *Semper Fidelis: the History of the United States Marine Corps* (New York and London: Macmillan–Collier, 1980), p. 204.
24 For the Soviet experience of insurgency, see Walter Laqueur, *Guerrilla: A Historical and Critical Study* (London: Weidenfeld and Nicolson, 1977), pp. 160–5.
25 For the Spanish experience, see Stanley G. Payne, *Politics and the Military in Modern Spain* (Stanford, Calif.: Stanford University Press, 1967); for the Portuguese, see René Pélissier, *Les Guerres Grises: Résistance et Révoltes en Angola* (1845–1941) (Orgeval, France; Pelissier, 1977) and Malyn Newitt, *Portugal in Africa: The Last Hundred Years* (London: C. Hurst, 1981).
26 Martin Kitchen, *A Military History of Germany from the Eighteenth Century to the Present Day* (London: Weidenfeld and Nicolson, 1975), p. 179.
27 See Ion M. Bridgeman, *The Revolt of the Hereros* (Berkeley, Calif.: University of California Press, 1981). L. H. Gann and Peter Duigan, *The Rulers of German Africa 1884–1914* (Stanford, Calif.: Stanford University Press 1977), pp. 104–30, and Helmuth Stoecker, *German Imperialism in Africa* (London: C. Hurst, 1986), pp. 39–113, also cover German colonial conflict.
28 For the use of airpower in colonial campaigns, see Charles Townsend, 'Civilisation and "frightfulness": air control in the Middle East between the wars', in Chris Wrigley (ed.) *Warfare, Diplomacy and Politics: Essays in Honour of A. J. P. Taylor* (London: Hamish Hamilton, 1986); Général A. Niessel, 'Rôle militaire de l'aviation au Maroc', *La Revue de Paris*, vol. 33 (February 1926), pp. 508–32.
29 The use of gas in colonial campaigns is covered in Edward M. Spiers, *Chemical Warfare* (London: Macmillan, 1986).
30 Pélissier, *Les Guerres Grises*, pp. 451–2.

Further reading: Chapter 2

Beckett, Ian F. W. (ed.), *The Roots of Counter-Insurgency* (Poole: Blandford Press, 1988).
Bridgeman, Jon M., *The Revolt of the Hereros* (Berkeley, Calif.: University of California Press, 1981).
Callwell, Colonel C. E., *Small Wars. Their Principles and Practice* (London: HMSO, 1906).
Gottman, Jean, 'Bugeaud, Galliéni, Lyautey: the development of French colonial warfare', in Edward Mead Earle (ed.), *Makers of Modern Strategy* (Princeton, NJ: Princeton University Press, 1943), pp. 234–59.
Gwynn, Major General Sir Charles W, *Imperial Policing* (London: Macmillan, 1939).
Jeffery, Keith, *The British Army and the Crisis of Empire, 1918–22* (Manchester: Manchester University Press, 1984)
Kiernan, V. G., *European Empires from Conquest to Collapse* (London: Fontana, 1982).
Millett, Allan R., *Semper Fidelis: the History of the United States Marine Corps* (New York and London, Macmillan–Collier, 1980).
Porch, Douglas, 'Bugeaud, Galliéni, Lyautey: the development of French colonial warfare', in Peter Paret (ed.), *Makers of Modern Strategy from Machiavelli to the Nuclear Age* (Oxford: Clarendon Press, 1986), pp. 376–407.

3

Blitzkrieg and Attrition: Land Operations in Europe 1914–45

G. D. SHEFFIELD

Traditionally, the European wars of 1914–18 and 1939–45 have been seen as representing two very different styles of war. The First World War was characterized by attrition, whereby circumstances dictated that attempts to defeat the enemy by manoeuvre were replaced by crude frontal assaults designed to physically destroy the opposing force. Technological developments and superior generalship, according to this view, allowed this crude and wasteful strategy to be replaced by one of manoeuvre during the Second World War. So deeply held is this belief that world wars represent two distinct types of war and eras of generalship that the official biographer of Field-Marshal Montgomery regarded it as a slur upon his subject that the undeniably attritional battle of Alamein should be seen as being 'in the mould of World War One'.[1] This chapter argues that this interpretation is misguided and that continuity, not change, was the hallmark of warfare at the tactical and operational levels during the period under examination, and further that it was the First World War, not the Second, that was the main period of innovation.

1914 – The end of mobility

The Boer War of 1899–1902 and the Russo-Japanese War of 1904–5, and even earlier conflicts such as the US Civil War (1861–5), demonstrated the destructive power of modern weapons and the strength of the defence. Although de Bloch, a civilian theorist, concluded from the evidence of these wars that future war would inevitably end in deadlock, many soldiers of all nations were convinced that

51

the offensive could still succeed. If high morale and the spirit of the offensive could be inculcated, even the conscripts of mass armies (which had been made possible by administrative, technological and social advances in the nineteenth century) could be made to cross the 'zone of death' and close with the enemy, although casualties would be heavy. Dense Napoleonic formations were abandoned in favour of looser skirmish screens, with the emphasis being placed on firepower rather than shock action. The French doctrine of the offensive *à outrance* was simply an extreme version of an approach that was common to most European armies. This theory, as propounded by Foch and Grandmaison, was based on a simplistic interpretation of Clausewitz, stressing the primacy of the offensive. As anticipated, this led to heavy losses in the encounter battles of August 1914, but on a strategic level the much criticized Plan XVII did have some virtues. Plan XVII failed to bring victory not because it committed the French army to the offensive, but because of its execution.[2]

The German version of the offensive fared little better in 1914. The Schlieffen plan was the product of Germany's geo-strategic position. Faced with a war on two fronts, the bulk of the German forces were to defeat France in a six-week campaign before using Germany's strategic railways to rush troops east to oppose France's ally, Russia, which was notoriously slow to mobilize. The Schlieffen Plan, which was named after the German Chief of Staff from 1891 to 1906, was a classic example of a *Kesselschlacht* (literally a 'cauldron battle', or battle of encirclement). It was an extension of German tactical theory, which sought to avoid the frontal assault. Seven armies were deployed in the west. An immensely strong right flank was to wheel through neutral Belgium to avoid the French defences along the common frontier; the right wing would then pass to the west of Paris and encircle the French armies. This plan broke down partly because it was over-ambitious, and partly because the tip of the right flank swung east, and not west, of Paris. This exposed the German flank to a counterstroke, which led to the German defeat on the Marne. There followed a last spasm of the war of movement, but by November lines of trenches stretched across the entire battle front. Far from being a war decided by a swift offensive, the defensive had proved dominant and a continuous front had come into being.

Thus by the end of 1914 a strategy of frontal assault and one of manoeuvre had both proved unsuccessful. Temporarily, the operational art of manoeuvre was put into suspended animation as the generals grappled with the unfamiliar problems of siege warfare. The German attempt to break the impasse by frontal assault at the First Battle of Ypres (October–November 1914) was repulsed with perhaps 100,000 casualties. The French offensive in Champagne in February 1915 cost the French about 240,000 men. This was to be the pattern of warfare on the Western Front. Attacking armies would incur huge losses for gains that could usually be measured in yards, or a few miles at the most. A decisive breakthrough, leading to the resumption of mobile warfare, was not achieved until March 1918.

Deadlock 1914–18

The Anglo-American view of the First World War is largely coloured by a folk memory of 1 July 1916, the bloodiest single day in British military history. On that day, Rawlinson's Fourth Army attacked on the Somme and suffered 57,000 casualties, 20,000 of which were fatal, for very little territorial gain. This action has given the impression that most infantry attacks on the Western Front suffered the fate of being similarly cut to pieces by machine gun and artillery fire in front of the enemy wire. In fact, throughout the war, infantry experienced relatively little difficulty in penetrating enemy positions when supported only by artillery. Even on the atypical 'First Day on the Somme', the British 18th and 30th Divisions and neighbouring French formations succeeded in taking all their objectives. The difficulty lay not in 'breaking-in' to enemy positions, but in 'breaking-out' or exploiting initial success.

The French assault on Vimy Ridge on 9 May 1915 admirably illustrates this problem. After a thorough artillery preparation, Pétain's XXXIII Corps succeeded in advancing 2.5 miles into the German lines in one and a half hours. Had reserves been immediately available to relieve the exhausted assaulting divisions the French could have converted a tactical success into a major victory. But it took six and a half hours for the reserves to arrive, by which time the impetus of the assault had been lost, and the Germans had stabilized the situation. In place of a decisive breakthrough the French had gained only a shallow salient in the German line from which they could be attacked on three sides. The battle for Vimy Ridge then degenerated into an attritional battle, which consumed 100,000 Frenchmen and 60,000 Germans. This was the fundamental problem: it proved easier for the defender to bring up reserves to plug gaps in the line than it was for the attacker to bring fresh troops forward to take over from the assaulting battalions.

The problem was largely one of communications. The First World War was fought with recognizably modern weapons but without the benefit of modern communications. The 'walkie-talkie' radio did not exist, and although by the end of the war primitive wireless sets had become more widespread, in earlier years infantry was reliant on visual signals or field telephones, which were for all practical purposes useless in the initial stages of an assault, when a breach was most likely to be achieved. Visual signals such as flags proved to be ineffective and indeed dangerous to the user. Thus the major means of communication was by 'runner', a soldier who had to recross No Man's Land to give a verbal report or present a written message. Hours might pass before a demand for reserves was received, and then the information had to be analysed. Once activated, reserves then faced a long and tedious journey across No Man's Land, probably under fire, before reaching the captured trenches – by which time the opportunity to break through had usually disappeared. The paradox was that it was possible for troops to travel very quickly by rail to the rear of the battlezone, but then they could only move at a snail's pace to the front line. There were some occasions when reserves were undoubtedly held too far back, as at the Battle of Loos in September 1915, but the case was more often simply one of poor communications hampering their use. On the occasions when reserves were held forward, as in the attack on Vimy Ridge by French Tenth Army in September 1915, they were prone to suffer heavily from enemy artillery fire. By contrast, the defender's telephone wires, buried deep beneath the ground, had a greater chance of survival, and thus their reserves could be summoned up with greater celerity. Naturally, the shorter distances involved and the fact that the reserves did not need to cross No Man's Land constituted an enormous advantage to the defender.

In their struggle to square the circle soldiers evolved, in the field, effective, modern tactics. Inevitably, many mistakes were made in the early, experimental stages. Battles on the Western Front were dominated by artillery: nearly 60 per cent of British casualties were caused by shell fire, and machine gun and rifle fire accounted for 39 per cent for instance. Therefore, the development of artillery tactics was of great importance. During 1915, the French and British had come to place their faith in massive bombardments, intended to destroy enemy positions and kill large numbers of enemy troops. Only when the artillery had done its job, would the infantry advance. This doctrine is summed up in the pithy phrase, 'artillery conquers, infantry occupies'. In 1916 the trends of the previous year were taken to extremes, as the war economies of the belligerents expanded and the supply of shells began to approach the demand. Perhaps the most extreme example of reliance on the sheer smashing power of artillery came at the opening of Somme offensive in July 1916. The British Fourth Army assembled the greatest number of guns they had yet seen, including 455 heavy guns and howitzers, or one heavy gun for every 57 yards of front to be attacked (although this concentration was puny compared to later bombardments). The artillery plan was simple. While field guns firing shrapnel cut the enemy barbed wire, the heavy pieces would destroy the German positions in a sustained bombardment, burying the enemy infantry in their dugouts. The British infantry were confidently informed that they would merely have to occupy empty trenches.

Such predictions proved wildly over-optimistic, and sufficient German infantry survived the shelling to wreak havoc on the advancing British. With hindsight, it is clear that the Royal Artillery had been set a hopeless task. Much of the available ammunition had been faulty, and of the 1,500,000 shells fired, about 1,000,000 were shrapnel, which were mainly useful for wire-cutting. As John Keegan has pointed out, the high explosive (HE) that was fired was pitifully inadequate for the task of destroying deep dugouts. Being mostly fused to explode on impact, 'a proportionately quite trifling concussion' was transmitted to the German dugouts beneath the surface: each 10 square yards received only one pound of HE. Having failed in their primary task, the Fourth Army's gunners also failed to give adequate support to the actual assault. The artillery was firing to a rigid timetable in clumsy 'lifts'. The guns would concentrate on a given objective, and then at a predetermined time would lift to a further objective, perhaps 500 yards away. These had been set in accordance with the expected rate of advance of the infantry. However, in the absence of adequate communications, there was no way of recalling the barrage, even if (as so often happened) the infantry failed to keep pace with it.[3]

Some British commanders, at least, reacted swiftly to the terrible lessons of 1 July 1916. One of the two divisions that enjoyed success on that day, Major-General Sir Ivor Maxse's 18th, had employed a 'creeping' barrage. This was a 'curtain' of shrapnel shells, which moved ahead of advancing infantry. This had numerous advantages over the clumsy use of 'lifts'. Because the blast propelled the shrapnel balls forward, infantry could move within 100 yards of the barrage. It also moved at the actual, rather than the theoretical, pace of the infantryman, 100 yards in 3 to 5 minutes. This was effectively used in the capture of Trones Wood on 14 July, and quickly became standard practice for British gunners.[4]

The alternative to using artillery to destroy enemy positions was to use it to neutralize them. In March 1915, at the Battle of Neuve Chapelle, the British had used a brief, 35-minute bombardment with some success. This method was soon discarded, and it was left to a German gunner, Col. Georg Bruchmuller, to demonstrate the potential of this type of bombardment. Bruchmuller, nicknamed *Durchbruchmuller*, or 'Breakthrough Muller', came to the conclusion that the most efficient use of artillery was in short, intense bombardments, in great depth. In Bruchmuller's own words, 'We desired only to break the morale of the enemy, pin him to his position, and then overcome him with an overwhelming assault'. The 'overwhelming assault' was to be made by infantry using infiltration tactics (see below) and it was to be supported by the *Feurwalze*, a form of creeping barrage. These tactics were successfully used on the Eastern Front at Riga, in September 1917, where Bruchmuller commanded the artillery of von Hutier's Eighteenth Army, and later against the British at Cambrai on 1 December 1917.

Bruchmuller's masterpiece was the bombardment of 21 March 1918, the first day of the German Spring Offensive that restored movement to the Western Front. He succeeded in achieving complete surprise, which multiplied the effectiveness of the barrage. Against some opposition from German High Command, German gunners became adept at opening a 'predicted' barrage without previously registering the guns on targets ('shooting by the map'), a method which placed great emphasis on the skill of the gunner. Bruchmuller's fireplan for 21 March lasted for only five hours. At 4.40 am about 6000 guns, including 2508 heavy guns, opened up, to the full depth of the British position. The targets chosen included points of particular importance, such as command posts and telephone exchanges, the disruption of which would have a disproportionate impact on the enemy's cohesion. The widespread use of gas shells forced the British to wear their respirators, which further lowered their efficiency. The guns ranged back and forth, sometimes lifting from one particular target only to come crashing down again later. Five minutes before the infantry assault went in, at 9.40 the barrage was brought to a deafening crescendo. The result was to dishearten and disorient the men of the defending British Fifth Army, who, hampered by thick fog, were overwhelmed by the infantry assault.[5]

By 1918, close co-operation between air and ground had become the prerequisite of successful gunnery. Aircraft had become the 'eyes' of the artillery, observing fall of shot and undertaking photographic reconnaissance missions. The struggle for command of the air was stimulated by the need to allow one's own reconnaissance aircraft to operate unimpeded, while denying the same facility to the enemy. Indeed, effective use of aircraft enabled the French and British to dispense with preliminary bombardments altogether in 1918. Thus the First World War saw a radical transformation in artillery tactics. In the final campaigns, all major armies were using predicted barrages, creeping barrages and neutralizing fire in place of the clumsy and ineffective tactics of earlier years.

Infantry tactics also underwent something of a revolution. In early 1915, one newly raised British unit in training in England was still using the tactics of August 1914, advancing in extended order, taking advantage of cover and then charging 'in a long, closely formed line'.[6] By late 1915 wartime volunteers were thought incapable of mastering such tactics. Thus, from the time of the Battle of Loos in September 1915, infantry advanced in 'waves'. A wave consisted of a line of men, each several paces apart, each wave being separated by 100 yards from the one in front or behind. These tactics were modified in the light of the experiences of 1916 in the Verdun and Somme campaigns. The introduction of the linear 'creeping' barrage, while giving the infantry greater support in the advance, was not without dangers of its own. Its very success ensured the survival of the linear approach, and thus delayed the development of more effective infantry tactics.

The French proved a little more flexible than the British in the field of infantry tactics, continuing to train their men to advance in short rushes, taking advantage of the terrain. At Verdun, in 1916, General Nivelle established his reputation by using infantry in small groups in several successful counter-attacks, but these were still essentially linear attacks subject to the tyranny of the 'creeper'. One French officer argued for a radically different approach. Captain André Laffargue drew upon his experiences in Pétain's attack on Vimy Ridge in May 1915 to suggest that infantry should be re-armed and reorganized to enable them to fight their way forward. He wanted mortars to be sent up with the assaulting infantry, and picked men – two groups in each platoon – to be armed with light machine guns. Assault infantry were to 'infiltrate' the enemy line, penetrating as deeply as possible, thus creating havoc behind the front. This would cause disruption to the enemy, and prevent him from organizing an effective riposte. To add to the disrupting effect, the preliminary barrage had to reach the depth of the position to be attacked. The assaulting infantry would bypass centres of resistance, which would be tackled by following waves. Laffargue's ideas were largely ignored by the Allied armies. Their enemy was rather more receptive.

The willingness of the German army to adapt and change made it the most formidable fighting machine on the Western Front. In contrast to the Allies, it had encouraged the cultivation of a high level of initiative among junior commanders, precisely the qualities needed for effective application of 'infiltration' tactics. Although Laffargue's ideas were not the only influence on German thinking, they did play an important role in the development of the successful infantry tactics of 1917–18. The infantry strength of each division was reduced, but its firepower was considerably augmented to include 50 mortars and 350 heavy machine guns. (The comparable British figures were 36 and 64.) 'Storm' battalions were organized around assault teams armed with light machine guns, mortars, flame-throwers and light artillery pieces. These units had a dual purpose: of providing the cutting edge of infantry attacks (and counter-attacking in defensive positions) and of training other units in their techniques. As they demonstrated at Riga, Caporetto and Cambrai in 1917, and against the British Fifth Army on the Somme in March 1918, the Germans produced an infantry tactic that, although far from infallible, did on occasion succeed in combination with artillery in breaking the deadlock of trench warfare.[7]

Although their relative lack of skill in comparison with the Germans can be exaggerated, the British army of 1917–18 was still at its most effective in static trench fighting and deliberate assaults. Thus the success of the initial, 'set-piece' opening of the Battle of Arras in April 1917 was not matched by the subsequent stages in which the fighting became more fluid. This was largely the fault of poor training and leadership. Major-General Sir Cecil Pereira, commander of 2nd Division, complained after the fighting at Miraumont in February 1917 that time after time 'a company gets to a certain point and is content to stay there. Possibly they dig in, they always fail to push outposts to their front for protection or to gain ground or to patrol to their flanks . . . ' In 1916 light machine guns in the form of Lewis guns became more widespread, although they tended to be centralized as a company weapon rather than allowing the development of Laffarguian platoon tactics. The introduction of weapons such as mortars and rifle grenades made more flexible tactics feasible, but the British were hampered by a lack of common doctrine. Although in 1918 many British infantry divisions were using what Maxse described as the 'worm' (platoon columns and sections, utilizing a modified form of fire and movement to fight their way forward), some were still using the 'wave', which had become even more inappropriate with the replacement of linear defence with defence in depth.[8]

When trench warfare had begun in 1914, trenches were sometimes little more than narrow holes in the ground, protected by perhaps a single strand of wire. In the course of 1915, trench systems developed in sophistication. As well as the forward, or 'fire' trench, parallel 'support' and 'reserve' trenches were constructed, connected by lateral communication trenches. Trench systems underwent further refinement in 1917. As a result of experience on the Somme, German defensive philosophy underwent a profound change. The policy of '*Halten, was zu halten ist*' or 'Hold on to whatever can be held' had proved extremely costly in men. It involved holding the front line in considerable strength, and promptly counter-attacking any enemy lodgements. It has been calculated that the Germans counter-attacked at least 330 times during the course of the battle.[9] In September 1916 the Hindenburg/Ludendorff team replaced Falkenhayn as the effective German commander-in-chief, and an extremely democratic process of consultation with the men in the field began. The result was the adoption of a policy of 'elastic' defence in depth. In place of linear defences, a thinly held outpost zone of scattered defences, 500–1000 metres deep, would serve to canalize an attacking force, who would first have to pass through the German barrage. Then they would run into the 'battle zone', which would be 2 km or more in depth. This consisted of a series of mutually supporting strongpoints capable of all-round defence, which were intended to continue to resist even if surrounded. If an attacker succeeded in fighting through this zone, he would face a further line of machine gun pits in front of the field artillery. The essence of this defence was the counter-attack. Squads dedicated to this role were stationed in the defensive zones, and units of storm troops were positioned in the rear to sweep the enemy back. In the winter of 1916–17, the Germans constructed the Hindenburg Line on these principles, and flexible defence was also adopted by the French and British, although the Allies tended to station large numbers of troops in the forward zone, with unfortunate results. However, by 1918 the principle that defences should be held in depth was firmly established. It was a lesson that would have to be painfully relearnt, on a much larger scale, in 1939–45.[10]

Other weapons played a less important role in the campaigns of 1914–18. Cavalry was of strictly limited value on the Western Front from 1915–18, although in the periods of open warfare in 1914 and 1918, and in the wider spaces of the Eastern Front, horsemen could still fulfil a useful role as reconnaissance troops. Gas, which had seemed to be a war-winning weapon when first used at Ypres in April 1915, proved to be little more than a useful auxiliary. Counter-measures, in the form of crude 'gas-masks', were quickly developed, and by 1918 relatively sophisticated respirators were in use. The main usefulness of chemical weaponry was in forcing opponents to wear respirators, with a consequent loss of efficiency. However, the use of gas 'had been effective locally and suggested a potential utility for future conflicts'.[11]

Perhaps the most important auxiliary weapon was the aircraft. In addition to their primary role, reconnaissance, and their use in the fighter mode, aircraft became increasingly important for ground attack.

The revolution in warfare that had occurred by 1918 is illustrated by the Battle of Amiens, which began on 8 August 1918, described by Ludendorff as the 'Black Day' of the German army. In this battle, the lessons so painfully learnt during the previous four years were applied with great success. Infantry, armour (see p. 64), artillery, aircraft and, to a lesser extent, horsed cavalry acted in close co-operation. This was made possible by the greatly improved communications that had been developed by 1918: wireless was the cement that bound the diverse elements of the Allied armies into a cohesive whole. The wireless of 1918 was still fairly primitive. Infantry battalions, aircraft and batteries could not contact each other, and the brigade tended to be the forward station of the wireless set, with the battalion still reliant on the field telephone, but in 1918 wireless 'came of age by permitting highly organised fire direction centres to function. They anticipated the shape of things to come in the Second World War'.[12]

Generally speaking, the tactical conditions of the Western Front were replicated in theatres such as Gallipoli and Italy. Warfare on the Eastern Front was somewhat more fluid than in the West. The vast size of the theatre of operations ensured that, unlike in France, armies could not be strong everywhere. Thus, both the Central Powers, in the Polish campaign of 1915, and the Russians, in the Brusilov Offensive one year later, were able to achieve considerable breakthroughs, and the front moved sometimes hundreds of miles. In addition to the considerable differences between warfare on the two major fronts, there were also certain similarities. In the East, the defender falling back on shortening lines of communication found it easier to bring up reserves than the attacker and, as in the West, the war was ended not by one climatic breakthrough followed by a battle of encirclement, but as the result of the cumulative effect of vast casualties on one belligerent's will and ability to fight on.

It is clear that to view the tactical problems of the First World War purely in terms of technological determinism, as some have done, is overly simplistic. Many other factors apart from that of technology, not least tactical doctrine, must also be taken into account. In theory, had either side made a major tactical breakthrough earlier in the war, the war could have been brought to a speedier conclusion. In practice, in 1918, the Germans came up against the problem familiar from the Eastern Front: how to convert tactical success into strategic success. Despite breaking the deadlock, all the Germans managed to do was to make the continuous front mobile. The Allies were thrust back and took heavy casualties, but their armies remained unbroken, partly because the Germans lacked an effective instrument of exploitation. Only in the second half of 1918 did modern tactics and technology combine with the exhaustion of a belligerent's will-to-resist to produce a decision. The lesson of the First World War, which was confirmed by the Second World War, was that, in a total war, evenly matched adversaries must batter each other until one can rise no longer.

Strategies of attrition, 1914–18

The popular view of offensive operations on the Western Front is that they were 'dull battering-ram efforts . . . that only served to demonstrate the incapacity of . . . [generals] whose mental processes were confounded by the deadlock . . . All they could think of was a policy of attrition and frontal attacks.'[13] In reality, attrition was not merely 'blind bashing', but part of a coherent strategy. When the war began, soldiers thought in terms of victories achieved by superior generalship, not attrition. The events of 1914 forced the generals to rethink their strategic plans. Falkenhayn, the German Chief of Staff, decided to go on to the defensive in the West. The end of the war of movement had left the Germans with an important advantage, that of being able to construct their defences on high ground overlooking that of the Allies, and they took full advantage of this in constructing formidable defences. Not unnaturally, the primary concern of the French army was the expulsion of the German invader from French soil. The British had traditionally made use of their naval power to pursue a 'Blue Water' strategy, to avoid committing a large army to Europe. However, the failure of the expedition to the Dardanelles discredited any further major attempt to break the deadlock by the use of seapower, so Britain too became committed to a 'Western' strategy.

In 1915, a series of offensives was launched against the German positions, attacks which were costly in lives, gained little ground and did not force the Germans to retreat. Why, then, did the Allies persist with them? Joffre, the French commander-in-chief, described his policy as one of 'nibbling' at the enemy. His aim was to attack the bulge in the German line, the Noyon Salient, by so weakening the Germans as to eventually cause a collapse at some point that the Allies could exploit. This was the meaning of 'attrition' in 1915. In 1916, attrition came to mean something rather different. On 21 February 1916 the Germans attacked at Verdun, in a battle primarily intended to bleed the French army white and force an exhausted France to the conference table. This plan failed, and the attritional struggle at Verdun cost the French 362,000 casualties and the Germans 336,000. The Allied offensives on the Somme in 1916 and in the Third Battle of Ypres in 1917 took things a stage further. Although they began with the aim of reopening mobile operations, they evolved into attempts to exhaust enemy reserves and inflict sufficient casualties on the German army to promote a collapse in morale. This was known as 'the strategy of the longest purse'. Put crudely, the Allies would ultimately prevail in a war of attrition because they had a larger population than the Central Powers. Haig, the British commander-in-chief from 1915, described this as the 'wearing-out battle'.[14] Naturally, this was a dangerous strategy, because the attacker could expect to incur higher casualties than the defender. As the fate of the French army in 1917 demonstrated, Allied morale might give way first, but Haig had enough confidence in his own army to take the risk. The German offensives of 1918, although designed to win the war through mobility, were at least as bloody as the positional battles of 1916 and 1917. In the autumn of 1918 the long-awaited event finally occurred. The German armed forces, having sustained around 1.8 million fatalities, lost their will to fight on. On the Eastern Front there was a similar tale, of indecisive battles and vast losses on both sides leading ultimately to the collapse of the Russian army.

Was attrition unavoidable? All warfare involves a degree of attrition. The Battle of Borodino in 1812 was a classic example of a Napoleonic battle of attrition. In one day, 65,000 men became casualties. The Western Front was essentially a siege, and thus the terrain was peculiarly favourable for the defender. It was impossible to achieve victory by superior manoeuvres, so – like Napoleon at Borodino – the Allies had to use frontal assaults. The mistake came not in the basic strategy, which had many historical precedents (and was to be repeated during the Second World War), but in the conduct of operations. Some of the most successful operations in the 1915–17 period were those whose objectives were deliberately limited; Plumer's methodical victories at Ypres in September 1917, or the capture of Messines Ridge in June of that year, for example. But for much of this period, commanders insisted on chasing the will o' the wisp of a decisive breakthrough, without having the tactical ability to achieve it. It was on these occasions, such as the opening of the Somme offensive, or the French 'Nivelle Offensive' in April 1917, that the most spectacular disasters occurred, which were compounded by the prolongation of the offensive after the original *raison d'être* had vanished. Not until August 1918 did the Allies begin to move away from attempts to achieve a breakthrough, and instead fought a series of shallow, attritional battles to maintain pressure at different points of the enemy line. Haig argued that the victories of 1918 could not have been achieved without the attritional battles of 1915–17.[14] There is a measure of truth in this. The attrition of the previous years undoubtedly played a major part in the disintegration of German military morale in 1918, as well as the effects of the British economic blockade. To that extent the commanders of 1914–18 were right to pursue a strategy of attrition. However, the Allied generals – and Haig in particular – deserve criticism for underestimating German resilience and failing to come to terms with the realities of siege warfare, in which the traditional *bataille de rupture* was no longer appropriate.

The interwar years

The story of armoured vehicles in the First World War forms little more than a coda to the development of infantry and artillery tactics. Tanks were developed by the British as a response to the problems posed by trench warfare. In their first battles in 1916 the few available tanks were mishandled by being used in 'penny packets'. By the time of campaigns in 1918, tanks were being used *en masse* and in conjunction with other arms achieved a number of successes, notably at Hamel in July. Although the tank of 1918 vintage was too unreliable for sustained action (after five days of fighting at Amiens only six out of 414 tanks were still 'runners'), progressive soldiers saw enormous potential for the use of armour. One such was J. F. C. Fuller, who as a staff officer had been involved in planning the successful Cambrai offensive of November 1917, in which massed armour had been used for the first time. In May 1918 he had devised a plan, which was never to be put into practice, for an armoured offensive to win the war.

'Plan 1919' was the antithesis of attritional battle fought on a broad front. Fuller's idea was to use massed tanks with close air support to launch a surprise attack on a narrow front. Having broken through, the tanks would race to the rear and overrun enemy command centres, thus destroying the 'brain' which controlled the 'limbs' of the enemy army, rather than hacking the 'limbs' off individually in a prolonged attritional struggle. Fuller's influence on German thinking should not be exaggerated, but he was able to write, with a degree of truth, that 'In modified form, this tactical theory was put to the test in 1939, and became known as *Blitzkrieg*'. Basil Liddell Hart, another British military analyst, drew broadly similar conclusions. But where Fuller concentrated on the role of the tank almost to the exclusion of other arms, Liddell Hart argued that it would be essential for infantry to accompany armoured forces. Thus it would be necessary to mechanize the entire army.

Official recognition of these theories came in 1927 with the creation of the 'Experimental Mechanised Force' (EMF), composed not only of tanks but also of motorized infantry and artillery, with air support.[15]

The debate on armour in Britain was paralleled in other European countries. Contrary to popular opinion, the French attitude to armour in the interwar years was not simply one of purblind reaction. In 1918, the French army had possessed nearly 3,000 tanks. General Estienne, who has been described as the 'father' of French armour, showed a healthy regard for the potential of the tank as a mobile weapon. In 1933 a light mechanized division (DLM) was established, 'in every thing but name . . . the 1934 version of an armoured division'.[16] In the Soviet Union, under Tukhachevsky, the Red Army evolved an advanced doctrine in which all arms were to fight a co-ordinated battle. Soviet operations aimed at encirclement and destruction, rather than a Fullerian blow at the enemy's 'brain'. Integration was not only envisaged at a tactical level. To defend 'socialism in one country', the USSR was to build an industrial base capable of supporting total war.[17]

In 1939 Britain possessed the only totally mechanized army in the world. However, in deciding on extensive mechanization, the concept of elite armoured forces had been lost. The EMF had been disbanded in 1928, and Fuller had retired to fight his corner from outside the army. By the outbreak of the Second World War, British tanks were divided into two categories, the 'I' (Infantry) tank used for infantry support, and the lighter 'Cruiser' tank. Formed into armoured divisions, in which the emphasis was on the tank rather than on all arms co-operation, the Cruiser took on the cavalry's role of reconnaissance and exploitation. Among the reasons for official resistance to the ideas of Liddell Hart and Fuller was a paradoxical (in view of the development of the heavily tank-oriented British armoured division) belief that any future war would see a repetition of the dominance of the defence; that new weapons, particularly the anti-tank gun, would make the offensive use of armour difficult. Thus, in 1932, the British official historian of the First World War, Sir James Edmonds, wrote to Liddell Hart: 'Any tank which shows its nose will in my opinion be knocked out at once . . . The wars you and Fuller imagine are past.'[18]

The interwar years saw the establishment of the doctrine of *couverture* in France, by which the nation would mobilize for total war behind the supposedly impregnable series of fortifications along the German frontier, the Maginot Line. The defensive-mindedness of the French can be exaggerated. It is possible to discern a certain continuity between the ideas of 1914 and 1940, but certainly the early optimism of the tank enthusiasts proved ill-founded. In 1934, Colonel Charles de Gaulle advocated replacing France's large conscript army with a small, professional force 100,000 strong, totally mechanized and capable of taking the offensive. De Gaulle's heresy of espousing the cause of an 'aggressive' weapon was compounded by his attacks on the professionalism of the army and the shibboleth of total war, and in the prevailing atmosphere his ideas failed to get a sympathetic hearing and may even have retarded the development of French armoured forces. In 1939, France had large numbers of tanks, which were in some ways superior to contemporary German models, but thought on their employment was basically defensive. The Red Army's armoured doctrine too had suffered a decline from the heyday of the early 1930s. The poor performance of Soviet armour in the Spanish Civil War of 1936–9 had dented the reputation of the tank arm, and Stalin's purges of 1937–8 effectively decapitated the army. Tukhachevsky was among those who perished, and the large tank formations were split up, the tank once more becoming an infantry support weapon.

By the end of the 1930s, the British also had accepted that another war in Europe would be total. Liddell Hart had argued strongly for 'limited liability', with Britain performing what he saw as her historical role in the event of a war in Europe: using a naval blockade to starve an enemy into surrender, and committing only limited forces to Europe. He espoused the cause of strategic bombing as a way of avoiding a repetition of 1914–18 and, in fact, for most of the interwar period the British did place their faith in strategic bombing as a way of waging war in Europe, while avoiding the unpleasant necessity of deploying a large army on the Continent. In April 1939, when war with Nazi Germany appeared inevitable, Britain reverted to the pattern of 1914. It was decided that the Royal Navy was to blockade Germany, while the French covered the mobilization of a mass British army. Fifty-five divisions would be available by 1942, when the allies would go on the offensive.

It was the German army that exploited the potential of mechanized forces most effectively. There has been some debate on the extent of German economic preparations for war,* but there is no doubt that the German armed forces' preparations were based on the assumption that war would not come until the mid-1940s, and they were essentially unready in 1939. But to an awed world, Germany's newly created Luftwaffe and Panzer divisions appeared to offer chilling evidence of German readiness for war. Although Hitler's foreign policy exploited this belief, it should not be thought that the economic, diplomatic and

* See Ian F. W. Beckett's Chapter 1, p. 13 in this volume.

military policies of Nazi Germany were meshed into a 'masterplan'. It is more accurate to say that the weapons of *Blitzkrieg* (lightning war) served to frighten potential enemies and the tactics of *Blitzkrieg* made the short, victorious war a possibility. Thus, fortuitously, *Blitzkrieg* suited Hitler's opportunistic foreign policy.

The development of German armour owed much to one officer, Heinz Guderian. Much has been made of the extent to which Guderian was influenced by British theorists, particularly Liddell Hart and Fuller. While Guderian certainly studied the works of Fuller in particular, British General Staff manuals on armoured warfare seem to have had a greater influence on German thinking on the use of armour.[19] Guderian did not introduce entirely new concepts to the German army. The commander of the army from 1919 to 1926, Hans von Seeckt, had been forced to operate within restraints on Germany's armed forces imposed by the 1919 Treaty of Versailles, which was repudiated in 1935. He had created a force which could compensate for inferior numbers by superior mobility. Although Germany had neglected the tank in the First World War, some experience had been gained as a result of clandestine co-operation with the USSR. Beck, the chief-of-staff from 1933 to 1938, saw the value of armour, but had rather conservative views on its employment. It was Hitler who ultimately decided the fate of German armour. 'Hitler was keenly interested; he not only acquired a remarkable knowledge of the technical problems of motorization and armor, but showed that he was receptive to Guderian's strategic and tactical ideas.'[20] At the end of the decade, with Guderian as Chief of Mobile Forces, the spearhead of the German army was its Panzer divisions: mobile formations built around the tank but including supporting elements. It should be remembered that these were elite forces, comprising only about one-tenth of the strength of the army. In contrast to the British army, non-Panzer divisions were reliant on the horse for transportation.

The early Blitzkriegs

German *Blitzkrieg* technique did bear some resemblances to Plan 1919, but it also was firmly in the tradition of the infiltration tactics of 1918 and the *Kesselschlacht*. For the *Blitzkrieg* to succeed, surprise was essential. Armoured forces were used to assault a narrow front, employing overwhelming numbers to ensure penetration. Two or three columns would break through and then race into the enemy rear, bypassing strongpoints and acting as pincers, encircling enemy forces or positions. Panzer Grenadiers (mechanized infantry) accompanied the tanks, while the infantry divisions mopped up remaining centres of resistance. Aircraft, especially the Ju 87 'Stuka' dive bomber, would act as flying artillery. The emphasis was on the disruption and paralysation of the enemy. By using fast-moving armour and aircraft, the major problem of the March 1918 offensive – the inability to convert tactical into strategic success – was overcome. Co-ordination of all elements was essential; the role of the anti-tank gun was particularly vital in protecting the flanks of an armoured breakthrough. Tank versus tank action was relatively rare, and against a well co-ordinated anti-tank defence the tank usually came off worst. This was a lesson that the British failed to heed. The early campaigns in the Western Desert in 1940–42 were characterized by attempts to fight battles with unsupported armour, with unfortunate results. Not only was infantry/armour co-operation poor, but the obsession of the RAF with strategic bombing had lead to the neglect of its tactical role. Both faults were still evident as late as the Normandy campaign in 1944.[21]

If *Blitzkrieg* at a tactical level owed much to the practice of 1914–18, there was another sense in which it belonged to an even older German military tradition. It has been argued that *Blitzkrieg*, far from bringing a revolution in operational art, simply turned the clock back to the era of Schlieffen.[22] Both the Polish and French campaigns of 1939–40 can be seen as falling firmly within the German military tradition, being further examples of the German obsession with the *Kesselschlacht*, in which destruction of the enemy and not mere defeat was the aim. Poland was attacked from three sides, and the Germans carried out a double envelopment, encircling and crushing the Polish armies. Even the speed of the advance was little different to 1914, when von Kluck's men had been expected to march 15 miles per day; the average daily rate of advance for the Panzers in Poland was only 11 miles. The original plan for the invasion of France in 1940, Case Yellow, was little more than a revision of Schlieffen. The problem of how to avoid the powerful French frontier defences produced roughly the same answer, a wheeling movement through the Netherlands and Belgium. The plan that was finally used was devised by a relatively junior officer, General Erich von Manstein, the chief-of-staff to Army Group A. This has often been hailed as a stroke of strategic genius, but in its essentials it was simply an example of a successful *Kesselschlacht*. Manstein's plan involved a feint through the Low Countries to draw off the main Allied forces, while the main blow would come in their rear, through the Ardennes. This would take the form of a deep strategic thrust, which would envelop the bulk of the enemy forces. Thus, both tactically and operationally, *Blitzkrieg* owed much to established German military practice.

Superficially, the early years of the Second World War appeared to show that armoured warfare had provided a way of avoiding the deadlock of 1914–18, but there were certain important differences between the campaigns of 1939–41 and those of the earlier war. On the Western Front, the morale, training, equipment and doctrine of the belligerents' armies had been approximately equal. By contrast, the Polish army of 1939 was poorly equipped and its forces were maldeployed. The French army suffered from poor morale and, more important, mishandled its armour. Significantly, French tanks such as the Char B were qualitatively superior to the German Panzer I and II, which formed the bulk of the Panzerwaffe. Superior doctrine and tactics, not superior technology, decided the battle for France. The French 'Dyle Plan' mirrored Plan XVII, just as Case Yellow mirrored Schlieffen. The bulk of the best French troops moved into Belgium to meet the German advance, leaving the sector opposite the Ardennes to be protected by linear defences. There were no mobile reserves to counter enemy forces that might break through the outer crust. Once von Rundstedt's Army Group A had crossed the Meuse on 14 May 1940, and thus pierced the French defensive cordon, the shock seemed to paralyse the French High Command, much as Fuller had predicted in Plan 1919. The French were then decisively defeated in a classic *Kesselschlacht*.

Blitzkrieg was not infallable. For success, it was dependent to a large extent on bluff; on achieving surprise, attacking weak points in the enemy defences, and on the enemy's being unable to mount an effective riposte. One incident in the 1940 campaign reveals one of the principal weaknesses of *Blitzkrieg*. Erwin Rommel's 7th Panzer Division was attacked in flank near Arras on 21 May 1940, and as Rommel reported: 'heavy fighting took place against hundreds of enemy tanks and following infantry . . . The enemy broke through the defensive line formed by our PAK [anti-tank artillery], the guns were put out of action or overrun and most of their crews were killed.' Rommel succeeded in beating off the attack, but it caused great alarm among the German High Command and caused the Panzer spearhead to be halted for 24 hours. The attack had been made by a mere 74 British 'I' tanks (58 of which were armed only with machine guns) and two infantry battalions.[23] There was a price to pay for the use of armour in deep strategic thrusts. That price was the vulnerability of the flanks, and the effect of a minor, ad hoc attack against the flank of an armoured column indicates the results that might have been achieved had the Allies made proper use of mobile reserves.

Barbarossa and after

The Polish and French campaigns seemed to indicate that technology had provided a method of winning wars swiftly and relatively bloodlessly: the six-week campaign in the west cost the Germans roughly 27,000 dead, compared with nearly 11,000 killed on the first day of the 1918 Spring offensive alone. The events on the Eastern Front were to show that the earlier campaigns had been an aberration, born of the vast inequalities in fighting power between the rival armies.

Operation Barbarossa, the German invasion of Russia, began on 22 June 1941. Initially this campaign, followed the pattern of the earlier *Blitzkriegs*. Once again, the Germans achieved surprise and, exploiting the Red Army's linear deployments, took huge numbers of prisoners in battles of encirclement. Five days after the invasion, 324,000 prisoners were captured at Minsk, while in October, 663,000 men, 1200 tanks and 5400 guns fell into German hands 125 miles from Moscow at Vyazma. The strength of the Red Army in the west had been 4.7 million men in June, but by October the total had plummeted to 2.3 million. Despite their successes the Germans did not succeed in inflicting a mortal wound on the USSR. The Germans themselves contributed to their defeat by failing to come to terms with the problems inherent in an invasion of Russia. The sheer size of the Soviet armed forces came as a considerable shock. Halder, the chief-of-staff, wrote in his diary in mid-1941: 'We under-estimated Russia; we reckoned with 200 divisions, but we have already identified 360'.[24] In addition, the Panzer divisions upon which so much depended were weaker in strength than they had been twelve months earlier. The total number of divisions had increased from ten to twenty-one, but this increment had been achieved by halving the number of tanks in each formation.

On campaign, the tank strength of the 1941-style Panzer division could dwindle rapidly. The 18th Panzer division was reduced from the 212 tanks with which it had begun the campaign to 83 by 9 July 1941, and only 12 by late July. However, it is arguable that this was not as grave a handicap as it might appear, for a Panzer division with a low number of tanks was the equivalent of a Motorized division, which was still greatly superior to an infantry formation. The poor roads in Russia inevitably limited mobility of the Panzer's wheeled transport, and mobility was the key to *Blitzkrieg*. Finally, the logistical problems of operating in the Soviet Union had been underestimated. In August 1941 Army Group Centre was forced to halt to allow supplies to reach its forward elements. It could, in fact, keep only two of its four armies in combat supplies at any one time. This was the very antithesis of *Blitzkrieg*, which finally foundered in the mud around Moscow in November 1941.[25]

The greatest contribution to the failure of Hitler's most ambitious *Blitzkrieg* was made by the Red Army itself. In 1937, Tukhachevsky had foreseen that a *Blitzkrieg* would only work against:

an enemy who doesn't want to and won't fight it out. If the Germans meet an opponent who stands up and fights and takes the offensive himself, that would give a different aspect to things. The struggle would be bitter and protracted . . . In the final resort, all would depend on who had the greater moral fibre and who at the close of operations disposed of operational reserve in depth.[26]

The Russians did stand and fight. They relocated their industrial base east of the Urals, and the sheer size of Russia allowed them to trade space for time to bring up reserves. This enabled them to survive Barbarossa and the German *Blitzkriegs* of 1942 and, when the time was right, to take the offensive themselves at Stalingrad.

In contrast to the First World War, the 1939–45 conflict did not stimulate a revolution in tactical thinking. The tactics that were used to counter the methods of *Blitzkrieg* were a direct development of the 'elastic' defences of 1918. Even in 1940, the French had begun to use *quadrillage*, a chequerboard system of defence in depth, to counter some armoured thrusts. The standard British defensive layout of 1940 was a trench designed to counter frontal assaults. As a result of bitter experience, this was abandoned in favour of the two- or four-man slit trench. Instead of being connected, these positions were sited in mutually supporting groups to provide all-round defence against attacks from the flank or rear. The prevalence of anti-tank weapons, including easily portable infantry weapons such as the German *Panzerfaust* and US Bazooka made such positions increasingly tough nuts for armour to crack. In the desert, the Germans became skilled at using their own tanks as bait to lure the British armour on to a concealed anti-tank screen. Later in the war, anti-tank defence evolved further with the appearance of mobile anti-tank guns such as the US M-10 Tank Destroyer and the German Jagdpanther.

By the mid-war period, 'elastic' defence had reasserted itself and defences many miles deep were constructed. In July 1943, 1900 German tanks were launched against the Kursk salient in an attempt to regain the initiative after the disaster of Stalingrad. Delays to the commencement of 'Operation Citadel' forfeited the element of surprise, and allowed the Russians to prepare an elaborate belt of defences, as much as 110 miles deep in places. Minefields channelled the panzers towards strongpoints of anti-tank guns, known as *Pakfronts* to the Germans. In sectors where the Soviets expected to be attacked by armoured forces, the density of anti-tank guns and anti-tank mines reached 25–30 and 1500–2000 respectively per kilometre of frontage. These defences were backed up by masses of artillery; in all, the Soviets deployed more than 20,000 pieces.[27] In eight days of attacking, the deepest penetration the panzers managed was only 20 miles. Then, in the style of the German stormtroops of 1918, but on a far greater scale, the Soviets threw in their reserves to push the enemy out of their lodgement. A 'Steppe Front' of five armies swept forward and the greatest tank battle in history commenced. For the loss of perhaps 1500 armoured fighting vehicles (AFVs), the Red Army destroyed 1000 tanks, losses that were, for the Germans, irreplaceable.

The Germans developed their own answer to Soviet armoured offensives. They frequently found themselves about to be enveloped, but turned this to their advantage by using their central position to defeat the enemy in detail. The 'manoeuvre on interior lines' was far from being a new concept, but the mobility of mechanized forces gave it a new application. Thus, German forces would be used to hit an armoured thrust in flank, and then moved rapidly to repeat the process on another sector. German virtuosity in these operations has been much admired but it should be seen in perspective. Such operations only succeeded in slowing, not halting, the remorseless Soviet advance.[28]

Offensive tactics were also developments of those of the Great War rather than startling innovations. In the German army, the descendants of the stormtroops of 1918 were panzergrenadiers: motorized infantry accompanied the tanks and were used (dismounted) to overcome obstacles and to exploit breakthroughs. Speed and the use of individual initiative were the essence of these attacks. As in the First World War, the German Army stood head and shoulders above their enemies in terms of doctrine, training and leadership. *Auftragstaktik* (mission-oriented command system) demanded initiative and drive, by placing the onus on junior commanders 'to devise and carry out their own schemes'.[29] US and particularly British troops were noticeably lacking in these military virtues. British tactics were therefore characterized by the deliberate, setpiece battle, just as they had been in 1917. After the salutary experience of France in 1940, greater emphasis was placed on instilling initiative, but in the Normandy campaign the British were still overly partial to setpiece attacks.

In the US army affairs were somewhat different. The German successes of 1939–40 had had considerable impact on US doctrine. The US army created an Armored Force in 1940, and its divisions were modelled on the German panzer formations. The emphasis was on mobility, with more than 400 tanks in each division and the infantry entirely mounted in half-tracked armoured personnel carriers (APCs). From 1943 the emphasis was changed, as the Americans absorbed the lessons of the British campaigns in North Africa and their own experience of the use of armour in the difficult terrain in Italy. The number of tanks in each division was reduced, but tanks were attached to infantry formations, which bore the brunt of battle. The Armored Division was now regarded as an instrument of exploitation. Small unit tactics were based on the use of fire and movement: once the enemy had been located, he would be pinned down by fire by one section while another advanced. A somewhat crude tactic sometimes used to maximize the use of fire was 'the marching fire offensive': infantry simply formed into a line, firing as they advanced.[30]

The Red Army took infantry tank co-operation furthest of all, with infantry frequently riding into battle on tanks. Like the British, the Soviet forte was the ponderous setpiece attack, in which firepower, in particular artillery, was relied upon to smash the enemy, support the infantry in their advance and then prevent the enemy bringing up reserves. Stalin's 'god of war' was concentrated in artillery divisions or even corps, with a consequent reduction in divisional artillery to only 40 or so guns. Typically, Soviet operations employed artillery bombardments that rivalled any of those used in the First World War. For Operation Uranus, the counter-offensive at Stalingrad on 19 November 1942, for instance, 13,541 guns were used, while 3500 guns and mortars amassed along the fourteen miles of front where the main effort was to be made. This density was considered low: thus the preliminary bombardment was of relatively long duration — 80 minutes. The Western armies were just as reliant on artillery as the Soviets and their predecessors in the First World War. The techniques of 1914–18 – 'hurricane' bombardments, rolling barrages and the like – were in common use in 1939–45. In some ways, the use of artillery was expanded. The Second World War artilleryman might be called upon to fulfil a new role, such as that of anti-tank or anti-aircraft gunner. Flexibility was increased with the introduction of self-propelled artillery and the assault gun, a turretless tank with a fixed gun, which could bring fire support up among the frontline infantry.

Although the use of airpower became more sophisticated than it had been in 1918, the fact remains that its basic roles were mostly unaltered, although the Second World War saw the tactical role of the aircraft extended to supplement the artillery. In July 1944, the attempt to break out of the Normandy bridgehead by US VIII Corps (Operation Cobra) was preceded by 1500 heavy bombers saturating the German positions with 3400 tons of bombs, many of which fell on to the forward positions of the US infantry. As with infantry tactics, the greatest advance over 1914–18 was in the field of communications. The widespread dissemination of radio gave the 1939–45 battle a degree of flexibility missing from the earlier war. Technological developments notwithstanding the Second World War was as much an artillery war as its predecessor.[31]

The poor performance of armour in an offensive role in battles such as Kursk, Alamein and Goodwood has led to an assumption that the latter years of the Second World War saw a decline in the usefulness of the tank. This interpretation ignores the Soviet experience, for, although British and American perceptions of the role of armour had certainly changed by 1944–45, the Soviets continued to use armour on a large scale. Marshal P. Rotmistrov, commander of 5 Guards Tank

Army at Kursk, was later to write that by July 1943 'armoured and mechanised troops had become the Soviet Army's main striking and mobile force'.[32] The difference in attitudes may be explained partly by the fact that, while Anglo-American tanks were generally inferior to German models by this stage of the war, the Soviet T-34/85 was not. The second, and more important factor, was that, unlike the Western Allies, the Soviets used armoured forces in accordance with the principles of 'operational art', by treating individual 'battles' as part of a single operational plan. It should not be forgotten that *Blitzkrieg* offensives were still possible in the latter years of the war. On 22 June 1944 the Soviets commenced Operation Bagration, deploying a total of 2715 tanks and 1355 SP guns. The results were spectacular. In a week, German Army Group Centre was virtually destroyed in a classic *Kesselschlact*. The Germans lost 900 tanks and 130,000 men, including, 66,000 taken prisoner, in three major pockets. By the end of the offensive in August their losses were close to 300,000 and the Soviets had advanced 350 miles. This disaster to German arms was followed by another in August, as the Anglo-Americans broke out of the Normandy bridgehead and captured 50,000 prisoners in the Falaise pocket. The Allies were then able to race east: Patton's US Third Army covered 400 miles in 26 days. Unlike those of 1939–41, these *Blitzkrieg* offensives were not conducted against inferior or ill-prepared opposition. The *Blitzkriegs* of 1944 were only achieved after prolonged attritional fighting had gravely weakened the enemy. In the East, three and a half years of conflict had taken their toll on the Germans. In Normandy, the breakout was preceded by two months of intense, static warfare. The case of 21st Panzer Division was not untypical. In the period 6 June to 21 August 1944, this formation lost all of its armour (127 Panzer IVs and 40 assault guns) and approximately 12,350 officers and men, leaving only 300.

This was the reality of most battles of the Second World War after 1941. They were mostly attritional battles fought on a broad front, not the rapid and limited campaigns envisaged by Fuller and Liddell Hart. The advent of armour gave some battles a greater degree of mobility, but one of the most common experiences of the fighting man in the Second World War was positional fighting from holes in the ground, or slogging from house to house in street fighting, or at best a slow advance, not lightning war. The Battle of Alamein, which ended with a 900-mile pursuit along the coast of North Africa, began with what Montgomery described as 'crumbling' attacks largely undertaken by

76   *Warfare in the Twentieth Century*

infantry. 'What else had Haig been trying to achieve at Passchendaele', one historian has asked, 'if not to "crumble" the German positions in this way?'[33] On the strategic level, too, the Second World War was an attritional struggle. Just as the German collapse in 1918 can be largely attributed to the attrition to which it had been subjected in previous campaigns, the demise of the German army in 1945 was a direct result of the 'wearing-out' battles of 1942–5. In the Second World War, it was the Eastern Front that was the decisive theatre of war: while the Anglo-American strategy until 1944 centred on strategic bombing and the Mediterranean, the Soviets were taking on the bulk of the Wehrmacht. Thus, in the Second World War, comparable battles to Verdun, the Somme and Third Ypres were Stalingrad, Kursk and Operation Bagration. Once again, Germany was defeated only after a bitter, prolonged, attritional struggle that left most of the victors almost as weak as the vanquished.

Seen from this perspective, most of the major innovations of the Second World War appear as peripheral to the mainstream development of war. Paratroops, although enjoying some success, proved ultimately to be nothing more than a useful auxiliary. Commando-style raiding forces had their critics even while the war was in progress and may, with hindsight, be seen largely in terms of a diversion of resources from more profitable activities. Only in the fields of nuclear weaponry, communications and intelligence (such as ULTRA, which falls outside the parameters of this chapter) were major advances made in the Second World War. This is of more than purely academic interest. The armies of Europe and the United States still train for essentially the same style of warfare that was developed on the Western Front in 1914–18 and honed on the Russian steppes twenty-five years later.

Notes: Chapter 3

1   Nigel Hamilton, *Monty: The Making of a General 1887–1942*, (London: Hamish Hamilton, 1981) pp. 804–5.
2   Michael Howard, 'Men against fire: the doctrine of the offensive in 1914' in Peter Paret (ed.), *Makers of Modern Strategy from Machiavelli to the Nuclear Age* (Oxford: Clarendon Press, 1986) pp. 522–3. See also Hew Strachan, *European Armies and the Conduct of War* (London: Allen & Unwin, 1983) for military developments before 1914.
3   John Keegan, *The Face of Battle* (Harmondsworth: Penguin, 1978) pp. 235–40; Martin Middlebrook, *The First Day on the Somme* (London: Allen Lane, 1971) pp. 277–8.

4 Shelford Bidwell and Dominic Graham, *Fire-Power: British Army Weapons and Theories of War 1904–1945* (London: Allen & Unwin, 1982) pp. 83–5, 111–12.
5 Timothy T. Lupfer, *The Dynamics of Doctrine: The Changes in German Tactical Doctrine During the First World War* (Fort Leavenworth, Kans: Leavenworth Paper No. 4, 1981) pp. 44–50. See also Martin Middlebrook, *The Kaiser's Battle* (London: Allen Lane, 1978) for a good account of 21 March 1918.
6 *West Sussex Gazette and South of England Advertiser*, 11 March 1915, p. 10.
7 Lupfer, *Dynamics of Doctrine*, pp. 37–58; G. C. Wynne, *If Germany Attacks* (London: Faber and Faber, 1940) pp. 55–8.
8 G. D. Sheffield, *The Effect of War Service on the 22nd Battalion Royal Fusiliers (Kensington) 1914–18, with Special Reference to Morale, Discipline and the Officer/Man Relationship* (unpublished MA thesis, University of Leeds, 1984) p. 52; Bidwell and Graham, *Fire-Power* pp. 121–30.
9 John Terraine, *The Smoke and the Fire* (London: Sidgwick & Jackson, 1981) p. 124.
10 See Lupfer, *Dynamics of Doctrine*; Wynne, *If Germany Attacks*; Tom Wintringham and J. N. Blashford-Snell, *Weapons and Tactics* (Harmondsworth: Penguin) pp. 167–71.
11 Edward M. Spiers, *Chemical Warfare* (London: Macmillan, 1986) p. 33.
12 Bidwell and Graham, *Fire-Power*, p. 144. For the evolution of air power, see Robin Higham, *Air Power* (London: Macdonald, 1972) and Malcolm Cooper, *The Birth of Independent Air Power* (London: Allen & Unwin, 1986).
13 Leon Wolff, *In Flanders Fields* (Harmondsworth: Penguin, 1979) p. 31.
14 J. H. Boraston (ed.), *Sir Douglas Haig's Despatches* 2nd edn (London: Dent, 1979) esp. pp. 319–21.
15 Major-General J. F. C. Fuller, *The Conduct of War 1789–1961* (London: Eyre & Spottiswood, 1961) p. 244; Brian Bond, *Liddell Hart: A Study of his Military Thought* (London: Cassell, 1977) pp. 23–9.
16 Brian Bond and Martin Alexander, 'Liddell Hart and De Gaulle: the doctrines of limited liability and mobile defense', in Paret, *Makers of Modern Strategy*, p. 608.
17 Condoleeza Rice, 'The making of Soviet strategy', in Paret, *Makers of Modern Strategy*, pp. 664–6; Strachan, *European Armies and the Conduct of War*, p. 159.
18 Stephen Brooks, *Armoured Warfare* (London: Imperial War Museum, 1980), p. 29.
19 The author would like to thank his colleague, Dr J. P. Harris, for sharing his unpublished research on this topic.
20 Major-General F. W. von Mellenthin, *Panzer Battles* (London: Futura, 1977), pp. xv–xvi.
21 Correlli Barnett, *The Desert Generals*, 2nd edn (London: Pan Books, 1983) pp. 85–110: Carlo D'Este, *Decision in Normandy* (London: Pan Books, 1984) pp. 293–7; Max Hastings, *Overlord* (London: Pan Books,

1985) pp. 312–24.

22   Elmar Dinter and Paddy Griffith, *Not Over By Christmas* (Chichester: Antony Bird, 1983) pp. 88–90.

23   Brian Bond, 'Arras, 21 May 1940: a case study in the counter-stroke' in Correlli Barnett, Shelford Bidwell, Brian Bond, John Harding and John Terraine, *Old Battles and New Defences: Can We Learn from Military History?* (London, Brassey's Defence Publishers, 1986) pp. 73–5.

24   B. H. Liddell Hart, *The Other Side of the Hill* (London: Pan Books, 1983), p. 260.

25   For the logistics of Barbarossa, see Martin van Creveld, *Supplying War: Logistics from Wallenstein to Patton* (London: Cambridge University Press, 1977), pp. 142–80.

26   John Erickson, *The Road to Stalingrad* (London: Panther Books, 1985) p. 17.

27   Major-General Ivan Parotkin (ed.) *The Battle of Kursk* (Moscow: Progress Publishers, 1974) p. 163; Geoffrey Jukes, *Kursk: Clash of Armour* (London: Macdonald, 1969) p. 79.

28   US Army Department, *German Defense Tactics Against Russian Break-throughs* (Washington, DC, US Army Department Pamphlet 20–233, 1951); Dinter and Griffith, *Not Over By Christmas*, pp. 97–101, 106–11; Liddell Hart, *The Other Side of the Hill*, pp. 321–8.

29   Martin van Creveld, *Fighting Power: German and US Army Performance, 1939–45* (London: Arms and Armour Press, 1983) pp. 36–7. Admiration of German military prowess has often led to a tendency to gloss over the darker side of German operations. For a corrective, see Omer Bartov, *The Eastern Front, 1941–45, German Troops and the Barbarisation of Warfare* (London: Macmillan in association with St Antony's College, Oxford, 1985).

30   For Allied tactics, see General Sir Anthony Farrah-Hockley, *Infantry Tactics 1939–45* (London: Almark, 1976); Russell F. Weigley, *Eisenhower's Lieutenants* (London: Sidgwick & Jackson, 1981) pp. 8–28; Russell F. Weigley, *History of the United States Army* (London: Batsford, 1968) pp. 472–5.

31   For a good introduction to the subject of Second World War artillery see Ian V. Hogg, *Barrage: The Guns in Action* (London: Macdonald, 1970).

32   Parotkin, *Battle of Kursk*, p. 168.

33   Paddy Griffith, *Forward into Battle* (Chichester: Antony Bird, 1981) p. 93. The author would like to thank Dr Griffith for reading and providing constructive criticism on an early draft of this chapter.

Further reading: Chapter 3

Bidwell, Shelford, and Graham, Dominic, *Fire-Power: British Army Weapons and Theories of War 1904–45* (London: Allen & Unwin, 1983).

D'Este, Carlo, *Decision in Normandy* (London: Pan Books, 1984).

Erickson, John, *The Road to Stalingrad* (London: Panther Books, 1985).

Erickson, John, *The Road to Berlin* (London: Panther Books, 1985).

Griffith, Paddy, *Forward into Battle* (Chichester: Antony Bird, 1981).
Keegan, John, *The Face of Battle* (Harmondsworth: Penguin, 1978).
Lupfer, Timothy T., *The Dynamics of Doctrine: The Changes in German Tactical Doctrine During the First World War* (Fort Leavenworth, Kans: Leavenworth Paper No. 4, 1981).
Mellenthin, Major-General F. W. von, *Panzer Battles* (London: Futura, 1977).
Travers, Tim, *The Killing Ground: The British Army, The Western Front, and the Emergence of Modern Warfare, 1900–18* (London: Allen & Unwin, 1987).

4

Naval Power

GEOFFREY TILL

Uncertainties and doubts

In 1890 a book was published called *The Influence of Seapower on History, 1660–1783*, written by an ageing, studious and frankly rather stuffy US naval officer called Alfred Thayer Mahan. Despite its dreary provenance and its uncompromisingly historical approach, it somehow captured the spirit of the times, sold all round the world in its tens of thousands and helped transform the habits of thought of a whole generation. The Kaiser said in 1904:

> I am just now not reading but devouring Captain Mahan's book and am trying to learn it by heart. It is a first class work and classical in all its points. It is on board all my ships and constantly quoted by my captains and officers.[1]

The success of Mahan and his ideas was greeted with some relief by naval men, because navies had undoubtedly been going through a bad patch over the previous quarter of a century. The furious rush of technology in the nineteenth century had transformed naval warfare. Sail had yielded to steam, iron had replaced wood; there had been a revolution in naval gunnery, and there were many new naval weapons, such as torpedoes, mines and submarines. It was clear to outsiders that many naval officers did not know what to make of all this.

Some naval conservatives believed that things would go on in much the same way as they had before, and have earned a good deal of scorn, then and since, for thinking so. Other professionals were excessively radical, and thought the new technology would transform the face of battle, the philosophy of warfare at sea, and the general place of seapower in national strategy. Radicals and conservatives alike pointed out the absence of real experience of naval warfare at this time. There had been important naval battles, such as Navarino (1827), Sinope (1853) and Lissa (1866) but no major maritime wars between significant naval powers. As a result naval opinion was as uncertain about the nature of warfare at sea in 1890 as it had ever been before or since.

Naval fumblings and uncertainties contributed to a widespread loss of confidence in the value and function of navies, and to a tendency instead to concentrate on the value of the great continental armies, especially as exemplified by Bismarck's Germany. In France and Russia the protagonists of seapower found it difficult to compete against their army counterparts. In the United States, the strategically important and technologically innovative navy of the civil war period went into a period of near terminal decline. Even in maritime Britain, recurrent anxieties about the country's vulnerability to invasion led to large-scale schemes for the raising of militia forces, the construction of coastal fortifications along the southern coast and to more being spent on the army than on the navy.

These doubts found expression in schools of thought that many professional sailors found unsettling. In France there appeared the *Jeune Ecole* led from the mid 1870s by Admiral Theophile Aube and the journalist Gabriel Charmes, who argued that new technology, especially in the shape of the torpedo and the torpedo boat, should revive and reinforce France's historic interest in the *guerre de course* (attacks on merchant shipping). Because large ships were now so vulnerable to sneak attacks by torpedo boats the British would no longer be able to make use of their traditional weapon, the naval blockade, against lesser fry. Instead, the smaller maritime powers would be able to use the new technology to make the *guerre de course* even more effective in the future than it had been in the past. By 1914, the correspondence columns of *The Times* showed that there were increasing numbers of people who believed that the advent of the submarine, in particular, meant that the weak naval powers could now bully the strong.

An even more fundamental challenge to seapower arose from a British geographer called Halford Mackinder, who gave a celebrated lecture to the Royal Geographical Society in 1904, entitled 'The geographic pivot of history', and whose ideas were later encapsulated in a book strangely called *Democratic Ideals and Reality*. His basic message was that in the past the maritime powers had been able to dominate the world by their exercise of seapower around the edge of the natural heartland of the world, namely the centre of the Eurasian landmass stretching from Eastern Europe to the Urals. But this would be true no more, for the age of Columbus was over. Now technology (especially in the shape of the railways) and political advance would combine to make it possible for the hugely superior human and material resources of the heartland to be mobilized and mobilized with such effect that the centre would now dominate the periphery. It was all summed up in the jingle:

> Who rules East Europe, commands the Heartland.
> Who rules the Heartland, commands the World Island.
> Who rules the World Island, commands the world.[2]

Since the heartland was the supreme expression of 'landpower', this effectively meant that the elephant would have its historic revenge on the whale. Landpower was increasingly impervious to maritime attack, but on the other hand could often exploit the vulnerabilities of the seapowers by using its army to threaten their naval bases and ports and by diverting some of its vast resources into producing a navy of the sea denial type – such as that proposed a little earlier by the *Jeune Ecole*. Although Mackinder's views were largely ignored in Britain, they were (and indeed are) quite influential elsewhere. They were certainly a source of aid and comfort to those who sought to challenge the proposition that in peace and in war the maritime powers would always win.

The faith reaffirmed

Because of all these doubts and heresies, navalists were relieved and inspired by the extraordinary success of the ideas of new prophets of sea power such as Mahan.

Alfred Thayer Mahan was born in 1840, the son, ironically enough, of a Professor at West Point Military Academy. A scholarly and not very successful naval officer, he developed a theory of seapower that showed what it was and how it worked, and clarified its importance in the scheme of things. He soon joined the staff of the new US Naval War College on Rhode Island, and in 1890 published the first of many major books in which he used the history of British seapower to produce a philosophy of war at sea. His ideas are scattered around all his books and articles, but many of them are summarized in *Naval Strategy*, published in 1911. Feted and lionized as the apostle of seapower, he died in 1914.

It is important though to see Mahan as a product of his times. The success of his ideas was at least as much a consequence of the revival of interest in seapower as a cause of it. By the time he became influential in the United States, the Navy had already begun to claw its way back from the nadir of rot and obsolescence into which it had fallen in the 1870s. Moreover, other apostles of seapower appeared in other countries at much the same time, such as Admiral P. H. Colomb in Britain, Admiral Baron Curt von Maltzahn in Germany and Akiyama Saneyuki in Japan. Although not all these navalists sang exactly the same tune, their view, roughly and briefly, was that seapower would continue to dominate the world because of the persistence of its manifest advantages in mobility and flexibility. National power, security and prosperity depended on foreign commerce across the oceans, which in turn called for a merchant fleet, bases, colonies and naval protection. Countries so endowed would continue to dominate the world just as they always had.

Navalists believed that control of the seas required a large and powerful battlefleet, intent on aggressively offensive operations against hostile battlefleets. The Command of the Sea so won could then be exploited by the protection of trade (and the destruction of the opposition's) and by the projection of military power ashore. Victory would inevitably follow.

A somewhat more judicious British view of the matter was taken by the other major naval writer of the period, Sir Julian Corbett. Born in 1854 into a comfortably middle-class family, Corbett trained as a lawyer and only came to the study of naval affairs in middle age. He lectured on maritime strategy at the Royal Naval College, Greenwich, finding it, he told a friend, 'very uphill work . . . I had no idea when I undertook it how difficult it was to present theory to the unused organs of Naval Officers'.[3] He was close to many of the great men of the Royal Navy of that period, and was actively involved in many of their reforming campaigns. His ideas, too, were based on historical research, and the quality of his thinking can readily be seen in his book *Some Principles of Maritime Strategy*, published in 1911.

Primarily interested in the British example, Corbett emphasized that seapower was no more than a means to a political end. It was important for Britain to have a maritime strategy that suited its political aspirations. Most likely this would be a balanced, amphibious type of strategy, where it would be possible to make the best use of the advantages offered by maritime superiority. Britain should be able to maintain ultimately irresistible economic pressure on its continental foes, support its allies, defend its trade, accumulate wealth to prosecute the war, seize colonies and project military power ashore against the enemy's most vulnerable points. Instead of yielding to the temptation to engage in continental adventures, Britain should maintain a navy second to none, and an army appropriate to an amphibious role.

But Corbett was very well aware that seapower on its own could not overwhelm a strong and resolute landpower. Seapower had its limits, and Britain would need continental allies with large armies in the future as it had in the past. He was also shrewdly conscious of the limitations of Command of the Sea and was prepared to argue very strongly that there was far more to maritime strategy than the pursuit of decisive battles.

The actual influence of these navalists is hard to deduce. They were both certainly quoted more than they were read. As Lord Esher remarked:

> Julian Corbett writes one of the best books in our language upon political and military strategy. All sorts of lessons, some of inestimable value, may be gleaned from it. No-one, except perhaps Winston, who matters just now, has ever read it . . . Obviously history is written for schoolmasters and arm-chair strategists. Statesmen and warriors pick their way through the dusk.[4]

However that may be, navalism, as represented by such writers as these, had recovered from its mid-century doldrums to become very strong in the first two decades of the century. The period leading up to 1914 featured an intense naval arms race, exemplifying and exacerbating the deteriorating relationship between Britain and Germany, and arguably helping to cause the First World War.

As far as the British and Germans were concerned, it was a naval arms race about two things, quantity and quality. In the first place, Germany was determined to win for itself the international status to which it thought its political, economic and cultural strength entitled it. The construction of a battlefleet seemed an attractive way of doing this, because it would weaken Britain, the country seen as most likely to get in the way of German ambitions overseas. Under the inspired leadership of Admiral von Tirpitz, the Germans embarked on a determined battleship construction programme.

At first this was justified on the grounds of Tirpitz's so-called Risk Theory, which aimed to produce an inferior fleet that was, nevertheless still strong enough to threaten the superior British fleet with such damage that Britain would feel vulnerable to later threats from other naval powers. Anticipating their consequent exposure to French/Russian pressure, the British, therefore, would be deterred from using their maritime superiority to pursue policies inimical to German interests. If genuine, this would have been a most imaginative peacetime use of naval power for the broadest purposes of state strategy.

But many historians now believe that these comparatively modest aims were not genuine, and sought simply to conceal Tirpitz's real aim, not for naval sufficiency but for outright superiority. Certainly the British believed this to be the case. As a result, they entered into collaboration with Japan (1902), France (1904) and Russia (1907). Thus the Risk Theory completely backfired, adding to Germany's enemies rather than reducing them. A redistribution of Britain's naval assets back to home waters and the unambiguous way in which these assets were pointed at an enemy across the North Sea (Scapa Flow, not Portsmouth, became the main naval base) reinforced the point.

Worse still from the German point of view, the British embarked on a determined and ultimately successful programme of naval counterbuilding. The two countries passed through periods of acute antagonism, but in general the British, aided by having fewer continental distractions, maintained their superiority. Although figures vary, the eve of war position was approximately as shown in Table 4.1.

Naval competition was not merely in terms of quantity and number, but also in the quality of naval assets. Naval technology was developing its own momentum, driving admirals and statesmen into policies of expansion. The most important aspect of this was quite clearly the growing power and range of the large naval gun. The increasing decisiveness of naval artillery put a premium on efficient fire-control, powerful armament and heavy armour, and in various countries the idea of an 'all-big-gun ship' began to emerge.

Britain's Admiral Jacky Fisher took the lead in this, and in 1906 launched a revolutionary battleship called the *Dreadnought* with ten 12-inch guns. Because six of these could fire ahead/astern and eight could be used for a broadside, *Dreadnought* was equal to three

Table 4.1 The naval balance on the eve of the First World War

Britain		Germany
20	Dreadnoughts	13
9	Battlecruisers	5
2	Nelsons	0
12	Dreadnoughts building	7
1	Battlecruisers building	3
3	Dreadnoughts building for other countries	0
39	Pre-Dreadnoughts	22

Source: A. J. Marder, *From Dreadnought to Scapa Flow*, Vol. 1 (London: Oxford University Press, 1961, pp. 439–42).

ordinary battleships ahead and two on the broadside. For this reason, said Fisher, the launch of *Dreadnought* would:

> mark the beginning of a new naval epoch. For . . . all existing battleships – even the most modern – will be practically obsolete . . . Today all nations start *de novo*.[5]

The trouble was that a good proportion of the world's existing battleships, now obsolete, were British, a point made with some force by Fisher's critics. But Fisher argued that Britain now had no choice. If the British did not produce the *Dreadnought*, then someone else would. Furthermore, Fisher followed the *Dreadnought* with his equally famous *Invincible* class battlecruisers, large 25,000- ton ships armed with eight 12-inch guns but lightly armoured. They were supposed to be able to fight their way through enemy cruiser screens to find the enemy fleet, and to be powerful enough to slow it down until the main battlefleet arrived. They should also be fast enough to run away from enemy battleships if necessary, and to hunt down detached cruisers. Once again, Fisher's lead was followed by the Germans and others.

This material advance was backed up in all the world's major navies by extensive programmes of naval reform, in the admission, training and employment of personnel, in staff work and organization, and in preparations for mobilization. The consequences of this for the conduct of naval operations remained to be seen, however, and so, for that matter, did the validity of the case proposed at this time by the navalists about the strategic advantages of power at sea.

The naval side of the First World War

British maritime strategy in the First World War was not 'maritime' as understood by the pre-war theorists. Such a strategy would have been based on the Royal Navy defeating the enemy, imposing a blockade, destroying Germany's overseas empire and firing the army like a projectile into the enemy's flank areas. Instead, a large proportion of Britain's war effort was aimed at the provision and support of a huge continental army, which was to play a central role on the Western Front. The effort devoted to this could not be given to a maritime strategy, and so the Royal Navy found itself operating with fewer resources and with more severe constraints than it had anticipated.

Britain's geographic advantages and battlefleet superiority meant that Britain had Command of the Sea, and could exploit that command to the extent of mounting a tight commercial blockade on German shipping, which more or less cut off Germany from the outer oceans. Provided that there were no catastrophes on land, it seemed, Britain would eventually be able to defeat Germany.

But this would be a very slow process, because the imposition of the blockade and efforts to neutralize the German High Seas Fleet took up so high a proportion of Britain's naval capacity that there was little left to be used on other things. Nor could the British afford to run the risk of imposing a close military blockade on Germany, and, even before the war, had decided that a distant blockade, which allowed the Germans more sea room, would have to do. And there was also the generally unrecognized possibility that some new naval development might come about to upset all these calculations.

In short, the situation was acceptable from Britain's point of view. Although the Royal Navy was anxious to seize every opportunity to destroy the High Seas Fleet rather than simply to neutralize it (because such a victory would hasten Germany's collapse), its leaders also knew they could easily lose the war in an afternoon. An outright victory would be welcome, but it was not essential; for this reason, the British were not prepared to force a battle on the Germans at any cost.

But when the extent of Germany's caution became clear, the British became more interested in schemes that would force the Germans into battle, such as deep probes into the German Bight, carrier air strikes on the German coast and, more remotely, amphibious attacks on Heligoland or Germany itself.

Germany's maritime strategy was cautious, not only because of the professional prudence brought about by its naval inferiority (although in the period between October 1914 and February 1915, refits and absences meant that the British lead was surprisingly small) but also for other strategic reasons. The army dominated Germany's strategy, and considered naval concerns of only secondary importance, except in so far as they protected Germany from amphibious assault. The politicians wanted to keep the fleet intact as a bargaining tool for end-of-war negotiations and were anxious about the effect a defeat would have on German and neutral opinion.

The German Fleet War Order of 1914 summed up the Germans' strategy well:

> Our object is to damage the British fleet by means of offensive advances against the forces and *watching or blockading the German Bight*, and also by means of a ruthless mining, and if possible a submarine offensive carried out as far as the British Coast.
>
> When an *equalisation of forces* has been attained by these measures, all our forces are to be got ready and concentrated and an endeavour will be made to bring our fleet into action under favourable conditions.[6] (My emphasis.)

The phrases emphasised are important. The reference to the 'equalisation of forces' showed that the Germans were only prepared to accept main battle with the British when a preliminary strategy of mine and submarine attack, with ambushes of isolated sections of the Grand Fleet, had reduced British seapower to manageable proportions. Until the great day came when the Germans could finally settle accounts with the British, it was sensible for them to keep their forces safe.

The reference to 'forces . . . blockading the German Bight' plainly assumed that the British would be maintaining a close military blockade on the German side of the North Sea. Such a blockade should offer satisfactory opportunities for equalization. The German Navy was dismayed to discover that the British were not after all prepared to charge into their own destruction, and gradually the need was recognized for a more offensive strategy to force the British into a battle on German terms. In February 1915 Admiral von Pohl took over from von Ingenohl as commander of the High Seas Fleet, and gave German maritime strategy a marginally more offensive air. The big change, though, came with the arrival of Admiral Scheer in January 1916; but by that time Germany's window of opportunity had closed.

For the first two years of the war there were various minor battles. In some cases these were clashes between isolated fleet detachments operating in the outer oceans (for example, the battles of Coronel and the Falkland Islands) but generally they were the results of probes by either side. In the Scarborough raid of 16 December 1914 and the battle of the Dogger Bank on 19 January 1915, the Germans sought to lure just a part of the British Fleet into action. In others, such as the succession of carrier-assisted forays into the German Bight (exemplified by the Cuxhaven Raid of Christmas Day 1914), the British tried to sting the Germans into action. Of these generally inconclusive battles, the action at the Dogger Bank was probably the most important. The German idea was to surprise British light cruiser screens in the area and then to ambush Admiral Beatty's Battlecruiser Force, based at Rosyth, as it came up to support them. Things did not work out that way and the Germans, who lost the battle, recognized certain technical deficiencies in battlecruiser design and fleet operation, which the British, who won, did not.

Both sides were disappointed in the way things had gone generally. The Germans had been unable to reverse a strategic trend that would ultimately lead, they thought, to their defeat at sea. The British had not yet won a new Trafalgar. One of the reasons for this had been that the military performance of both sides' battlefleets was less impressive than people had anticipated before the war. Submarines, for one thing had proved a real constraint. After the Disaster of the Broad Fourteens in September 1914, when one U-boat had sunk three antiquated cruisers as though potting ducks in a shooting gallery, the British swung from scepticism about the submarine to something approaching hysteria. The mere suspicion of a periscope caused several 'battles' at fleet anchorages, with destroyers rushing about dropping depth charges like confetti at a wedding.

But in fact the Germans were consistently disappointed in their submarines' capacity to attack major British units, or even to report their activities accurately. The same could be said of other new weapons, such as torpedo boats, mines, aircraft and airships. They were occasionally successful, but only to the extent of making the fleet commanders on both sides accumulate more integral defences (torpedo-boat destroyers, minesweepers, ship-borne fighter cover, and so on) and operate their battlefleets with an additional caution that simply made it more difficult for either to succeed in forcing a battle on their terms.

Moreover, both battlefleets had proved unwieldy, sluggish and short-legged. Throughout the war, finding the opposition, even in the restricted waters of the North Sea, proved very difficult indeed, despite the best efforts of Zeppelins and other reconnaissance aircraft, submarine picket lines and naval intelligence. In addition, the gunnery accuracy of battlefleets was very poor. At Jutland, the Germans were thought to have done quite well in the circumstances to have achieved a hit rate of 3.44 per cent (compared with 2.17 per cent for the British). Battlefleets, in fact, were the ultimate in blunt instruments.

Even so, the German High Seas Fleet, under the energetic leadership of Admiral Scheer, was anxious to overcome these difficulties and even up the odds a little by destroying Admiral Beatty's Battlecruiser Force. The increasing effect of the British blockade and Britain's growing numerical superiority convinced Scheer that the situation at sea, and therefore on land, could only get worse. Already Britain proved to have had enough surplus capacity to mount and support major amphibious operations in the Dardanelles in 1915. The fact that the campaign was a dismal failure was not the point. It might well have succeeded in its intention of undermining the German coalition in just the way that Corbett and others had prophesied; at the very least it was an earnest of what Germany might have to face in the years to come, unless something was done to improve the situation.

It was Scheer's desire to improve the odds by ambushing Beatty's Battlecruiser Force that led to the Battle of Jutland on 31 May 1916.[7] The result of this, the largest ever clash between opposing battlefleets, was disappointing for the British. They suffered the loss of 14 ships, totalling some 111,000 tons, and 6784 casualties against German losses of 11 ships (62,000 tons) and 3058 casualties. A host of minor things had gone wrong for the British. There were signal and intelligence failures, deficiencies in the quality of their armour protection, shells and fire control. The Grand Fleet had been difficult to handle as a tactical unit. Like a brontosaurus, its size had sapped its strength.

Although, tactically, the German fleet had won a minor victory and had effected an escape so that its leaders could live to tell their tale, strategically the situation remained at least as bad as it had been before, and arguably worse. Scheer realized that the German effort to wrest naval supremacy away from the British by these orthodox means was bound to fail and so abandoned it. It is true that, despite the legend, the High Seas Fleet did go to sea once more, but in an even more gingerly fashion than it had before.

There were those who argued that this was an unnecessary battle. Churchill put it like this:

Although the battle squadrons of the Grand Fleet have been denied all opportunity of decisive battle, yet from the beginning they have enjoyed all the fruits of a complete victory. If Germany had never built a Dreadnought, or if all the Dreadnoughts had been sunk, the control and authority of the British Navy could not have been more effective . . . There was no need for the British to seek battle at all . . . A keen desire to engage the enemy impelled, and a cool calculation of ample margins of superiority justified, a movement not necessarily required by any practical need.[8]

Corbett, who wrote the first three volumes of the Official History of the war, later got into trouble with the Admiralty for agreeing with Churchill to the extent of saying that there were other more important things to which the British should have devoted their maritime efforts, not least the protection of trade and the projection of power ashore.

If Mahan had still been alive at the time, he would almost certainly have sided with the other school, which argued that a more decisive victory would have made a significant difference to the outcome of the war. It would have been a devastating blow to German morale and at the same time encouraged Britain's allies and the neutral powers. It would have released destroyers and other resources from the Grand Fleet for convoy escort work, and so forth. It would have made possible Anglo-Russian efforts in the Baltic. It would have allowed the British to impose a really crippling close military and economic blockade of Germany, cutting that country off even from Scandinavia. And it would have allowed the British to seal the U-boats into their harbours.

Despite their differences, these two schools of thought were agreed that battlefleet supremacy was the key to victory in the war at sea, and therefore to the ultimate outcome of the whole confict. But not everyone agreed, then or since.

When Scheer returned from Jutland he reported to the Kaiser that further such efforts would be futile. Instead:

> A victorious end to the war at not too distant a date can only be looked for by the crushing of English economic life through U-boat action against English commerce.[9]

The Germans then bent their efforts to an unrestricted submarine war, which by the Spring of 1917 was leading to the sinking of between 500,000 and 750,000 tons of shipping per month. This was quite devastating, and a gloomy Admiral Jellicoe (First Sea Lord) told the Government that Britain would have to seek an armistice by November, if losses continued at this rate.

On the face of it, the U-boat war seemed to show that the French *Jeune Ecole* had been right after all. New technology in the shape of submarines (and mines) had shown the battlefleet to be basically an irrelevance. The war had been won and lost by little ships and submarines on the distant oceans, not by the great ships swinging uselessly at their anchors in the Jade and at Scapa Flow. As things turned out, would it not have been better for Tirpitz to have built a fleet of submarines, not Dreadnoughts and battlecruisers?

Orthodox opinion dismissed such heresies quite easily, by going back to what might have happened if Jutland had turned out differently. If the German fleet had won, British trade would have been quite indefensible, and Britain would have collapsed in weeks. Because the great ships of the Grand Fleet had stopped that from happening, they had achieved a level of command of the sea that the small ships could exploit to win the first submarine war.

The U-boat campaign was more successful than it should have been because the British had not used their trade defence assets properly (in particular by being reluctant to convoy merchant ships). The U-boat campaign was defeated by a combination of better tactics, and better equipment, but this success in no way required the material down-rating of the battlefleet. As far as the orthodox were concerned, it all simply went to show that Mahan and Corbett were right. Unless it was based on Command of the Sea, any attack on maritime communications would eventually fail.

Orthodox opinion also concluded that the war demonstrated once more the contribution that seapower could make to victory. Although it was true that the extent of British Command of the Sea was less than the British wanted (and so, for example, the Germans were able to operate in the Baltic by disrupting links between Russia and her Western allies), maritime supremacy was a vital ingredient in the final success. It had the negative value of preventing the Germans from successfully exploiting any of Britain's maritime vulnerabilities.

Maritime supremacy, the orthodox argued, had many positive advantages. It allowed the British to seize all German colonies. Because of it, huge numbers of soldiers and mountains of equipment (e.g. 1 million French soldiers and 2 million American soldiers over a period of 17 months) could be transported to the scene of military operations. Only by seapower could the military power of the Americans and British be brought to bear in the relevant theatre. British and allied seapower kept going the huge flow of supplies needed to fuel the war economy. Seapower played an important part in the destruction of Turkey, and crippled Germany through the imposition of a stringent blockade. And the ultimate cause of these and other strategic benefits was the battleship. As Admiral Kato reported to the Japanese Parliament, after the war:

> the more we study the experience gained in the war, the stronger grows our conviction that the last word in a naval campaign is still with the capital ship and the heavy gun.[10]

Renewed doubts in the interwar period

The interwar period was another era of very rapid technological change, which seemed likely to upset traditional patterns of thought about the conduct of naval warfare. Submarines were developed steadily both as a means for the attack of shipping and as an adjunct to the battlefleet. Although the U-boat had been defeated in the First World War, and although the arrival of ASDIC was expected to help its defeat in any subsequent conflict, Britain was anxious that the submarine should be banned. It was a measure of their continued faith in the future of the submarine that the French, among others, resisted any such idea. Even so, orthodox sailors in the British, German, Japanese and American navies tended to be over-sanguine about their ability to cope with this threat.

There was tremendous controversy about the future of the battleship, which was generally regarded as the capital ship of the time, that is, the backbone of the battlefleet. Progressives, such as Liddell Hart, maintained that orthodox sailors had the same attitude to battleships as bishops have to cathedrals and were not realistic about their growing limitations. There were two major issues:

(a) How vulnerable was the battleship to submarine and air attack? Although the strength of their 'conservatism' is usually much exaggerated, most naval officers failed to gauge the extent to which new technology would threaten battleships and the established types of naval operation to which they contributed.

(b) There was almost as much controversy about what the size of the battleship should be. Defending them against the new threats meant more deck armour, anti-aircraft gunnery and anti-torpedo measures. This resulted in a tendency to make battleships ever bigger. As they became bigger, they became more expensive, individually more valuable in strategic terms (so that naval commanders would be less inclined to risk them) and less mobile (as they needed such large docks and there were few of these). Doubts grew, therefore, as to their cost-effectiveness. Since in most people's view battleships and seapower were synonymous, this amounted to a major challenge to the continued strategic centrality of conventional navies.[11]

The other great controversy of the period was the extent to which airpower (and perhaps even the land-based variety of the sort represented by the RAF) could take on roles traditionally carried out by groups of ships. In Britain, for example, the air staff argued that the aircraft's increased capacity to sink ships – an impression much exaggerated by very loaded experiments carried out by General Billy Mitchell in the United States in 1921[12] – meant that airpower could take over much of the traditional role of defending Britain and its overseas dependencies, such as Singapore, from invasion.

There was also the narrower, but equally intense controversy over what balance should be struck between the navy's own airpower and other traditional naval weapon systems. Would naval aircraft perform simply ancillary duties (spotting, reconnaissance, anti-submarine patrols) or might they take on the primary task of attacking the enemy's battleline? In Britain, as elsewhere, opinion was divided, with most inclining to caution in their acceptance of change.

The conclusions that individual navies came to about all of this varied. Generally speaking, the Americans and Japanese navies took the lead in the development of naval aviation (although the extent of this is usually exaggerated) but were out-of-touch in the matter of the submarine and trade defence. The Germans, surprisingly enough, were very sceptical about the future importance of submarines. In nearly all these issues the British steered a middle course, being neither very right nor very wrong.

But nearly all sailors were agreed that the new technology had not undermined the future importance of seapower. There were, though, few major theoretical explorations of maritime strategy at the time. Two of the most influential were the works of Admirals Sir Herbert Richmond in Britain and Raoul Castex in France. These both considered the experience of the First World War and the likely impact of new technology, and concluded with a fairly conventional reaffirmation of the faith.[13]

Richmond and Castex tended to argue that seapower would absorb the new technology so that it would become a part of the naval arsenal. The aircraft, for example, would become a naval weapon, which would help the battleship to perform its tasks. At some future date, aircraft carriers (or the submarine) might even become the new capital ship instead of the battleship. Because new technology simply made possible new naval weapons and tactics, none of this in any way implied a reduction in the importance of seapower.

Around the world, sailors argued that the supreme expression of seapower remained the balanced battlefleet, a mixed and integrated unit capable of performing all the functions of battle. Although there were different emphases from navy to navy, the battlefleet was widely thought likely to operate on these broad lines:

Finding the enemy This would be the first task, which would be the responsibility of light cruiser screens, submarine picket lines, and/or shore- and sea-based reconnaissance aircraft. Once the enemy was located, the battlefleet would deploy from a cruising disposition into a battleline.

Fixing the enemy   In the event the enemy sought to escape he would need to be slowed up until the main part of the battlefleet arrived. Submarines, torpedo or bomb-dropping aircraft, or detached battlecruisers could be used to do this.

Strike   Fleet submarines, destroyers and aircraft might all be used to help disrupt the enemy's formation of a battleline and thereby his attempts to concentrate his firepower. The enemy's attempts to do likewise would be defeated by the defensive action of destroyers, fighters and anti-aircraft fire. The main devastation of the battleline would be wrought by the heavy guns of the battleline, aided by spotter aircraft. Further aircraft, destroyer and submarine attack on the enemy's fleet would add to the general effect.

The degree of Command of the Sea enjoyed depended on the battlefleet's actual or anticipated success in such battles as this. The more Command of the Sea, the easier it would be for the victor to defend his merchant fleet and attack the opposition's, and to project military power against the shore.

Some navies tended to lay more stress than others on particular parts of this generalized picture of naval warfare. The Americans and the Japanese put more stress on the aerial component of the battlefleet than the British felt able to. The British are often accused, moreover, of concentrating too much in the interwar years on preparing for the decisive battle and not enough on the techniques of trade protection and amphibious operation. The Second World War was to show there to be some justice in this charge.

The naval side of the Second World War

In the Second World War, the British found themselves confronting adversaries who generally preferred to avoid decisive battle, for the best of all possible reasons, namely that they would probably lose it. Both the Italians and the Germans instead practised a kind of fleet-in-being strategy. Recognizing that they had inferior surface fleets, they sought to extract as much strategic benefit as they could from their naval forces by keeping them intact and using them only with caution.

The role of the battleship *Tirpitz* illustrates the policy well. Its wartime career was spent largely at anchor in one of the fjords in Norway. But the fact that it could, and sometimes did proceed to sea, and that it was intrinsically a very powerful ship, meant that the British had to escort every convoy going to Russia strongly enough to deal with the *Tirpitz*, should it seek to interfere. In the nature of things, this tied down a sizeable part of the Home Fleet and reduced the Royal Navy's capacity elsewhere. This explains why the British devoted such effort to the destruction of a ship which, on the face of it, did virtually nothing at all throughout the year.

It was plain that the German and Italian navies were forced to work to a rather different philosophy of naval warfare, where they engaged in activities without first gaining the level of Command of the Sea which orthodox opinion said they needed in order to be successful. Thus the Germans almost immediately launched another U-boat campaign against Britain's Atlantic shipping, and in 1940 invaded Norway in the teeth of British naval supremacy, which Admiral Raeder admitted 'is contrary to all principles in the theory of naval warfare'.[14]

The Germans nevertheless succeeded because they were able to show that shore-based airpower gave them a measure of control over the sea which partly compensated for their naval weakness. The same lesson was drummed home during the British evacuation of Crete, where British losses were equivalent to those of a good-sized fleet action. In actions like this the British discovered that the battlefleet needed more in the way of defensive fighters and anti-aircraft guns than prewar estimates suggested. The subsequent Mediterranean campaign, amphibious operations in Europe and the Pacific campaign all showed that, when these became available, the fleet was able to move more confidently back into such narrow waters.

The idea of conducting naval operations without first seeking to gain or maintain Command of the Sea through decisive fleet actions was taken still further in the naval war between Germany and the Soviet Union. Both in the Black Sea and Baltic Sea there were significant naval actions, mainly in direct support of army operations ashore. Generally, though, neither side sought confrontation at sea with the other's main naval forces. There were several reasons for this. The Germans kept most of their naval forces for the struggle with the

Western allies; the Soviet Navy suffered from poor leadership, and its concerns were dominated by the army. The much greater emphasis given to land operations meant, for example, that too few naval assets and little shore-based aircover were available for more ambitious naval operations designed to secure Command of the Sea.

No doubt Mahan would have said that, since neither side had much in the way of naval supremacy, neither side could make as much strategic use of the sea as it might have done. The fact that the Germans were able to evacuate lost territory almost without interference shows that, especially towards the end of the war, the Soviet Navy let slip many opportunities to contribute to the destruction of the German war effort, which it might have been able to exploit if it had achieved a higher level of Command of the Sea.

The situation was quite different in the Pacific where, rather in the spirit of the Anglo-Dutch wars of the seventeenth century, both protagonists bent every effort to the struggle for naval supremacy. Accordingly, they sought and fought a great series of major naval battles across the face of the world's biggest ocean, in exactly the manner prophesied by Mahan. Of course, the style of battle was different and, in such encounters as the Battle of the Coral Sea and the Battle of Midway, it gradually became clear that the new capital ship of the world's navies was now the aircraft carrier. For the first time in history, the protagonists of a battle fought without their main forces catching sight of each other. In a celebrated passage Samuel Morison described the battleship encounter in October 1944 between Admirals Nishimura and Oldendorf as 'firing a funeral salute to a finished era of naval warfare. One can imagine the ghosts of the great admirals from Raleigh to Jellicoe standing to attention as the battleline went into oblivion.'[15] But, although technology took radically different forms in the carrier battles of the Pacific, the strategic principles of seapower seemed to be the same.

The extent of the technological change, though, should not be exaggerated. While there were five great carrier battles in the Pacific war, there were also twenty-two other major surface naval actions. As late as 17 June 1944, there appears in Admiral Spruance's orders for the Battle of the Phillippine Sea little that would have seemed remarkable ten or fifteen years earlier:

> Our aircraft will first knock out enemy's CVs [aircraft carriers] as operating carriers, then will attack enemy battleships or

cruisers, to slow or disable them. Task Group 58.7 [Admiral Lee's battleship gun-line] will destroy the enemy fleet by fleet action if enemy elects to fight or by sinking slowed or crippled ships if enemy retreats.[16]

There were battles centred on aircraft carriers in the European war too. Indeed, the very first one ever was the great Battle of Taranto on 11 November 1940, when a force of twenty-one Swordfish aircraft from HMS *Illustrious* sank three Italian battleships in the Mediterranean and quite transformed the strategic situation. But, generally, naval actions in this theatre took a more traditional form, not least because neither the Germans, Russians nor the Italians had operational carriers in their fleet. In such encounters as the battle of Cape Matapan, the destruction of the *Bismarck* and the *Scharnhorst*, and the battle of Cape Spartivento, there were many very familiar features to the conduct of operations. Perhaps the best example was the action off Calabria in July 1940. Admiral Cunningham described it like this:

> First we had the contact of long-range reconnaissance aircraft: then the exact position of the enemy relative to our own Fleet by the FAA [Fleet Air Arm] aircraft from the carrier, and the informative and accurate reports of their trained observers. Next the carrier's striking force of torpedo bombers went in to attack, though on this occasion, through no fault of their own, they were not successful. Meanwhile, the cruisers, spread on a line of bearing, pushed in to locate the enemy's battlefleet, and finally the heavy ships themselves came into action.[17]

The whole thing bore an almost uncanny resemblance to numerous exercises and table battles of the interwar period, even to the extent of the cruiser *Neptune* making once more the traditional signal 'Enemy battlefleet in sight'.

Moreover, in such encounters the battleship proved just as difficult to sink as its prewar advocates said it would. The *Bismarck* for example only succumbed after receiving the attentions of 8 British battleships or battlecruisers, 2 carriers, 11 cruisers, 21 destroyers and 300 aircraft sorties. A total of 60 torpedoes were launched at her and she was bombarded for several hours by the heavy guns of the British battleline. 'There could hardly be any better proof of the modern battleship's staying power.'[18]

Although it is plainly necessary, therefore, to enter some qualifications about the claim, it is nevertheless clear that by the end of the Second World War a major change had taken place in the nature of naval battle. Although both remained essential, the gun had yielded to the naval aircraft as the major naval weapon system, and the appearance and composition of the balanced fleet would now be significantly different to what it had been.

To discuss briefly how the sea was used, the navies of the belligerents were once more engaged in strenuous battles for control of the sea communications on which the transportation of men and materials and the functioning of the allied war economy depended. Clearly the war would have ended differently if the German U-boat campaign had proved successful. But, once again, it was defeated by a whole combination of measures, including convoy-and-escort, air patrols, construction programmes, operational intelligence, support groups, and so on. Mahan would have said, no doubt, that such an outcome was inevitable (though it certainly did not look like this to the protagonists) because the Germans did not have the required level of Command of the Sea. No doubt, too, he would have argued in contrast that the brilliant success of his own navy's submarine war against Japan was based on naval mastery, just as it should have been.

Because the British and Americans and their allies were in the main separated from their adversaries by large stretches of waters, amphibious operations were bound to take a much more prominent position in this war than in the last. To start with, these most difficult of operations were not conducted well, but by the end, the Western allies' capacity for amphibious warfare at a strategic level was one of the central features of the war and seriously alarmed the Soviet Union, their erstwhile ally.[17]

To conclude, seapower was once more a vital component of the British and American conduct of the war. There were those who argued that perhaps its contribution was somewhat less this time than it had been in the First World War, because the centrality of the major clash of huge continental armies, especially on the Eastern front, was relatively more important and because the Reich was much less susceptible to blockade than had been the Kaiser's Germany. Nevertheless, it seems hard to quarrel with Corbett's conclusion that, although navies on their own do not defeat continental landpowers, they make it possible for armies to do so. In the Second World War in Europe, seapower was a necessary but not sufficient cause of allied victory. In the Pacific, arguably, it was the decisive form of military action.

Navies in the nuclear age

Even before the Second World War ended, the explosion of atomic bombs over Hiroshima and Nagasaki heralded a new era of technological change. Since 1945 the world has changed in many political and economic ways too. Some experts have argued that changes in the law of the sea will reduce the value of navies by undermining their traditional mobility and flexibility.[19] Others have concluded that political changes have reduced the utility of applied force of all varieties, naval ones included. Since, as we shall see, navalists pride themselves on the political usefulness of navies in peacetime, this charge is a serious one.[20]

But it is undoubtedly in the technological area that change has threatened to bring about the most profound transformations in the general importance of seapower, in the roles that navies perform and in the way they perform them. The revolution in weaponry stands out, particularly with the development of nuclear weapons and their possible application to war at sea. The sinking of the Israeli destroyer *Eilat* by the Egyptian Navy in 1967 confirmed the age of the naval missile, as did the Indo-Pakistan war of 1971, the Falklands War of 1982 and the current Iran–Iraq war. These new weapons are more lethal, more accurate, of longer range, apparently capable of infinite development, and launchable from the smallest of naval platforms.

Perhaps, by narrowing the gap between large and small naval forces, naval missiles will at last justify the historic claims of the *Jeune Ecole*? Maybe, the claims of the air school of the interwar period have now finally turned out to be right? On the other hand, missiles give the large surface ships such as the Soviet Navy's nuclear battlecruiser *Kirov* or the US Navy's *New Jersey* battleships more defensive and offensive power than they have ever had before.

The large nuclear-propelled fleet carrier, with a complement of 90-odd aircraft and a bewildering array of defensive and offensive armament, when operating within what the US Navy calls a Carrier Battle Group, still represents an awesome accretion of power. For that very reason, it also represents a tempting target, not least to nuclear weapons. In many quarters the same criticisms are made of the continued strategic validity of the fleet carrier as were made of the battleship in the interwar period.

The lethality of modern weapons has increased the advantages of hiding, and many would argue that its particular combination of effective firepower, relative concealment, high speed and long endurance through nuclear propulsion has raised the submarine to a status above that of the surface ship. It seems to many that it is no longer the aircraft carrier, still less the battleship (even with cruise missiles and nuclear weapons) but the nuclear-propelled submarine that is the capital ship of the late twentieth century.

Nevertheless, the surface ship would still seem to be an essential ingredient in any attempt to use the sea for the transport of men and materials or for the projection of power ashore. The fact that the surface ship operates at once above the water (with its helicopters, missiles and electronics), on the surface, and below it (with its anti-submarine weaponry) also makes it uniquely flexible, both in peace and in war.

Moreover, the surface ship still enjoys huge advantages in that other main dimension of technological change in modern warfare: the revolution in communications, sensors and command and control. The volume of potential reconnaissance and battle information has enormously increased during the past several decades thanks to the advent of surveillance and communications satellites, sensor technology and computer data processing. The problems that these advances also bring are more manageable on surface ships than anywhere else. As the French Admiral Hubert Moineville has recently concluded:

Thus missiles, data processing and helicopters have restored standard surface ships to their rightful place in combat at sea – something that would have seemed unlikely some years ago.[21]

In recent years the US Navy has reactivated its *Iowa* class of battleships (58,000 tons) and the Soviet Navy has built the 32,000-ton *Kirov* nuclear battlecruiser class and the 13,000-ton *Slava* class of heavy cruiser. All around the world, in fact, ships of all classes have shown an apparently unstoppable tendency to get bigger. This all suggests that earlier, once fashionable views of the imminent demise of the large surface ship have proved completely illusory.[22] The conclusion of the orthodox majority is, therefore, that the balanced fleet must still retain a wide variety of different types of weapon platforms, just as it has always done, Perhaps, however, the mix of the components has altered a little, with relatively rather more emphasis now being given to submarines and to small combatants with missiles.

However, the radicals remain. Their argument is, briefly, that the technological, political and economic changes described here have tended to reduce the value of seapower, or have at least changed its historic procedures out of all recognition. Two arguments are commonly advanced. First, naval defence inflation has changed the relationship between the various forces concerned with the sea. In particular, weapons platforms required for positive use on the sea (e.g. large surface ships, carriers, amphibious warfare ships, merchant ships and their escorts) have become relatively more expensive than the forces that seek to deny that use (submarines, mine-warfare vessels, aircraft). This is because they are technologically more vulnerable, and therefore need ever more expensive layers of defensive armament. Increasingly, it would seem, the useful and positive side of seapower will become too expensive for more and more countries, at least in situations where such power is or might be threatened.

Secondly, it was claimed that the advent of nuclear weapons would reduce the relative value of navies because future conflicts between the great powers would either be short because nuclear weapons were used or be kept short for fear that they might be. Either way, the war would be over before navies had time to exercise a decisive influence on its outcome, because, as all the traditional theories agreed, the exercise of maritime power is essentially a slow-acting business. This caused something of a crisis of confidence even in the strongest navies, analogous to the one in the nineteenth century. As Admiral Gorshkov remarked:

> It turned out unfortunately that we had some very influential 'authorities' who considered that with the appearance of atomic weapons, the Navy had completely lost its value as a branch of the armed forces. According to their views, all of the basic missions in a future war allegedly could be fully resolved without the participation of the Navy.[23]

This prophecy of naval doom turned out to be wrong as well. The defence policies of the two superpowers now have a much greater

Warfare in the Twentieth Century

maritime orientation than they have had for decades. Moreover, during the past twenty years, there has been a surprising number of wars with a significant naval component, including the Arab–Israeli wars of 1967 and 1973, the Vietnam War, the Indo–Pakistan war of 1971, the Turkish invasion of Cyprus in 1974, the Falklands War of 1982 and the current Iran–Iraq war.

Among the various reasons for all this, no doubt, is the expectation that the catastrophic consequence of going nuclear would greatly inhibit the use of such weapons, and by making unavoidable wars long, limited or both, would render conventional military operations perfectly possible. The non-nuclear powers, moreover, have no alternative to preparing for conventional conflict. In point of fact, and despite changes in their political, economic and technological environment, the world's navies have found themselves conducting a range of activities both in peace and in war that are intrinsically familiar and are themselves carried out in a rather familiar way.

Admiral Sergei Gorshkov, lately Commander-in-Chief of the Soviet Navy, is the nearest the postwar world has produced to a Mahan, Corbett or Richmond, and his book *The Seapower of the State* is a convenient guide to the current and anticipated functions of navies. His views are of interest not only for this reason but also because he also acts as a spokesman of one of the world's very newest navies. As such, Admiral Gorshkov is an ideal example of a very modern mariner. Further, as will be shown later, his views have more general applicability than might at first appear to be the case.

To Admiral Gorshkov and other Soviet writers, the concept of sea dominance is at least analogous to what Corbett would have understood by Command of the Sea. It means 'the capacity to attain military or economic aims in the ocean, independent of the countermeasures of the adversary.'[24] The more favourable this 'operational regime' the more can the sea be used for positive purposes in furtherance of the war effort, and the more can it be denied to the adversary. Modern technology, however, means that the attainable and perhaps necessary level of sea dominance will be lower; it will probably prove to be more localized and less permanent than in the past.

The neutralization rather than destruction of the adversary's main naval forces through the maintenance of the fleet-in-being and the imposition of blockade remains possible. Indeed, the Soviet Navy imposed a blockade in the 1973 Arab–Israeli war, and in its exercises shows itself to be interested both in maintaining and breaking blockades. Nevertheless, sea dominance is still best based on victory in a decisive sea engagement. 'The battle always was,' wrote Gorshkov, 'and remains the main means of solving tactical tasks.'[25]

Regarding the conduct of battle, this is how Admiral Chernarvin, Gorshkov's successor as Commander-in-Chief, put it fairly recently:

> Under modern conditions, a naval battle represents a combination of strikes by heterogeneous forces . . . [with] . . . regard to target, place and time, and the precision of the cooperation of these forces acquires ever greater and greater significance in battle.[26]

Soviet writings suggest, and a look at the size and shape of the Soviet Navy confirms, that the Soviet understanding of a balanced fleet is a rather traditional one. Although there is perhaps greater stress on the relative importance of submarines and land-based naval aircraft than in the US Navy, for instance, considerable importance is attached to providing as many different types of attacking systems as possible, including large surface ships and aircraft carriers. This diversity is necessary because it affords the naval commander operational flexibility and makes it easier for him to conduct the diverse, geographically dispersed but integrated sequence of strikes on enemy forces understood to be the essential part of a naval battle.

In all probability these battles would not be independent events as Jutland was, but would be part and parcel of larger naval operations intended to make use of the sea for the attack/defence of shipping and/or the land. In fact, this was generally the case even in the Second World War.

Soviet writers, and Soviet exercises, devote much attention to the defence of all forms of sea-borne attack, and it is in connection with these operations that they seem to believe naval battles most likely to occur. During the years since 1945 various types of threat have been identified. In the late 1940s the Russians tended to be very concerned about the threat implied by the Anglo-Americans' demonstrated capacity for amphibious warfare on an oceanic scale. In the 1950s the nuclear-armed aircraft of US Navy carriers seemed very threatening. In the 1960s the menace of the ballistic-missile-firing submarine came to the fore, and more recently there have been anxieties about the threat posed by cruise missiles fired from naval aircraft, submarines and surface ships.

Defending Soviet territory against such threats clearly requires the establishment of a notional defensive perimeter as far forward as possible. In recent years, exercises show this perimeter to have been moving out from the Soviet Union. Now its outer edge, which would probably take the form of a submarine screen, has passed through the Greenland–Iceland–UK gap, and is somewhere to the south-west of it. Land-based aircraft would supplement defences against any invaders as they came north. Closer still to the Soviet Union, the invaders would encounter the main units of the surface fleet, and finally the Soviet Navy's myriad forces of coastal defence.

Strategic defence against ballistic-missile-firing submarines (SSBNs) is nowadays a rather different kind of operation because the great range of modern submarine-launched missiles means that submarines do not need to come anywhere near the Soviet Union. To deal with this threat, Soviet anti-submarine forces would have to move very far forward indeed, and many would doubt this to be a practical proposition in the present circumstances. It is interesting that Soviet writers have always argued that this is a perfectly legitimate task; they do not appear to sympathize with views heard in the West that hunting SSBNs may prove destabilizing.

There is not much doubt that the Soviet Navy's main wartime role would be the deployment and defence of its own SSBNs. Most analysts believe the Soviet Union would not use these submarines in the early stages of a world conflict, but would try to keep them in reserve. Consequently there is a strong requirement to defend them from Western attentions for as long into the war as necessary. For this reason, such submarines are usually kept in home waters, where they can be guarded by the rest of the fleet.

Less apocalyptically, Soviet writers and exercises demonstrate a strong and continued interest in amphibious operations, not least because this is an area where seapower may make its biggest and most direct impact on the outcome of the war on land. They do not appear to think that the advent of new technology, even nuclear weapons, has in any sense undermined the historic importance of the task.

It is true, however, that their ships and their concepts imply a more localized and tactical understanding of amphibious operations than applies, for example, in the US Marine Corps. Their interest in the use of hovercraft in this role suggests they stress speed more than range in the conduct of amphibious operations. Soviet amphibious warfare ships tend to be smaller and more range-limited than their Western equivalents, and the Soviet Navy's aircraft could not yet provide much in the way of air support for forces ashore. All this suggests a less ambitious concept of amphibious operations than applies in the US Navy.

A prolonged assault on reinforcement and re-supply shipping (not to mention economic shipping) plainly implies a war of some duration. For most of the 1960s and 1970s, Soviet writers tended to be sceptical about whether a total war between West and East could be a long one, and so tended to pay less public attention to this historic function of seapower than did their possible victims. In so far as it was a necessary task, it could be performed once more by localized action within European waters, and especially against European ports. More recently, there have been signs of a shift away from this line of thinking towards the orthodox Western view that the essentially maritime nature of the North Atlantic alliance makes the defence of shipping as important now as it always has been. The general expectation is that this would primarily be a role for torpedo-firing submarines and for shore-based naval aviation.

The dire consequences of major war in the nuclear age has had the effect of reducing incentives to resort to force. In this circumstance, Admiral Gorshkov has argued, the usefulness of the historic peacetime role of navies as instruments of diplomacy has been much reinforced:

> Demonstrative actions by the fleet in many cases have made it possible to achieve political ends without resorting to armed struggle, merely by putting on pressure with one's own potential might and threatening to start military operations . . . Thus the fleet has always been an instrument of the policy of states, an important aid to diplomacy in peacetime.[27]

Their flexibility and geographic reach gives navies great advantages over the other services in the execution of this role. The Soviet Navy clearly believes itself to be of value in this 'peacetime task' of deterring war and defending the forces of peace and progress from Imperialist encroachments. This is a global role, requiring large ships, replenishment vessels for distant operations, and might provide an important rationale for the new Soviet aircraft carrier.

Finally, technology has in recent years made the commercial value of the waters surrounding a country's shoreline immensely more important than it used to be. For this reason, as the current United Nations Convention on the Law of the Sea shows clearly, countries are expanding their jurisdiction over the seas and paying more and more attention to their defence against outsiders. The defence of coastal waters has always been one of the main functions of navies. Soviet writers and Soviet activities demonstrate beyond doubt the view that this function is getting more important still. The task of defending local waters is performed by small combatants, fast attack craft, coastal submarines, fishery protection squadrons and mine warfare vessels.

While Admiral Gorshkov may have produced the most comprehensive statement of the purposes and methods of modern sea power to have been published since the Second World War, many comparable views have been expressed elsewhere. The United States, for example, has produced two generalized statements of contemporary maritime strategy, the first by Admiral Stansfield Turner in 1974,[28] which gained a certain currency, though rather more outside the US Navy than inside it. Turner's was a modest statement of the naval case, which put a good deal of emphasis on the diplomatic or 'presence' role of seapower in times of peace. The US Navy's role in the conduct of naval deterrence was also claimed to be of obvious importance. Somewhat more controversially, though, Turner was sceptical of the more grandiose concepts of sea control then popular among the carrier admirals, and argued instead for a type of sea control that was concerned much more narrowly with the defence of NATO's sea communications across the Atlantic.

At the time, this fitted in well with the post-Vietnam mood of disenchantment with the military and seemed sensible in the light of current doubts about the future viability of large aircraft carriers. The US Navy's doubts about this approach were confirmed by its opinion that successive administrations were using such views as an excuse to cut back on naval construction generally, and on carrier construction in particular. The result of all this was seen to be a decline in naval strength to something like 450 ships by the end of the Carter administration.

Since that time, however, the administration of President Reagan and his energetic Navy Secretary John Lehman has reversed this tendency. Now the American aim appears to be to recapture that naval mastery, which the administration believes to be essential for the prosperity and security of a maritime nation like the United States and a maritime alliance like NATO. And the vehicle for doing this is a 600-ship navy complete with new nuclear supercarriers.

Not surprisingly, perhaps, this naval renaissance has also been accompanied by a theoretical statement of the case, rather unimaginatively entitled *The Maritime Strategy*.[29] In this, the authors (mainly John Lehman and Admiral James D. Watkins, then Chief of Naval Operations) argued that only by the fullest exploitation of its ability to command and use the sea could a maritime power hope to seize the initiative from a land power, and especially from a land power with a large navy like the Soviet Union. A dominant navy would allow the defence of Western interests around the globe in peacetime, and in war would redress imbalances, such as that prevailing on the Central Front, by exploiting the Soviet Union's vulnerability to sea-based assault. The many campaign options discussed included a determined campaign against Soviet SSBNs, the destruction of the Soviet surface fleet and its shore bases, and strikes against Soviet territory. Such a policy required the provision of much new equipment and the perfection of ambitious operational techniques. Most publicity has gone, firstly, towards the provision of highly sophisticated nuclear-propelled submarines capable of operating under the ice of the Arctic and, secondly, towards the development of carrier battle groups capable of prevailing in the most hostile of environments. It should not be thought, however, that *The Maritime Strategy* is without its critics;[30] nor is it altogether new, or neglectful of the need for more humdrum activities such as convoy escort and mine-sweeping. *The Maritime Strategy*, in fact, is a vigorous and generalized statement of contemporary maritime strategy that shows how the US Navy has responded to the technology of the late twentieth century.

Although this brief survey of contemporary naval activity has focused on the theory and practice of the two superpowers, a good deal of what has been said applies to most other navies also. The perceptions of large navies and small ones are of course different, but this is mainly a function of scale. Consequently, small navies simply have rather less ambitious versions of most of the roles performed by large ones. For this reason, the theories expounded by navalists such as Admirals Gorshkov and Watkins apply to small navies too – at least to some degree.

Conclusions

Despite the onrush of new technology, many of the functions of seapower and indeed its general place in the overall order of things have not changed as much as might be expected. Stripped of its Marxism-Leninism, modern jargon and matériel, a good deal of what Admiral Gorshkov has to say about the importance and functions of seapower, for instance, would be perfectly recognizable to Mahan and Corbett. No doubt this is because new technology provides not just problems, but also, eventually, solutions. Writing in the arguably equally challenging early 1920s, Admiral Richmond put it like this:

> Everything . . . that has come up has had its counter. It is against science that it should not be so . . . the science that develops one weapon will be equally competent to find out its antidote.[31]

In short, despite the oscillating effect of technological move and countermove, things have stayed more or less where they were.

An awareness of the many continuities in the exercise of seapower makes Soviet writers in particular pay considerable attention to the naval past, since they believe it profoundly relevant to the present and future. They do not, however, take this comfortable sense of continuity too far, believing that the value of historical reflection about the role of seapower in the twentieth century is that it tells us not just what has remained the same, but also what has not. It is certainly true that the challenge of technology to the established truths of naval warfare is now stronger than ever. It would be dangerous for naval professionals just to assume that they will overcome these technological challenges simply because the naval history of the twentieth century shows them always to have done so before.

Notes: Chapter 4

1 Quoted in M. T. Sprout, 'Mahan, evangelist of sea power,' in E. M. Earle (ed.) *Makers of Modern Strategy* (Princeton, NJ: Princeton University Press, 1943), pp. 442–3.
2 Sir Halford Mackinder, *Democratic Ideals and Reality* (London: Constable, 1919), p. 194.

3 Sir Julian Corbett, quoted in D. M. Schurman, *Julian Corbett 1854–1922* (London: Royal Historical Society, 1981) p. 44.
4 Quoted in D. M. Schurman, *The Education of a Navy* (London: Cassell, 1965), p. 190.
5 Fisher, quoted in A. J. Marder, *The Anatomy of British Sea Power* (Hamden, Conn.: Archon Books, 1964) p. 538.
6 This is taken from the British naval staff translation of the German Official War History. A more accessible version may be found in Admiral Reinhard Scheer, *Germany's High Sea Fleet in the World War* (London: Cassell, 1920), p. 25.
7 The best account of Jutland is still Arthur J. Marder, *From Dreadnought to Scapa Flow*, Vol. III, 2nd edn. (London: Oxford University Press, 1980).
8 Winston Churchill, 'The war by land and sea', *London Magazine*, October 1916. But compare his *The World Crisis* (London: Butterworth, 1927) pp. 108–13, and the commentary by Marder, *From Dreadnought to Scapa Flow*, Vol. III, pp. 263–9.
9 Admiral Scheer's Report to the Kaiser, in Marder, op. cit., p. 206.
10 Kato, quoted in *Der Krieg zur See* (Admiralty translation 1919, Naval Historical Branch Library).
11 For more on British attitudes to battleships, see G. Till, *Air Power and the Royal Navy* (London: Jane's, 1979), pp. 153–161, 193–4.
12 ibid., pp. 156–9, and G. Till, 'Airpower and the Battleship', in Bryan Ranft (ed.), *Technical Change and British Naval Policy 1860–1939* (London: Hodder & Stoughton, 1977) pp. 117–19. The point was that the ship in question, the German battleship *Ostfriesland* was old, defenceless, and in any case had nearly sunk on the way to the trials in which it was triumphantly dispatched by General Mitchell's bombers.
13 Richmond's best-remembered and broadest works were his *Statesmen and Sea Power* (Oxford: Clarendon Press, 1946) and the unfinished *The Navy as an Instrument of Policy 1558–1727* (London: Cambridge University Press, 1953). Castex's five-volume *Théories Stratégiques* (Paris: Société d'Editions, 1929–35) was the major work on maritime strategy in this period.
14 Raeder, report to the Fuehrer, 9 March 1940 (Fuehrer Naval Conferences, Admiralty translation 1947, Naval Historical Branch Library).
15 S. E. Morison, *History of United States Naval Operations in World War II*, Vol. XII (Boston: Little, Brown, 1958), p. 241.
16 Quoted in Vice-Admiral E. P. Forrester, *Admiral Raymond A. Spruance* (Washington: Director of Naval History, Department of the Navy, 1966), p. 136.
17 Admiral of the Fleet Viscount Cunningham, *A Sailor's Odyssey* (London: Hutchinson, 1951), p. 260.
18 S. Breyer, *Battleships and Battlecruisers, 1905–70* (London: Macdonald, 1973), p. 87.
19 An argument of this sort is advanced by Elizabeth Young in 'New laws for old navies', *Survival*, vol. 16, no. 6 (1974).

20 For example, Sir James Cable, *Gunboat Diplomacy 1919–1979* (London: Macmillan, 1980).
21 Hubert Moineville, *Naval Warfare Today and Tomorrow* (Oxford: Blackwell, 1983), p. 73.
22 For a celebrated exposition of this case, see P. Cohen, 'The erosion of surface naval power,' *Foreign Affairs*, vol. 49, no. 2 (1971).
23 Admiral S. G. Gorshkov quoted in R. W. Herrick, *Soviet Naval Strategy* (Annapolis, Md: Naval Institute Press, 1968), p. 68.
24 Admiral K. A. Stalbo, 'The strategy of the United States on the World Ocean', *Morskoi sbornik*, no. 10, 1983.
25 Admiral S. G. Gorshkov, *The Sea Power of the State* (London: Pergamon, 1979), p. 224.
26 Admiral V. N. Chernarvin, *Morskoi sbornik*, no. 11, 1982.
27 Gorshkov, op. cit., p. 248.
28 Admiral Stansfield Turner, 'Missions of the US Navy', *Naval War College Review*, March–April 1974.
29 Admiral James D. Watkins *et al.*, *The Maritime Strategy*, Supplement to *Proceedings of the US Naval Institute*, January 1986.
30 For a good example of such criticism, see John Mearsheimer, 'A strategic misstep', *International Security*, vol. 11, no. 2 (1986).
31 Admiral Sir Herbert Richmond, evidence to Bonar Law Enquiry (on the future of battleships), 5 January 1921, Cab. 16/37 (London: Public Record Office.)

Further reading: Chapter 4

Booth, Ken, *Navies and Foreign Policy* (London: Croom Helm, 1977).
Booth, Ken, *Law, Force and Diplomacy at Sea* (London: Allen & Unwin, 1985).
Brodie, Bernard, *A Guide to Naval Strategy* (New York: Praeger, 1965).
Gorshkov, Sergei G., *The Sea Power of the State* (Oxford: Pergamon, 1979).
Hagan, Kenneth J., ed., *In Peace and War: Interpretations of American Naval History 1775–1982* (London: Arcenwood Press, 1978).
Kennedy, Paul M., *The Rise and Fall of British Naval Mastery* (London: Allen Lane, 1976).
MccGwire, Michael, ed., *Soviet Naval Policy* (New York: Praeger, 1975).
Marder, A. J., *The Anatomy of British Sea Power* (London: Frank Cass, 1940).
Marder, A. J., *From the Dreadnought to Scapa Flow*, 5 vols (London: OUP, 1961).
Martin, L. W., *The Sea in Modern Strategy* (London: Chatto & Windus, 1967).
Roskill, Capt. S. W., *The Strategy of Sea Power* (London: Collins, 1962).
Till, Geoffrey, *Maritime Strategy and the Nuclear Age*, second edition (London: Macmillan, 1984).

5

The Theory and Practice of Strategic Bombing

JOHN PIMLOTT

To many, the concept of strategic bombing – the aerial bombardment of the enemy's homeland, hitting industrial and civilian targets in hope of destroying the capacity and willingness to wage war – is symbolic of 'total war' in the twentieth century. More than any other aspect of modern conflict, it epitomizes the ruthlessness and totality of war, bringing civilian populations, their homes and places of work, firmly into the front-line, while paying scant respect to the traditional restrictions of time, space and (many would argue) morality. Indeed, the last point has occasioned deep controversy, raising a host of questions about the legitimacy of waging war specifically against civilian targets, and this has been fuelled by the lack of any clear-cut strategic bombing victory, at least in terms of purely conventional (as opposed to atomic) weapons. As this chapter will endeavour to show, the gap between theory and practice in strategic bombing is wide and, unless the aggressor is prepared to use the inherently suicidal destructiveness of atomic or nuclear weapons to achieve instantaneous devastation, he is forced to use an instrument of war that is expensive (in both manpower and material terms), heavily dependent on new technology and extremely time-consuming. Despite the promises made by the early theorists of airpower, strategic bombing is by no means a simple or decisive route to victory.

The early years

The chief characteristic of strategic bombing is the fear it induces among people not traditionally associated with the waging of war – the ordinary civilians working in or living around the target areas. Their concept of aerial bombardment was important in the evolution of a theory of strategic bombing before 1939: a concept based upon a mixture of imagination and experience. The former had its roots in popular fears of attack from the wide-open element of the air, which largely predated the discovery of the secrets of flight. As early as 1670, the Jesuit priest Francesco Lana de Terzi had foretold with amazing perspicacity the consequences of air attack upon civilian centres, describing a design for an air machine that would rain explosive devices and incendiaries on to an unsuspecting and unprotected population.[1] In more modern times, the British writer H. G. Wells, in his popular book *The War in the Air*, first published in 1908, followed a similar line, painting a fearful picture of destruction, chaos and death delivered from the air.[2] Images such as these had been made infinitely more realistic when, in December 1903, the Americans Orville and Wilbur Wright made the first manned flight in a heavier-than-air machine.

But imagination alone does not produce viable strategies of war. Of much more importance was the actual experience of aerial bombardment, reinforcing the fiction of an earlier time. Civilians in Britain were the first people in the world to come under sustained aerial attack, and their experiences between 1915 and 1918 were to act as a basis for a variety of theories of strategic bombing that emerged in the aftermath of the First World War.

The original idea for mounting air raids against the British homeland seems to have come from Major Wilhelm Siegert of the Imperial German Army. In October 1914, only two months after the outbreak of hostilities, he received permission to train a squadron of single-engine Taube aircraft for operations against the ports of southern England then being used by the British Expeditionary Force. His plan had to be abandoned when projected airfields in north-eastern France were not captured by ground forces, but a seed had been sown in the German mind. It was nurtured and brought to partial fruition by Admiral Hugo von Pohl of the Imperial German Navy, who suggested using Zeppelin airships because of their relatively unrestricted range. His campaign began in January 1915.

Problems were encountered from the start. Zeppelins required the right sort of weather before they could be launched on raids, which could take up to twelve hours to complete; navigation was exceptionally difficult, particularly over the North Sea or if clouds covered the sun or stars; even when targets were discovered, they proved almost impossible to hit with accuracy from an operating altitude of 3600 m (12,000 ft). Within weeks, the Germans had been forced to admit that they could hit nothing more precise than a city, but when, in May 1915, the airships destroyed urban housing in London's dockland, the popular conception of aerial bombardment suddenly became reality.

The Zeppelins continued to mount spasmodic, mostly night-time raids on English targets until November 1916. In terms of actual damage they achieved little, but their effects went much deeper. Although only fifty-one Zeppelin raids took place, civilian reaction was sharp. People responded to the apparently indiscriminate nature of the attacks by rioting in the streets, absenting themselves from factories (which they regarded as likely targets) and demanding, through the press and Parliament, some form of retaliation or at least defence.[3] The Government hastily organized defensive measures, deploying searchlights, anti-aircraft guns and fighter aircraft around the target cities, but results seemed poor. Despite the destruction of two airships by anti-aircraft fire on 28 November 1916 – an event which, ironically, caused the Germans to suspend Zeppelin operations – the British public became firmly convinced that the attacker would always get through to drop bombs on to unprotected cities. It was to prove a remarkably tenacious belief and one that was to dominate future theories of strategic bombing.

This was reinforced by subsequent German actions, for by late 1916 the Germans had begun to shift the emphasis of their attacks from airships to aircraft. A squadron of 30 Gotha G-IV twin-engine biplanes, each capable of carrying up to 454 kg (1000 lb) of bombs to England from bases in occupied Belgium, had been created under Captain Ernst Brandenburger and, although training took time, this 'England Squadron' was ready for operations by mid-May 1917.

The first Gotha raids highlighted a number of problems. Flying accidents and mechanical defects enabled only twenty-one aircraft to take off for London on 25 May, and cloudy weather forced them to divert to secondary targets. Nevertheless, the sudden shift from night-Zeppelin to day-bomber attack caught the British defences unawares and, when a second raid took place on 5 June, killing thirteen people in Sheerness, all the previous fears of the British public reappeared. They were reinforced when, on 13 June, fourteen Gothas finally made it through to London, flying unmolested over the capital to bomb targets around Liverpool Street Station and the dockyards. A total of 162 civilians (including 18 small children in a school in Poplar) died, with 432 injured. A similar attack, carried out on 7 July, killed a further 57 people, with 193 injured.[4]

Public reaction in Britain was immediate and predictable. Mobs ran riot in London, smashing 'German' property and demanding retribution, workers absented themselves from factories, and war production, particularly of munitions, declined significantly. The situation was not helped by the obvious failure of existing defences – in the two London raids, only one Gotha had been destroyed, probably by anti-aircraft fire – and it was this as much as the outburst of public hysteria that forced the Government's hand. On 11 July, Prime Minister David Lloyd George created a special 'Committee on Air Organisation and Home Defence against Air Raids', composed of himself and the South African statesman Jan Christian Smuts. The findings of this committee, usually called the Smuts Committee as Lloyd George rarely found time to attend, were to lay the foundations of strategic bombing theory.

Smuts worked under considerable pressure, presenting his first Report to the Cabinet in early August. This dealt exclusively with the organization of an effective air defence system around London – the London Air Defence Area (LADA) – and was put into effect immediately. It involved some remarkably sophisticated innovations, with belts of anti-aircraft guns covering the approaches to the capital from north, south and east, and squadrons of fighters flying at pre-set patrol altitudes, ready to intercept the daylight raiders. By late 1917, London had been transformed from an open city into a defended location.

But this was only a short-term solution to the problem, and it was Smuts's second Report, submitted on 17 August, that contained the more dramatic recommendations. In this Report, Smuts advocated a complete reorganization of Britain's air services, currently split unsatisfactorily between the Navy and the Army and incapable of unified action. Unlike many of his contemporaries, Smuts recognized the potential of strategic airpower, even going so far as to predict that:

> The day may not be far off when aerial operations, with their devastation of enemy lands and destruction of industrial and populace centres on a vast scale, may become the principal operations of war, to which the older forms of military and naval operations may become secondary and subordinate . . .[5]

In other words, Smuts was seeing in the manned bomber a potential war-winner, capable of achieving so much destruction and demoralization that its efforts alone would force the enemy to sue for peace. He obviously regarded the Gotha raids as the beginning of just such an offensive against Britain, and went on to discuss possible ways of countering its effects. Defence, he argued, could be either 'passive', as in the case of LADA, or 'active', taking the form of a strategic counter-offensive against German cities, which would be so devastating that the enemy would be forced to divert aircraft away from his own offensive or even to negotiate for peace. As such a counter-offensive required a degree of co-ordination that existing military–naval rivalries precluded, Smuts went on to advocate the creation of a unified, separate air service, charged solely with responsibility for strategic counter-bombardment. They were radical proposals.

The government refused to take such a drastic step immediately, preferring to place the emphasis upon LADA, but events soon increased the pressure. In early September 1917, the Gothas began to mount night attacks in an effort to avoid the LADA defences and, by the end of the month, had been joined by a squadron of awesome R-type bombers, appropriately known as 'Giants'. Originally developed for long-range operations on the Eastern Front, the first of these Staaken RVIs – four-engine machines with a wing-span in excess of 40 m (130 ft) and a bomb-carrying capacity four times greater than the Gothas – joined the 'England Squadron' in what became known as the 'Raids of the Harvest Moon'. Every night between 25 September and 2 October 1917 London was hit, with predictable results. As panic-stricken civilians fled the city and war production declined, the Government hastily drew up an Air Force (Constitution) Bill, passing it into law on 29 November. Thirty-four days later, on 2 January 1918, the Air Ministry was formed and three months after that, on 1 April, an independent Royal Air Force (RAF) came into existence, charged primarily with the mounting of a strategic counter-offensive against the enemy homeland.

A combination of factors, ranging from political problems at the Air Ministry to a lack of suitable long-range aircraft, delayed the formation of an Independent Bombing Force until June 1918, and by that time the German raids had died out. High losses from flying accidents and, as techniques improved, from the LADA defences, coupled with mechanical problems that all but grounded the 'Giants', had prevented the Germans from maintaining the pressure of the Harvest Moon raids. Nevertheless, they had been able to introduce a number of innovations, notably the use of the 1016 kg ('one-ton') bomb and the concept of incendiary attack, which had increased public fears for the future. The last German raid actually took place on 19 May 1918, when twenty-eight Gothas crossed the English coast, straggling over Kent and Sussex for nearly two hours as they fought their way to London through a remarkable barrage of 30,000 anti-aircraft shells and numerous patrolling fighters. Six of the bombers – representing a prohibitive loss-rate of almost 20 per cent – failed to return and the German High Command withdrew the survivors to tactical support. There were thus no raids to prevent when the RAF began its attacks on German cities in June and, as the war ended five months later purely through military–naval activity, nothing was proved about the efficacy of the counter-bombardment policy. It was an unfortunate turn of events.

The evolution of theory

The British experience of bombing provided several 'lessons' which, in the absence of alternative evidence, necessarily formed the basis for future thought. Unfortunately, they were interpreted in different ways by different groups of people. To the ordinary civilians, the German raids had merely reinforced prewar fears of air attack: the bombers were indiscriminate in their assaults, capable of inflicting horrific damage and, most significantly of all, impossible to stop. Similar conclusions were drawn by the Government, with an additional belief that ordinary people could not sustain aerial bombardment, being prone to panic, demoralization and anarchy, with attendant ill effects on war production. To both groups, strategic bombing was therefore to be feared and, if at all possible, avoided, either through disarmament or, as it later developed, appeasement. The only people who felt that it was possible to live with the new threat were the strategists of the fledgling RAF and their supporters in other air services abroad. They advocated Smuts's idea of defence through aggressive action: threatening or actually carrying out counter-bombardment to deter or blunt an enemy attack. Factors such as the growing success of LADA from late 1917 or the enormous practical problems experienced by the Germans in maintaining a bomber offensive were either ignored or not appreciated. It was a basis for muddled thinking.

A precise 'theory' of strategic bombing began to emerge in the 1920s, relating to the evidence of the First World War and speculating on its significance. The most important writer on the subject was the Italian, Giulio Douhet. Born in 1869, he had entered the Italian Army in 1890 as an artillery officer and moved into the air arm twenty years later. During the First World War he saw service in the campaigns against Austria-Hungary, gradually formulating ideas about the strategic potential of airpower. His most influential work, *The Command of the Air*, was published in Italy in 1927.[6]

Douhet appreciated the revolution in strategy that airpower implied, pointing out its capability to destroy the heart of an enemy nation without the need for costly campaigns to break through the defensive land or sea walls that, in traditional strategic terms, protected it. But he was not so naive as to imagine that this would be easy. The enemy too would possess an air force, equally capable of offensive action, so his main concern was with the gaining and maintenance of 'command of the air', a concept defined as the ability 'to prevent the enemy from flying while retaining the ability to fly oneself'. This was important, he argued, because:

> To have command of the air means to be in a position to wield offensive power so great it defies human imagination. It means to be able to cut an enemy's army and navy off from their bases of operation and nullify their chances of winning the war. It means complete protection of one's own country, the efficient operation of one's army and navy, and peace of mind to live and work in safety. In short, it means to be in a position *to win*. *To be defeated* in the air, on the other hand, is finally to be defeated and to be at the mercy of the enemy, with no chance at all of defending oneself.[7]

Such beliefs implied two things. First, that aircraft, through their ability to use the three-dimensional setting of the air, were capable of attacking any target on the face of the earth, subject only to limitations of range and opposition. Second, that airpower was now an integral and essential element of war, to which the traditional methods of military and naval operations, tied as they were to movement on a flat plane, had to be subordinate. Furthermore, as Douhet believed that air opposition was inevitable, this command of the air had to be fought for, principally through offensive action in the enemy's air space. This would be achieved partly through the deployment of fighter aircraft to escort the bomber fleets, but primarily through striking 'mortal blows' at the enemy's sources of airpower – airfields, depots and factories – and selective strikes against civilian population centres. Such centres in fact assumed a central importance to Douhet as he grew convinced that 'the effect of such aerial offensives upon morale may well have more influence upon the conduct of the war than their material effects'. He further postulated that, under aerial bombardment, 'normal life would be impossible' and that 'the time would soon come when, to put an end to horror and suffering, the people themselves, driven by the instinct of self-preservation, would rise up and demand an end to the war'.[8]

But Douhet was not the only theorist to emerge in the interwar period. In the United States, for example, Brigadier-General William ('Billy') Mitchell, a serving airman, was so vociferous about the war-winning capabilities of the manned bomber and the need for an independent air service on the pattern of the RAF that he was eventually court-martialled and forced to resign. He too was of the opinion that, in an age of airpower, military and naval campaigns were obsolete, particularly so far as the United States was concerned. He pressed for the defence of his country to be put in the hands of an independent air force, demonstrating that the navy no longer had a role to play in this respect by destroying the ex-German battleship *Ostfriesland* from the air in July 1921. At the same time, Mitchell saw no reason why, in the event of war, the United States should not depend upon strategic bombing – it was much more immediate in its impact and would, when compared with the costly and time-consuming business of forming expeditionary forces for overseas service, be cheap to carry out. According to his theory, waves of self-defending bombers, gaining command of the air as they flew through it, would operate during the hours of daylight to hit vital parts of the enemy's war machine, undermining the capacity to continue the conflict. There would be no need to attack civilian centres, chiefly because the United States, with its industrial potential and lack of vulnerable land frontiers, would be able to continue the campaign for long periods and not be dependent on a swift victory. Despite his court-martial, Mitchell laid the seeds of a distinctly American theory of strategic bombing, which were to come to fruition during the Second World War.[9]

Neither Douhet nor Mitchell had a discernible effect on the RAF, which produced its own distinctive theory, based on its experience in the First World War. Under the leadership of Lord Trenchard, Chief of the Air Staff throughout the 1920s, RAF strategists had their own views about the question of air defence.[10] Whereas Douhet, and to a lesser extent Mitchell, recognized and catered for the inevitability of opposition to their bomber fleets, the RAF persistently underestimated its effect, regarding complete command of the air as unnecessary and a diversion of resources away from the main aim – offensive strikes against the heart of the enemy. The first move by the RAF in the event of war would therefore be concentrated attacks not against elements of the enemy's air force but against the industrial life-blood of his state – his factories, resource areas, internal communications and transport systems. There was, significantly, no emphasis on the deliberate bombing of civilian centres, it being felt that the demoralization resulting from industrial attacks would be sufficient to create a 'climate of collapse'. By 1939, this theory had been refined to the extent that potential air opposition had virtually disappeared from the equation. Exploiting the vastness of the air, RAF bombers, like the Gothas of 1917, would evade the enemy air force to strike like a lance straight at the industrial heart of the state, cutting it out neatly and cleanly by finding and destroying precise industrial targets during the hours of daylight. Such a belief gained official credence when, in 1932, a leading politician, Stanley Baldwin, felt obliged to warn his fellow countrymen that 'the bomber will always get through'.

Such an admission, however, illustrated a major flaw in RAF thinking, for if British bombers could guarantee their passage to the target in this way, it was only logical to presume that the enemy air force could do the same, appearing over British cities, free from opposition, to rain explosives and gas on to an unprotected public. This was exactly the prospect feared by the civilian population in Britain, which spent the interwar period developing its own views on strategic bombing. Indeed, the 'popular' theory that emerged was in many ways at variance with the 'academic' one put forward by the Air Staff, painting a picture of death and destruction that no amount of RAF counter-bombardment could relieve.

These fears appeared to be well founded. Although the casualties inflicted by the Germans between 1915 and 1918 were slight (1413 people killed and 3407 injured) it was appreciated that this was merely a foretaste of future horror. As aircraft design improved, bomber range and carrying capacity increased, and as the countries of Europe began to build up their air strength, the German raids, amounting to no more than 200 airship and 430 aircraft sorties over a three-year period, paled into insignificance. As early as 1925, the military thinker Basil Liddell Hart, in his book *Paris, or the Future of War*, was predicting that the French Air Force, composed of '990 aeroplanes', could cause 'a greater weight of bombs to be dropped on London in one day than in the whole of the Great War'. As the French threat receded, to be replaced in the 1930s by that from Nazi Germany, equipped with a large and modern Luftwaffe, the feeling of vulnerability increased. On 30 July 1934, Winston Churchill described London as 'the greatest target in the world, a kind of tremendous, fat, valuable cow, fed up to attract beasts of prey'. Four months later, he returned to the theme, predicting that as a result of bombing raids on London, 'three or four million people' would flee the city in panic, spreading chaos and anarchy throughout the land. It was a picture that seemed all too believable.

This was reinforced during the interwar period by the compilation of various statistics by the British authorities, based on the casualties of 1915–18. During that period, the Germans had dropped approximately 300 tons of bombs on to British soil, producing a casualty rate of 11.5 dead or injured for every ton. It was therefore presumed that this figure would remain true at all times, so that as the tonnage increased the casualties would do likewise, in neat multiples of 11.5. The resultant statistics, ignoring the fact that bombs rarely fall in precise patterns and that many would drop into areas already hit, causing no additional casualties, were terrifying. In 1924, it was estimated that during the first 24 hours of a raid on London, 5000 people would be killed or injured, followed by a further 3750 during the next 24 hours and 2500 each day thereafter for as long as the attacks continued. As bomber capabilities increased, so did the figures. By 1938, it was expected that Germany would be able to deliver 600 tons of bombs a day on to British cities, causing 70,000 casualties a week. A year later, when war was inevitable, a quarter of a million casualties in London alone was the figure for the first three weeks of air attack, with more than three million psychiatric cases, three million refugees and up to 50 per cent destruction of property. One of the first official acts of the Ministry of Health once war had been declared was to issue a million burial forms to local authorities.[11]

By 1939, therefore, the theory of strategic bombing was potentially muddled and subject to widely differing views. To the air force strategists, not only in Britain but also in selected countries abroad, the impact of airpower seemed assured: as soon as the war began, fleets of bombers would fly by day to hit precise industrial or population targets in the enemy homeland, ending the conflict quickly and avoiding the heavy ground-force casualties of the First World War. However, to many civilians – the new front-line in total war – the cost of such a strategy was prohibitively high, substituting their lives for those of the soldiers of the earlier war. In such circumstances, few governments were going to be willing to risk initiating a strategic bombing campaign for fear of the consequences of counter-bombardment, particularly as the ability of the bomber to survive and to carry out its attacks was apparently assured. Those air forces dedicated to the theory clearly had a long way to go before they would be able to prove their point.

The RAF bombing of Germany, 1939–44

This confusion was shown most forcibly in the role and capabilities of the RAF at the outbreak of the Second World War in September 1939. The Air Staff was still advocating the 'academic' theory of strategic bombing, arguing the case for a single, concentrated 'knock-out blow' against selected enemy targets, but they lacked both government backing and the necessary weapons. Because of the fear that any attack on Germany would give Hitler the excuse he needed to release the Luftwaffe against targets in Britain, leading to widespread civilian panic and heavy casualties, the government of the day imposed strict controls on the use of the bombers, denying them the opportunity to carry out their favoured strategy and dispersing their strength by sending a proportion to France with the British Expeditionary Force.

Even if this had not happened, Bomber Command was not really in any position to initiate a campaign. In September 1939, it had a paper strength of six Bomber Groups, but could muster no more than 300 aircraft for strategic attacks. No. 1 Group, equipped with Fairey Battles, was sent to France, with No 2. Group, fielding Bristol Blenheims, earmarked as the second echelon of the Advanced Air Striking Force attached to the BEF. No. 6. Group was a reserve formation, designed to act as a training command rather than a front-line force. This left Nos 3, 4 and 5 Groups, equipped with Vickers Wellingtons, Armstrong-Whitworth Whitleys and Handley-Page Hampdens respectively, but their strength was dissipated immediately by a government decision to use the Whitleys for night-leaflet raids over Germany. Although the Blenheims of No. 2. Group could be used to replace them until reinforcements were needed in France, the total force available for anything approaching a strategic bombing campaign was small. Moreover, the aircraft themselves were hardly impressive. The Blenheims, although reasonably fast, were rapidly approaching obsolescence and were incapable of carrying a large bomb-load; the Wellingtons soon displayed an alarming tendency to burn when hit; the Hampdens were cramped and poorly defended. None of the bombers had self-sealing fuel tanks and all faced the dilemma of imbalance between bomb-carrying capacity and fuel-load: if they were loaded up with fuel enough to reach deep into Germany, they had to sacrifice bomb-weight; if they were given a reasonable bomb-load, they could only be fuelled for short-range attacks.[12]

In the event, these problems were masked by the decision consciously to restrain the bombers, restricting them to daylight raids against German shipping in the North Sea, far from civilian targets that might prove provocative. This turned out to be a disastrous policy. As early as 4 September, when 15 Blenheims were sent to attack German battleships in the Schillig Roads, new problems emerged: five of the aircraft failed to find the targets at all and, of the remaining ten, five were shot down by alert German naval gunners. Nor was this an isolated case. By December 1939, as the enemy deployed *Freya* early-warning radar sets to cover the North Sea and squadrons of Messerschmitt Bf-109 and Bf-110 fighters to defend the naval locations, bomber casualties became prohibitive. On 14 December, five out of a force of 12 Wellingtons failed to return; four days later, 12 out of 22 fell to a combination of radar and fighter defences.[13] As the British were to discover during the following year (yet chose to ignore for some time), air defence could prevail against the manned bomber.

Such losses in late 1939 led to an urgent reassessment of the bombing campaign by the RAF. An obvious solution to the sudden emergence of viable air defence was to fly by night, avoiding the fighters, and when the apparent success of the Whitley leaflet-dropping raids was analysed (by January 1940 more than 65 million leaflets had been deposited over Germany, with no aircraft losses to enemy action) such a switch became inevitable. The aim of the campaign would remain the same – the precise destruction of industrial targets in the enemy homeland – but the method would alter significantly in the face of unforeseen practical problems. It was a pattern that was soon to be repeated.

Fortunately for Bomber Command, few raids were carried out at all during the early months of 1940. Bad weather kept the bombers grounded for most of January and February, although in March the government restraints began to be lifted. On 16 March, the Luftwaffe carried out a raid on Scapa Flow in which a civilian was killed. Regarding this as the beginning of a strategic campaign against the British population, the Government authorized a retaliatory raid on the night of 19–20 March against the German seaplane base at Hörnum on the island of Sylt. According to the crews who took part, 'significant damage' was inflicted. In truth, the base escaped attack entirely, implying new problems of navigation and bombing accuracy foreseen by Air Commodore A. Coningham, Air Officer Commanding No. 4. Group, when he described the switch from day to night bombing as starting a 'never-ending struggle to circumvent the law that we cannot see in the dark'.[14] Indeed, in a period before the development of radar aids to navigation, the best that the crews could do was to follow rivers or rail-lines towards their chosen targets. As this only worked on moonlit nights, few of the problems of daylight operations had in fact been solved: after all, if the bombers could see to this extent, so could the fighters sent against them.

It took time for these problems to be fully appreciated, partly because the German attacks on Scandinavia, France and the Low Countries diverted government (and RAF) attention from strategic bombing, but also because, once the BEF had been defeated, the RAF remained the only offensive weapon available if the war against Germany were to continue. As early as 15 May 1940, the Government began to lift its restrictions even more, reacting to reports of Luftwaffe 'terror attacks' on Rotterdam, and between then and 15 June, a total of 27 night raids were carried out, principally against industrial targets. A pattern was beginning to emerge.

But it would be wrong to imagine that a concentrated bombing campaign resulted, for during the period between June 1940 and November 1941 the fortunes of Bomber Command declined dramatically, reflecting the muddle and uncertainty of the interwar period.

This was shown most forcibly by the plethora of Bombing Directives issued by a Government clearly unsure how to use the weapon at its disposal, for although throughout the period the main aim was to destroy oil targets, on the assumption that this was one of the weakest parts of the German war economy, in reality a concentration of effort was impossible to achieve. Oil targets could only be hit with any likelihood of precision during moonlit nights, leaving the majority of each month to be devoted to 'secondary targets' which, by virtue of their availability, received the most attention. In addition, as a series of crises emerged in the wider war, the bombers kept being diverted to other aspects of the German war machine: in July 1940, invasion barges on the Channel coast took precedence; in March 1941, U-boat bases and construction yards, as the Battle of the Atlantic reached a new level of threat.[15] As bomber production could barely keep pace with losses, the available force remained small, and although new 'heavy' bombers such as the Short Stirling, Handley-Page Halifax and Avro Manchester gradually entered squadron service, there were never enough of them to have a decisive effect.

Nevertheless, by late 1940, the Air Staff was claiming some success, citing reports compiled by a number of government experts which implied that the attacks on oil installations had begun to bite. On 16 December, for example, Geoffrey Lloyd reported that German oil production had been reduced by 15 per cent since June, even though only 539 tons of bombs had been dropped on appropriate targets. This was sufficient evidence to ensure a continuation of the campaign, but in truth the situation was dramatically different. Doubts about bombing accuracy began to creep in when the first of the Photo-Reconnaissance Spitfires were deployed in November 1940 to carry out post-operation sweeps, for little of the damage so optimistically presumed could be discerned. When air cameras began to be fitted to the night bombers, taking photographs of the target as the bombs were dropped, the full extent of failure quickly became apparent.

These air photographs provided David Butt, a government scientist, with the evidence he needed to assess the accuracy of night bombing in August 1941. His report was a shocking indictment of prevailing bombing policy. On the basis of 600 photographs, taken by night bombers in June and July, he concluded that far from the aiming point being the 46 m (50 yds) around a target that precision bombing required, it was anything up to 8 km (5 miles) in diameter, and that in only about one-third of the cases he had studied. He even came across examples of targets more than 121 km (75 miles) away from those specified being attacked, implying that most of the bombs being transported so laboriously to Germany were being distributed far and wide, having little effect on either industrial potential or civilian morale.[16] Churchill described the Butt Report as 'a very serious paper' and began to express doubts about the efficacy of a continued campaign. In this he was joined by members of the Army and Navy, who resented the devotion of valuable aircraft to operations of only marginal effect, and by politicians and churchmen who queried the morality of the whole campaign. The situation was not helped by heavy RAF casualties – on the night of 7–8 November 1941, 37 aircraft were lost on raids over Berlin and Mannheim – and on 13 November Churchill ordered the RAF to curtail its operations, ostensibly for the winter months only but with the clear implication that he doubted the value of a continued campaign.

The Air Staff refused to give up. With bomber production increasing and the first of the radar aids ('Gee') already past the experimental stage, they felt that too much had been done to stop there: what was needed was a new, more realistic approach, reflecting the problems already encountered. Clearly, night-precision bombing had failed, chiefly because of navigation difficulties, but this did not mean that industrial targets could not be destroyed. If, in the light of the Butt Report, the RAF was only dropping bombs in the general vicinity of a factory, it seemed logical to make the target area much larger, taking in the urban infrastructure of housing and communications that supported it. Experiments in city bombing had already been conducted – on the night of 12–13 March 1941, a force of Blenheims had hit Bremen with apparent success – and, during the enforced moratorium of winter 1941–42, plans were finalized for a new Bombing Directive. It was issued on 14 February 1942, specifying a number of cities in Germany that were now to be bombed in their entirety, with particular emphasis upon the morale of the civil population and industrial workers. A note attached to the Directive by the Chief of the Air Staff, Sir Charles Portal, highlighted the nature of the new offensive when it stated that in the urban attacks 'the aiming points are to be the built-up areas, *not*, for instance, the dockyards or aircraft factories'.[17] Area bombing had arrived.

Thus, after only 30 months of war, the original theory of strategic bombing had been stood on its head. Because of practical problems in carrying out a campaign, the prewar emphasis upon daylight precision attacks had been altered to one of area bombing by night, substituting the destruction of urban workers for the destruction of precise industrial targets. Far from being a sharp scalpel, designed to remove key parts of the enemy war economy, Bomber Command had been forced to assume the attributes of a bludgeon, crude in its application and effects.

Such a shift of emphasis did not solve the problems of the campaign, for if cities were to be destroyed, the bombers needed to be capable of applying enormous, sustained pressure night after night. In early 1942, this was just not possible, and it was to take a further two years before anything approaching a viable weapon could be created. The job of doing so fell to Air Marshal A. T. Harris, appointed Commander-in-Chief of Bomber Command on 22 February 1942.[18] His first task was to halt the decline in official support for the bombing campaign, persuading Churchill and the politicians that the campaign was not only worth pursuing but also that it was capable of achieving victory. This was not going to be easy, chiefly because it required the creation of an entirely new weapon, which the politicians were not likely to authorize before they had received proof of its validity. Harris soon found himself in the centre of a vicious circle: expansion was dependent on success, but success could not be achieved without expansion.

His response was to mount a series of attacks, using the full potential of new aircraft and techniques developed during the previous phase of the campaign, with the aim of producing spectacular results. By early 1942, Bomber Command could still only muster about 400 front-line aircraft, but many of the twin-engine designs that had proved so unsatisfactory in the past had been replaced by purpose-built 'heavy' bombers. Some of these, such as the Stirling with its low ceiling and the Manchester with its unreliable Rolls-Royce Vulture engines, had not been a success, but the Halifax had potential and, once the twin Vultures on the Manchester had been replaced by four Merlins to produce the Lancaster, it was obvious that a very special aircraft had emerged. With a maximum speed of 462 km/h (287 mph) and an ability to carry 6350 kg (14,000 lb) of bombs over a range of 2670 km (1660 miles), the Lancaster was clearly a useful machine, ideally suited to city bombing. Nor were twin-engine designs completely ignored: as the first Lancasters entered squadron service in late 1941, they were joined by examples of the de Havilland Mosquito, an aircraft with a top speed of 644 km/h (400 mph) and a bomb-carrying capacity of 454 kg (1000 lb). The potential was enormous.[19]

At much the same time, the first of the radar aids to navigation had been introduced. Known as 'Gee', it consisted of a series of pulses, transmitted by a master station and re-radiated by two 'slave' stations to produce precisely timed signals which, when monitored by an aircraft, gave an indication of its position in relation to the stations. Accurate to within 3.2 km (2 miles) in 564 km (350 miles), 'Gee' had the range to reach as far as the Ruhr.[20] Issued to specially trained crews, who would act as illuminators and target-markers for a main force of 'followers' in a technique known as 'Shaker', the 'Gee'-equipped bombers took some getting used to, but by early 1942 it was obvious that skills were improving. So were the methods of city destruction as shown on the night of 28–29 March when the North German port of Lübeck, deliberately chosen as a target because of its preponderance of timber-framed buildings, was hit by incendiaries. The heart of the Old City was burnt out.

But Harris was aware that such success could not be repeated at will. Another 'Lübeck' would require special conditions that could not always be presumed, so he looked for even more dramatic evidence of his command's capabilities. He found it in the decision to mount a '1000 Bomber' raid, which was made possible only by using the entire front-line and reserve strength of Bomber Command. On the night of 30–31 May a total of 1047 aircraft flew against Cologne, and although the results in terms of destruction were poor – the city had recovered within six weeks – the reality of massed bombing could no longer be ignored. As the British press trumpeted forth the news, area bombing caught the public imagination and made full-scale commitment to it as a war policy inevitable. At a cost of only 41 aircraft, Harris had ensured the political backing he so desperately needed.[21]

This was only the beginning, however, for Bomber Command now faced a long and difficult haul. The strategy of area bombing may have been established and political support achieved, but the process of creating an instrument powerful enough to inflict telling damage on the enemy was by no means straightforward. As successive '1000-Bomber' experiments in 1942 proved, the bombers were still not capable of achieving the concentration of force needed to swamp civil defences and start uncontrollable fires. Too many of the crews were finding it difficult to navigate with accuracy, even when equipped with

'Gee', and were having to face German air-defence systems which, by 1942, were remarkably effective. Based on the so-called 'Kammhuber Line' of radar-guided night-fighters, the defenders were able to seize and maintain a worrying initiative that was to last until 1944.

During that period, some bombing success was achieved, but the going was hard and the casualties among the bomber crews cripplingly high. In an effort to ensure bombing concentration, Harris introduced the 'Pathfinder' concept, using experienced crews equipped with the latest radar aids to lead the 'Main Force' to the target, which would then be illuminated with special flares. Created on 11 August 1942, the Pathfinder Force was not without its critics, many of whom doubted the efficacy of creaming off the best crews for a dangerous job, but as new navigational aids such as 'Oboe' emerged, enabling the marker aircraft to fly along a precise radar beam until instructed to drop its flares or bombs directly over the target, the technique more than justified its development. By 1943, it was not unknown for an 'Oboe'-equipped Mosquito or Lancaster to illuminate the aiming point and then act as 'Master Bomber', remaining over the target to guide the Main Force in and correct its bombing errors.[22] When techniques such as this had been perfected, a viable instrument had begun to be created.

But successful city destruction remained the exception, resulting more from luck than design. The 'fire-storm' that devastated Hamburg in late July 1943, for example, undoubtedly owed much to the first use of 'Window' (aluminium strips designed to blind the radars of the German air-defence system), which allowed the bombers to arrive over the target in a concentrated pattern, and was aided by the accurate navigation achieved using H_2S – the first radar set to provide a 'picture' of the ground to the bombers flying over it – but if it had not been for the dry summer weather, the inferno would not have developed. If fire-storms could have been created at will, the sustained 'battles' of the Ruhr, Hamburg and Berlin, fought by Harris between March 1943 and March 1944 would have crippled the enemy; as it was, the Germans were able not only to absorb the damage inflicted but also to impose grievous losses on the bomber fleets. The process culminated in the disaster of 30–31 March 1944, when 95 aircraft (out of a force of 795) failed to return from a raid on Nuremberg.[23] After more than four years of war, the offensive had still to enjoy the sort of war-winning success claimed by the interwar theorists.

The combined bomber offensive, 1944–45

Nor was this an exclusively RAF problem, for by 1944 the Americans had also tried and failed to create an effective bombing strategy. When they entered the war in late 1941, they were determined to make their own distinctive contribution to the campaign against Germany, based on the Mitchell theory of daylight precision attacks. By August 1942, squadrons of 'self-defending' B-17 Flying Fortress and B-24 Liberator bombers had been flown to bases in Britain, promising a reinforcement to Bomber Command that could have proved decisive. At the Casablanca Conference of Allied war leaders in January 1943, a co-ordinated Anglo-US bomber offensive was clearly envisaged, aiming for 'the progressive destruction and dislocation of the German military, industrial and economic system, and the undermining of the morale of the German people to a point where their capacity for armed resistance is fatally weakened'.[24]

This Combined Bomber Offensive (CBO) did not emerge easily. By 1943, the RAF was dedicated to a form of bombing that the Americans refused to support, convinced as they were that accurate daylight attacks were possible, using a combination of 'self-defending' aircraft and the revolutionary Norden bomb-sight. At first, as the Eighth United States Army Air Force (USAAF) carried out short-range attacks over occupied Europe, this approach did not seem disastrous, but when the bombers went for targets deep inside Germany, the well organized air defences had a field day. On 17 August 1943, 376 B-17s flew in broad daylight to attack ball-bearing and aircraft factories at Schweinfurt and Regensburg: in a series of battles with defending fighters and under accurate anti-aircraft fire, 60 of the bombers failed to return – a loss rate of 16 per cent. When the same happened on 14 October against the same target of Schweinfurt, it was obvious that Mitchell's theory was not particularly apt.[25]

It was to take the Americans until early 1944 to achieve the sort of air superiority essential to daylight operations – they did so by fitting the P-51 Mustang fighter with a Rolls-Royce engine and drop-tanks, increasing its range and enabling it to escort the bombers on raids deep into Germany – but this did not mean that the CBO was an immediate reality. Between April and September 1944, the main weight of the Allied air effort was shifted to raids in direct support of the Normandy landings, with only spasmodic attacks on German industrial and population centres. In the process, the remains of the Luftwaffe in the West were virtually destroyed – 13,000 Luftwaffe aircrew were lost between June and October 1944 – and the elaborate infrastructure of ground-based radar defences was shattered as key early-warning stations on or near the French coast were captured, but the respite enjoyed by the Germans in terms of true strategic bombing enabled them to continue war production at hitherto unprecedented levels. Indeed, in terms of industrial output, the German war economy peaked in September 1944, five years after the beginning of the conflict and despite the enormous commitment of Allied resources to the bombing campaign.

Nevertheless, once the bombers were released from the need to support ground operations, the CBO could begin in earnest, and there can be no doubt that, for the last eight months of the war in Europe, significant damage was inflicted on the enemy state. Free from the danger of Luftwaffe attack, the USAAF was able to send its B-17s and B-24s the length and breadth of the Reich, searching out and destroying precise targets (particularly those associated with the production and distribution of oil) and contributing to the more general city attacks initiated by the RAF. It was even possible to achieve the ultimate aim of the CBO – RAF attacks on a particular target by night, followed by USAAF attacks by day – and, as the fire-storm that devastated Dresden on 13–14 February 1945 showed, the results could be awesome. In this particular case, an estimated 100,000 people died, implying that, in terms of crude power, the instrument of strategic bombing had been created.[26]

But it would be wrong to conclude from this that the interwar air theorists had been proved right, for it had taken more than five years of war to produce such an instrument and its essential nature as a bludgeon was far removed from the ideal of a scalpel, envisaged by Douhet, Mitchell or Trenchard. As the experiences of both the RAF and USAAF demonstrated, the idea of daylight precision raids, tearing the heart out of the enemy in a swift and decisive campaign, was just not practicable, forcing the air strategists either to shift the emphasis to area bombing by night – something which required the creation of an entirely new weapon – or to devote all their energies to the battle for air superiority. Either way, the result was a diversion of resources away from the main aims of the offensive – the destruction of war industries and the undermining of civilian morale – and a delay in the development of a true strategic campaign. Even when this campaign began in September 1944, its outcome was by no means clear-cut, for although no one could deny that the bombers made a significant contribution to the ultimate defeat of Germany, they did not do so alone, nor did they preclude the need for ground or naval operations. By May 1945, key sectors of the German war economy had been destroyed, notably oil facilities and communications, and a large number of cities had been devastated, but it is difficult to see how this on its own could have led to the 'unconditional surrender' that total war demanded. In addition, despite experiences such as Hamburg or Dresden, German civilian morale had not been broken – as the British had discovered during the Blitz in 1940–41, most civilians proved to be remarkably resilient under aerial bombardment, belying the prewar beliefs that panic would quickly ensue – and German armies had been able to put up considerable resistance until quite late in the war. The promise of easy victory through the element of the air had not been realized.[27]

The pattern of strategic bombing

From the example of the air offensive against Germany – described in some detail in order to show the nature and extent of the problems involved – a pattern of strategic bombing may be discerned, which other examples merely reinforce. The attraction of victory through the air is clearly strong, for most campaigns begin with high hopes being expressed about the effects of the bombers and their ability to destroy the enemy's capability to wage modern war. In 1939, the RAF was convinced that a single concentrated 'knock-out blow' would lead to the early defeat of Germany, and a similar sentiment was expressed by the leaders of the USAAF in 1942, despite the obvious problems experienced by the British in the meantime. When the Americans planned a campaign against Japan soon after the attack on Pearl Harbor in December 1941, they imagined that it would constitute a means of decisive victory, and as late as March 1965, when they initiated a similar offensive against North Vietnam (Operation Rolling Thunder), their optimism had not diminished.

In all cases, however, such claims were quickly shown to be exaggerated, for two main reasons. The first was that the politicians who controlled the war showed a marked reluctance to release the bombers with the concentrated force envisaged by the strategists. In the case of the RAF in 1939, this was understandable in terms of the widely held fear of a German counter-bombardment of British cities, but in more recent times it has come from a desire to prevent unnecessary escalation. In Vietnam, for example, the American campaign against the North between 1965 and 1968 was deliberately restrained to avoid provoking a reaction from Hanoi's allies in the communist world. As part of a strategy of limited war, the aims of the offensive were restricted to blocking Northern supply routes into the South and imposing a penalty on Hanoi for its continued support of insurgency below the Demilitarised Zone on the 17th parallel. In the process, the full weight of American airpower was not used – the massive B-52 Stratofortress bombers, each capable of carrying up to 24,500 kg (54,000 lb) of high explosives, were not released over the North during Rolling Thunder – and the targets were carefully controlled by the White House. Far from a concentrated blow being inflicted in March 1965, the campaign gathered pace only slowly, allowing the North Vietnamese to absorb the damage and survive the attacks.[28]

The second reason for a lack of immediate success was more practical, for in all the examples of strategic bombing that may be cited, the air forces involved found it exceptionally difficult to create the sort of weapon needed to carry out their attacks. This was shown most forcibly in the case of the RAF in 1939, for it was to take almost five years of war and massive changes to the nature of the envisaged campaign before anything like a viable instrument had been created. The same was true of the USAAF both in Europe, where the myth of the self-defending bomber was shattered in the skies over Schweinfurt, and in the Far East, where the campaign began without the Americans possessing the aircraft capable of reaching Japan from existing air bases. Indeed, the campaign against Japan was a classic case of resources having to be devoted to the creation of a viable weapon, for it was to take nearly two years and a massive injection of technological skill to produce the B-29 Superfortress bomber, as well as special amphibious operations to capture bases in the Mariana Islands from which the aircraft could reach the Japanese homeland. Even then, the practical problems of carrying out a bombing campaign were immense. As had been the case in Europe, the effectiveness of enemy air-defence systems soon undermined the concept of the 'self-defending' bomber and forced the planners to alter their methods of attack. Over Japan, where the need to contribute to a CBO was not a factor, the Americans were free to experiment with other approaches; it is interesting to note that by March 1945, having suffered significant daylight casualties, they shifted to what were effectively night area attacks, hitting Japanese cities with incendiaries in a deliberate attempt to destroy civilian morale.[29]

Nor was this the full extent of the practical problems involved, over Japan or elsewhere. In all campaigns, the nature and extent of enemy air defences has tended to disrupt the concentration of the bombers, forcing them either to alter their methods of attack or to accept high casualties. The RAF's shift from daylight to night precision bombing in early 1940 was a direct result of the losses imposed by radar-assisted fighters over the North Sea, and similar shifts occurred in the Luftwaffe during the raids on Britain in 1940 and, as already noted, in the USAAF over Japan five years later. Even over North Vietnam, in an age of more sophisticated technology, the losses inflicted by surface-to-air missiles (SAMs), fighters and anti-aircraft guns were substantial – during Rolling Thunder the Americans lost 922 aircraft to enemy action – forcing a diversion of effort to deal with the threat. As Douhet had foreseen, but other theorists had ignored, the need to gain and maintain air supremacy was an essential precondition of strategic bombing, requiring attention before the true campaign could begin.

This failure to concentrate the bombing force has been exacerbated in most campaigns by a need to divert aircraft to other, more pressing operations. During the RAF offensive against Germany this was a constant problem, apparent in 1940–41 as the bombers were sent against targets connected with the naval war, and the process culminated in the decision to use both British and American heavy bombers over Normandy between April and September 1944. The campaigns against Japan and North Vietnam were less subject to this weakening of effort, although they did suffer to a certain extent from the equally debilitating effect of poor intelligence assessment of targets and of levels of destruction achieved. As the Allies discovered when they analysed the effects of the bombing on Germany in 1945, many lucrative targets were either missed, because the planners had no way of knowing where they were, or were left to recover from raids that did take place, because it had proved impossible to gauge with any accuracy the true extent of damage caused. In such circumstances, the temptation must be high to go for bludgeon attacks, flattening the city on the assumption that it contains many valuable targets that are not on the planners' lists. When, in the absence of a weapon capable of hitting anything smaller than a city, the bombers cannot even take out precise targets, this temptation becomes operational necessity if the campaign is to continue.

These problems have undoubtedly blunted the impact of strategic bombing, enabling enemy states to survive and denying to the attacker all the advantages promised by the airpower theorists. As the campaign against Germany shows and other operations reinforce, war industry is a particularly difficult target to destroy and civilian morale does not always crack. But it would be wrong to leave the analysis there, for there is evidence to suggest that, in certain circumstances, the bombers can have a significant effect. The most obvious example of this lies in the use of atomic or nuclear weapons: although it is possible to argue that the Japanese did not surrender in August 1945 purely as a result of the attacks on Hiroshima and Nagasaki, there can be little doubt that the instantaneous devastation created on those occasions was the nearest that the bombers have ever come to satisfying the original theory of strategic bombing. As an integral part of the 'triad' of nuclear delivery systems currently deployed by the Americans and, to a lesser extent, by the Soviets, the manned bomber still has a role to play.

But the use of such weapons is likely to be suicidal in an age of MAD (Mutually Assured Destruction), leaving the theory still unproven in terms of conventional weapons. Nevertheless, evidence may be cited to suggest that, with new generations of highly accurate air-to-ground weapons, more selectively destructive rather than strategically decisive bombing can be considered. During the second phase of the American attacks on North Vietnam in 1972 (Operation Linebacker), for example, the use of 'smart' munitions, based on laser and TV guidance, had a devastating effect, shattering the oil storage facilities of the North and destroying key communications choke-points that had survived the less accurate Rolling Thunder strikes. When, in December 1972, these techniques were combined with a decision by President Nixon to release the B-52s over Hanoi (Operation Linebacker II) in a short but unrestricted campaign of city bombing, the effects were quite dramatic, forcing the communists to accept the American demand for more meaningful peace talks. The Israeli attack on the Iraqi nuclear reactor outside Baghdad in June 1981 (Operation Babylon), in which the levels of accuracy were remarkably high, implies that the creation of a scalpel rather than a bludgeon may now be possible.[30]

The fact remains, however, that strategic bombing has failed to live up to the expectations expressed by the theorists of the 1920s and

1930s chiefly because of the enormous range of practical problems involved in mounting a successful campaign. In the vast majority of cases, the best that can be created is a bludgeon of crude power, the creation of which is invariably expensive and time-consuming, allowing the enemy to absorb the attacks. In the process, it is the ordinary people who suffer, taking their place in the front line of total war.

Notes: Chapter 5

1 Count Francesco Lana de Terzi, *Prodromo overgo saggio di alcune invenzione nuovo* (1670). For quoted passages, see Air Marshal Sir Robert Saundby, *Air Bombardment. The Story of its Development* (London: Chatto & Windus, 1961), p. 6.
2 H. G. Wells, *The War in the Air: and Particularly How Mr Bert Smallways Fared While it Lasted* (London: George Bell and Sons, 1908). For other prophesies of the period, see I. F. Clarke, *Voices Prophesying War 1763–1984* (Oxford: Oxford University Press, 1966).
3 For an interesting account of public reaction to the threat of Zeppelin raids, see Basil Liddell Hart, *The Memoirs of Captain Liddell Hart*, Vol. I (London: Cassell, 1965), pp. 17–18.
4 Full details of all German air raids on Britain during the First World War may be found in Christopher Cole and E. F. Cheesman, *The Air Defence of Britain 1914–1918* (London: Putnam, 1984) and in Francis Mason, *Battle Over Britain* (London: McWhirter Twins, 1969), pp. 17–40.
5 Quoted in Neville Jones, *The Origins of Strategic Bombing* (London: William Kimber, 1973), p. 136.
6 Giulio Douhet, *The Command of the Air*, trans. by D. Ferrari (New York: Coward-MacCann Inc., 1942).
7 ibid., pp. 23–4.
8 ibid., p. 58.
9 Alfred F. Hurley, *Billy Mitchell: Crusader for Air Power* (Bloomington, Ind.: Indiana University Press, 1975).
10 Andrew, Boyle, *Trenchard* (London: Collins, 1962).
11 Statistics drawn from Tom Harrisson, *Living Through the Blitz* (London: Collins, 1976), Chapter 1.
12 For details of the organization of Bomber Command in September 1939, see Denis Richards, and Hilary St George Saunders, *Royal Air Force 1939–1945*, Vol. I, *The Fight at Odds* (London: HMSO, 1953), p. 41 and Appendix III, p. 406. Technical information on aircraft of the time may be found in Owen Thetford, *Aircraft of the Royal Air Force since 1918* (London: Putnam, 6th edn, 1976).
13 For details of operations, see Martin Middlebrook and Chris Everitt, *The Bomber Command War Diaries, An Operational Reference Book 1939–1945* (London: Viking, 1985), pp. 22, 26–7.

14 Sir Charles Webster and Noble Frankland, *The Strategic Air Offensive Against Germany 1939–1945*, Vol. I, *Preparation* (London: HMSO, 1961), p. 189.
15 ibid., Vol. IV, Appendix 8, pp. 112–33.
16 ibid., Appendix 13, pp. 205–13.
17 ibid., Appendix 8, pp. 143–8, transcribes the Directive of 14 February 1942; Portal's note, dated 15 February, appears in Vol. I, p. 324.
18 See Air Marshal Sir Arthur Harris, *Bomber Offensive* (London: Collins, 1947); Dudley Saward, *'Bomber' Harris* (London: Cassell, 1984).
19 Bruce Robertson, *Lancaster – The Story of a Famous Bomber* (Hemel Hempstead: Harleyford, 1974); Michael Bowyer, *Mosquito* (London: Faber & Faber, 1967).
20 Brian Johnson, *The Secret War* (London: BBC Publications, 1978), pp. 84–6.
21 Ralph Barker, *The Thousand Plan* (London: Chatto & Windus, 1965).
22 Full details of these radar aids are published in Johnson, *Secret War*, Chapter 2.
23 Martin Middlebrook, *The Nuremberg Raid* (London: Penguin, 1973).
24 Quoted in Noble Frankland, *Bomber Offensive. The Devastation of Europe* (London: Macdonald, 1970), p. 53.
25 John Sweetman, *Schweinfurt. Disaster in the Skies* (London: Macdonald, 1971).
26 David Irving, *The Destruction of Dresden* (London: William Kimber, 1969).
27 For a useful analysis of the CBO, see Richard Overy, *The Air War 1939–1945* (London: Europa, 1980), Chapter 5.
28 Carl Berger (ed.), *The United States Air Force in Southeast Asia 1961–1973* (Washington DC: Office of Air Force History, 1977), Chapter IV, pp. 69–100; also Guenter Lewy, *America in Vietnam* (Oxford: Oxford University Press, 1978), Chapter 11, pp. 347–417.
29 Carl Berger, *B-29 The Superfortress* (London: Macdonald, 1970).
30 Linebacker II is covered in Berger, *US Air Force in Southeast Asia*, pp. 95–9; see also Roger Freeman, 'Boeing B-52s in battle. The US Eighth Air Force's 11-day war in Vietnam', *Air Pictorial*, March 1987. The Israeli attack on the Iraqi nuclear reactor is covered in Amos Perlmutter, Michael Handel, and Uri Bar-Joseph, *Two Minutes Over Baghdad* (London: Corgi Books, 1982).

Further reading: Chapter 5

Berger, Carl, *B-29 The Superfortress* (London: Macdonald, 1970).
Berger, Carl (ed.), *The United States Air Force in Southeast Asia 1961–1973* (Washington DC: Office of Air Force History, 1977).
Cole, Christopher, and Cheesman, E. F., *The Air Defence of Britain 1914–1918* (London: Putnam, 1984).

Freeman, Roger, *The Mighty Eighth. A History of the US 8th Army Air Force* (London: Macdonald & Jane's, 1970).

Harris, Air Marshal Sir Arthur, *Bomber Offensive* (London: Collins, 1947).

Harrisson, Tom, *Living Through the Blitz* (London: Collins, 1976).

Hastings, Max, *Bomber Command* (London: Michael Joseph, 1979).

Jones, Neville, *The Origins of Strategic Bombing* (London: William Kimber, 1973).

Liddell Hart, Basil, *Paris, or the Future of War* (London: Kegan Paul, 1925).

Middlebrook, Martin, and Everitt, Chris, *The Bomber Command War Diaries. An Operational Reference Book 1939–1945* (London: Viking, 1985).

Overy, Richard, *The Air War 1939–1945* (London: Europa, 1980).

Webster, Sir Charles, and Frankland, Noble, *The Strategic Air Offensive Against Germany 1939–1945*, 4 vols (London: HMSO, 1961).

6

Nuclear Strategy

COLIN McINNES

On 6 August 1945 the first atomic bomb was dropped on the Japanese city of Hiroshima. Although by today's standards quite a small device (equivalent to 20,000 tons of TNT), the event seemed to usher in a new age when the traditional Clausewitzian idea of war as a continuation of politics by other means would be challenged. After all, if the result of a nuclear war was the annihilation of the two sides fighting it, how could this be seen as a rational tool of policy? The suddenness and scale of destructive power was such that traditional ideas of war no longer seemed applicable. In the words of Bernard Brodie:

> Thus far the chief purpose of our military establishment has been to win wars. From now on its chief purpose must be to avert them. It can have almost no other useful purpose.[1]

Strategy had moved away from how to win wars to how to stop them occurring in the first place, away from notions of victory towards those of deterrence.

The theory of deterrence

Deterrence rests upon the threat that the costs of aggression will outweigh the gains. In its simplest form, nuclear retaliation would act as a punishment to aggression, and the fear of nuclear attack would therefore deter aggression. In this sense the concept of deterrence is neither new, nor exclusive to the military: the idea of threatening a punishment to deter an action lies, for example, at the heart of most legal systems. Murder is deterred through the threat of a long prison sentence, or even capital punishment.

But such threats are not always successful. In the case of murder, the murderer may feel he can get away with the crime and avoid the punishment, he may be willing to accept the possibility of punishment, or perhaps most important, he may not be level-headed and rational, calmly working out the costs and benefits of his action, but a human being governed by emotions. Each of these cases could equally apply to nuclear deterrence. What is new, however, is that the nature of the nuclear threat is such that it cannot afford to fail: the costs of deterrence failing could be nothing less than annihilation.

How then do you ensure against the failure of deterrence? Central to its working is that the threat offered must be a credible one. The state must have both the political will and technical capability to carry out its threat. In terms of political will, a nuclear threat might be credible when the state threatening it is the only one with such weapons, or when retaliation is to deter massive nuclear attack alone. Thus, the American threat in the late 1940s might be deemed credible because the Soviet Union had no weapons with which to retaliate; similarly, the British independent deterrent is credible against an attack destroying the major cities in Britain. Once the Soviet Union acquired nuclear weapons, however, they could deter American retaliation with the threat of a counter-strike against US cities. This problem became particularly acute for extended deterrence, where the USA extended her deterrent umbrella to cover threats against her allies (particularly NATO) as well as herself. In this situation, the question was asked whether the USA would be prepared to use nuclear weapons against a Soviet invasion of western Europe, knowing that the result might be a Soviet strike against US cities. Is nuclear retaliation a credible threat against a limited attack, given that the result might be the destruction of your own cities? In these circumstances the willingness of a leader to use nuclear weapons is by no means guaranteed.

On the technical side, mere possession of nuclear weapons is insufficient to guarantee deterrence. To be credible, deterrent forces require the ability to survive an enemy attack (what is termed a second strike capability), penetrate enemy defences, and cause sufficient damage no matter what protective measures are employed. Ironically, to defend military assets can therefore be stabilizing in that it adds to the prospects of survival of the retaliatory force, while to defend civilians can be destabilizing in that it threatens the ability of retaliatory forces to inflict punishment.

Judging the credibility of a deterrent threat is far from easy. Probably the more straightforward assessment is of technical capability, because here at least we are dealing with tangible assets such as numbers of bombers and missiles. Yet calculations of missile survivability, bomber penetration, and so forth, are all dependent upon assumptions about how well (or badly) systems will perform. As a result, estimates can vary widely. Assessing political will appears even more difficult, because we are dealing with the reactions of individuals to novel situations when they will be under extreme stress. From this three things are apparent. First, credibility can never be 100 per cent certain, since it is heavily dependent upon assumptions about the behaviour of individuals and the performance of weapons. Secondly, it is essentially a subjective measurement. Finally, what matters is not whether you have the will and capability to carry out the deterrent threat, but that your enemy believes you to have that will and capability. Deterrence is therefore a perceived state of mind, rather than an absolute state of being.

For a number of reasons this strategy appears quite odd. It is essentially unmilitary in that it has very little to do with fighting and winning a war. Indeed, it has almost reached the point where strategy stops when war begins. Should deterrence fail, the role of military forces would be to engage in what Herman Kahn described as 'wargasm'. Moreover, there is something inherently dissatisfying about a strategy that emphasizes the vulnerability of civilians to nuclear attack, particularly when it also argues that defending military forces is a good idea. Aside from the moral question of whether it is right to threaten the lives of millions of innocent people (on both the enemy's side and your own, if the enemy has a retaliatory capability), and whether this is a proportionate response in accordance with traditional ideas of what constitutes a 'just war', this threat runs against traditional ideas of the role of a government in protecting its peoples and lands. Instead, governments are emphasizing the vulnerability of people and land, arguing that because this vulnerability is mutual no rational state would attack, and therefore peace is maintained.

This raises another difficulty with this particular concept of deterrence: that it is dependent upon rational behaviour. Some states, however, seem to be highly irrational. This may be because they are indeed irrational, but there are other more subtle reasons why they might appear so. First, they may lack the information on which to make rational judgements. To deter, a state must communicate its threat effectively. If it fails to do this, there is an information gap, which may lead to 'irrational' behaviour. Secondly, ideas of rational behaviour tend to be highly ethnocentric. What might appear to be a highly rational assessment of the costs and benefits of a particular action to one state, to another may seem highly irrational. Deterrence by punishment relies upon threats against valued assets. Yet the value placed upon a given asset (say, a proportion of a state's population) may vary considerably between states. For example, it might be suggested that, if the gain were the triumph of communism and the destruction of capitalist imperialism, the Soviet Union might be willing to sacrifice a large percentage of her population, as she did in the Second World War to defeat Nazi Germany.[2] Finally, a state might deliberately pretend to be irrational to force the other side to back down out of fear that its deterrent threats might not be heeded. In an analogy with the game of 'chicken', when American youths would race their cars towards one another and the first to pull away was 'chicken', Kahn suggested a possible tactic might be to appear drunk before the game, and throw out the steering wheel. This appearance of irrational and uncontrollable behaviour would so scare the other driver that he would be the first to pull away.

Perhaps the most worrying aspect about nuclear deterrence, however, is the consequence of failure. If the threat fails, then the result could be mutual annihilation, particularly if the response is a single 'spasm' strike. When added to the problems of credibility over extended deterrence and of reaction to limited threats, a more flexible and limited nuclear strategy seems desirable. Instead of a single massive strike aimed at punishing aggression, nuclear weapons might be employed against military targets, both to affect the enemy's warfighting capability and to encourage limitation in the conflict. Such a strategy would have two major advantages. First, avoiding attacks on cities would mean that these cities are held as hostages to encourage limitation by the other side. Therefore, since first use is not necessarily suicidal, credibility is boosted. Secondly, the strategy offers the hope of negotiating an end to the war (war termination) before annihilation occurs.

Of the many ideas for limited nuclear war, three key strands can be identified. The first is the introduction of nuclear weapons that would act as stepping stones between conventional and strategic nuclear forces – principally tactical nuclear forces. Thus a ladder of escalation could be created, with clearly definable steps between conventional war and all-out retaliation. Secondly, strategic nuclear forces could deliberately avoid cities, holding them as hostages against future strikes – what is termed the 'no-cities' or counterforce strategy. Finally, damage limitation measures could be introduced, either to protect the population directly by the use of air defences and shelters, or by a pre-emptive strike aimed at destroying as many of the enemy's military forces as possible before they could be launched, thus reducing the damage they could cause. Such ideas, therefore, move away from 'wargasm' towards more traditional warfighting ideas of the use of military power.

Ideas of limited nuclear war, however, face a number of practical difficulties. The idea of American and Soviet leaders carefully assessing what each other has done and choosing between a variety of options for reply, like two players in a game of chess, seems somewhat removed from reality. Apart from the stress and emotion involved, there are very serious doubts about whether either side has, or could ever have, the means for commanding and controlling a nuclear war. Not only the practical problems of communication in a nuclear environment but also more serious organizational problems have been identified.[3]

In addition, these ideas tend to imply both the existence of an agreed ladder of escalation and a willingness on both sides to accept limitation. The problem is that neither seems to exist. Although it might be argued that, in a war, if the alternative to limitation is mutual annihilation, then there will be natural pressures for limitation, this tends to ignore the issue of what exactly constitutes limitation. Unless there is a clear conception of what can and cannot be hit, then there is a very real danger of misunderstanding and of the war getting out of control.

The existence of independent nuclear deterrents belonging to governments that might have different perspectives on a war, is a further complicating factor. What Americans might see as a limited attack against military facilities in Britain could be seen in a very different light by a British government with millions of their citizens dead or dying. Moreover, nuclear weapons are essentially indiscriminate: their effects cannot be limited merely to military assets, but will include everyone and everything, civilian and military alike, within their destructive area. The idea of 'surgical' nuclear strikes against purely military targets cannot overcome the fact that millions of civilians might be killed. If this is the case, then a leader might ask in what sense is such a war limited?

Ideas of limitation also assume that there will be some process whereby political leaders can end the war. How leaders would actually negotiate with each other, what terms would be acceptable, and whether political leaders could actually maintain or reassert their control over military commanders are all issues that have received little or no attention until quite recently, and appear to pose problems that are not easily solved.

To some extent, though, this is merely a product of a more general problem: the lack of experience in nuclear warfare. It is very difficult to plan for something when there is no body of experience to act as a guide. Assumptions have to be made on the flimsiest of evidence, and problems may appear that had not been identified in advance. The effects of a limited nuclear strike on morale, on the environment and on political perception are all uncertainties of which warfighting theorists have no experience.

Substantial practical difficulties therefore exist with strategies of limited nuclear war. Arguably more important are the doubts about whether such a strategy is desirable, even if it were possible. The principal problem here is that, if war can be limited, then the costs of aggression are limited. The equation between costs and benefits is substantially altered, therefore, possibly making war once more a rational policy option. In addition, if a limited nuclear war is fought between the superpowers, the place for that war would probably be Europe. For Europe, this war would scarcely be limited. If war is more likely, but the consequences for Europe almost as severe, then the desirability of a warfighting strategy can be questioned by Europeans. The dilemma, however, is that a warfighting strategy might be necessary to reinforce the credibility of extended deterrence. For European NATO, therefore, a delicate balance has to be struck between ensuring that a war cannot be kept limited and that the credibility of the American nuclear guarantee is maintained.

Regarding the strategy of pre-emption, again there are questions about whether it is practical or desirable. Given the size of nuclear arsenals and their destructive power, even a highly successful pre-emptive strike would leave sufficient retaliatory forces to cause enormous damage. What may be adopted, however, is a coercive strategy, whereby retaliation against a pre-emptive strike is deterred by the threat of further strikes against cities. Thus, the enemy would be placed in a position where he could either do nothing, or commit suicide by retaliating.

Such a capability would be highly destabilizing, particularly if possessed by both sides. Indeed, the situation has been compared with a western gun duel, when the first to fire and shoot accurately would win. In such a situation, pressure would be intense to launch nuclear weapons at the slightest provocation, lest the enemy be about to do the same.

In conclusion, the simple punishment model of deterrence is highly unsatisfactory without a nuclear monopoly. Problems, however, surround both the practicability and desirability of limited nuclear war. This is the dilemma that has dominated US nuclear strategy.

US nuclear strategy

Although the USA was the first state to develop nuclear weapons, and the only one to use them in anger, initial American strategy was marked by an unwillingness to rely on them, and in particular to place them at the centre of any strategy for dealing with the Soviet Union. After the failure of attempts at international control, President Truman appears to have seen nuclear weapons as terror devices of the last resort, and therefore produced no strategy or conceptual plan for their use in war. Operational planning, and in particular the choice of targets, was left to the military, with only the very broadest of war objectives outlined from above. Under the leadership of Air Force General Curtis Le May, the man who had planned the fire-bombing raids on Japanese cities in the Second World War, planning by Strategic Air Command (SAC) focused on the laying waste of the Soviet Union and her allies. Lacking both the intelligence and numbers of weapons for attacks on military targets and war-supporting industries, targeting concentrated on large cities and centres of government.

As the American nuclear stockpile expanded rapidly in the wake of the Korean War and the 1949 Soviet atomic test, so the target list also began to grow. In 1950, SAC began to draw up an operational plan with three different categories of target. Top of the list were so-called Bravo targets – pre-emptive strikes against Soviet nuclear forces aimed at *blunting* their effectiveness. Next came Romeo targets, which would slow (or *'retard'*) the progress of Soviet forces into western Europe. And finally, the destruction of Delta targets would *disrupt* Soviet warmaking capacity.[4] With SAC dominating the targeting process, and without a clear strategy from the political leadership, a high emphasis on pre-emption emerged. Whether Truman knew of or understood this is uncertain. Truman left office without establishing a nuclear strategy, or even the principles for guidance in nuclear war planning.[5]

It was therefore left to the Eisenhower administration to formulate the first declaratory American nuclear strategy, although a pre-emptive strategy had been emerging at the employment level for some years.

On 12 January 1954, in a speech to the Council on Foreign Relations in New York, Eisenhower's Secretary of State John Foster Dulles announced the decision to 'depend primarily upon a great capacity to retaliate, instantly, by means and at places of our own choosing' to deter aggression.[6] In its crudest form, this strategy of massive retaliation envisaged conventional forces acting as little more than a tripwire to detect aggression. Once aggression had been detected the response would be a massive nuclear strike. This deterrence by punishment appeared in its gross simplifications not only highly inflexible, but also incredible and dangerous against limited threats. Once the Soviet Union gained its own retaliatory capability, so the United States would be unable to defend its allies conventionally, and unable to use its nuclear weapons for fear of Soviet retaliation against American cities. The US President would be placed in a situation of 'suicide or surrender', thus undermining the credibility of western defence.

Yet Massive Retaliation was never the caricature some of its critics portrayed it as being. As early as April 1954, in an article in *Foreign Affairs*, Dulles himself hinted at greater flexibility, stating that large-scale nuclear retaliation was neither the sole nor the most appropriate American response under all circumstances.[7] What the alternatives were, however, remained undisclosed, ostensibly to create uncertainty and as a result, caution in the mind of a potential aggressor. More important, Massive Retaliation fitted neatly into SAC's ideas of strategic pre-emption. The early years of the Eisenhower administration were marked by a belief, never made public, that SAC could execute an effective first strike against Soviet nuclear weapons. This would remove the Soviet retaliatory threat, and cause sufficient chaos in the Soviet Union to paralyse the country.[8]

As in the days of Truman, employment policy was left largely in the hands of the military, and of SAC in particular. Thus, while Dulles was declaring deterrence by punishment, SAC seemed more interested in being able to fight and win a nuclear war through a massive pre-emptive strike. The size of the strike, which included war-supporting industries and targets in other communist countries (Albania would effectively be destroyed because it possessed an air defence radar), led to the strategy being termed one of overkill.

With the expansion of the Soviet arsenal and the development of missile technology (offering little or no warning of attack), an American first strike began to look less and less feasible. Indeed, by the late 1950s, with the bomber gap, missile gap, and a series of scare reports about SAC vulnerability, the debate appeared to be moving to whether a Soviet first strike was possible. The Navy in particular compared the vulnerability of bombers to the invulnerability of the new Polaris submarines, arguing for a counter-city (or 'counter-value') policy rather than counter-force against airfields whose bombers would probably have been launched already.[9] This debate was resolved in 1959 by the proposal for an 'optimum mix' of military targets, which would also yield high civilian casualties. The emphasis on pre-emption was retained, though with increasing doubts about its feasibility from those outside the Air Force.

Although Massive Retaliation was far from the stereotype its critics portrayed it as being, the moral implications of overkill, and in particular the problems of credibility against limited threats, led to widespread dissatisfaction among civilian defence analysts. With the new Kennedy administration in the early 1960s, and in particular under Secretary of Defense Robert McNamara, nuclear strategy was reviewed, and the criticisms of civilian strategists (many of whom acquired roles in the making of policy) were taken to heart. The result was a shift away from pre-emption and overkill towards flexibility and limitation.

Announced in 1962, first at a meeting of NATO defence ministers in Athens, then in an address at the University of Michigan in Ann Arbor, McNamara's new strategy of Flexible Response marked a fundamental change in US declaratory policy. Cities were to be avoided, and emphasis was to be placed instead on a series of limited counterforce strikes aimed at encouraging negotiation and war termination. The United States would be capable of fighting a variety of different wars, from the conventional upwards, reacting to enemy aggression at the same level. The threat of escalation and the continuation of negotiation introduced an element of bargaining into the process. McNamara also emphasized the ability to defend America against attack (damage limitation) as a necessary part of his strategy, and positive political control over the use of nuclear weapons to enable both bargaining and control over escalation. The strategy, therefore, was one of deterrence by warfighting rather than punishment.

This new strategy was far from universally popular, however. European hesitancy was revealed by the five years from McNamara's initial outlining of the strategy in 1962 to the formal NATO acceptance of Flexible Response in 1967. The Soviet Union was similarly uncertain, both about whether restraint were possible, and, more important, in its fears that counterforce targeting could serve as a guise for a

US first strike policy. Soviet agreement that restraint was desirable was a necessary condition to the success of McNamara's strategy, but did not appear to be forthcoming. Within the United States as well, doubts were raised about the possible first strike implications of the policy, and whether collateral damage would be so high that limitation was not feasible. Most important of all, McNamara himself began to doubt the strategy. Damage limitation appeared expensive and ineffective, restraint seemed impossible, and the requirements of counterforce appeared merely an excuse for the military to demand more weapons.

By 1964–65, McNamara was beginning to move to another strategy, that of Assured Destruction. Returning much more to the punishment model of deterrence, this offered as a deterrent to nuclear attack the corresponding threat of unacceptable retaliatory damage (a figure which fluctuated between one-third and one-fifth of the Soviet population, and three-quarters to one-half of its industry). Since McNamara envisaged this situation would apply to both superpowers, Donald Brennan was able to coin the acronym MAD (Mutual Assured Destruction) for the strategy.[10]

In many ways, MAD reflected more McNamara's frustration with nuclear strategy than a satisfactory policy. For its critics, not only was the strategy intellectually redundant, but somehow immoral in its emphasis on the threat of mass genocide as the only means to stability. Moreover, its lack of flexibility would leave the US President with a 'suicide or surrender' response to Soviet nuclear attack. As Richard Nixon argued in his 1970 Foreign Policy Message to Congress:

> Should a President, in the event of a nuclear attack, be left with the single option of ordering the mass destruction of enemy civilians, in the face of the certainty that it would be followed by the mass slaughter of Americans?[11]

Although the President actually had rather more options than this, Nixon considered them too inflexible and unsubtle. Soon after the speech, therefore, studies were begun into building more options into the nuclear targeting plan, the SIOP (Single Integrated Operational Plan). In mid-1972 Nixon directed his National Security Adviser, Henry Kissinger, to head a top-level group to develop more options at the strategic nuclear level, and a similar panel started work in the Pentagon. These studies eventually led to the strategy of Limited Nuclear Options, the so-called 'Schlesinger Doctrine' (named after the then Secretary of Defense), the key document of which, NSDM (National Security Decision Memorandum) 242, was signed by Nixon on 17 January 1974.

The key idea of the Schlesinger Doctrine was that of escalation control – the ability to control escalation *at* the strategic level by a series of limited, selective strikes. By thus increasing the flexibility and range of options open to a President, it was hoped to avoid the 'suicide or surrender' decision highlighted by Nixon, and thus to enhance credibility. In the pauses between these selective strikes, the two sides could attempt to negotiate a ceasefire, while by avoiding certain high-value targets, hostages would be created to deter further escalation ('withholds'). Targeting focused on counterforce and the Soviet recovery economy (the Soviets' ability to recover quickly from the effects of a nuclear war, and therefore be in a position of superiority after the holocaust). This reflected the strategy's emphasis on restraint in the use of nuclear weapons, selectivity in their targeting, and above all their usability.[12]

Despite an initial interest in returning to a form of Assured Destruction, planning under the Carter Administration soon reverted along the lines of the Schlesinger Doctrine. In the summer of 1977, Carter ordered another review of strategic nuclear targeting. The result was the Countervailing Strategy, announced by Secretary of Defense Brown in 1979 and implemented in the signing of Presidential Directive (PD) 59 by Jimmy Carter on 25 July 1980. The emphasis of the strategy was on deterring aggression by convincing the Soviet Union that 'no war and no course of aggression by them that led to use of nuclear weapons – on any scale of attack and at any stage of conflict – could lead to victory'.[13] Through the ability to respond in a limited and selective manner to a wide variety of threats, the strategy sought to ensure that victory would be denied to the Soviets, or that unacceptable costs would be incurred.

The Countervailing Strategy was essentially an evolutionary development from what had gone before, prompted by new assessments of Soviet perspectives on nuclear war. These assessments indicated that not only did the Soviet Union believe in the possibility of a prolonged strategic exchange over a period of weeks, but that the Soviets considered victory a theoretical possibility in such an exchange. As such, what the Soviet leadership valued were its strategic nuclear forces and its ability to maintain control of the Soviet state in times of crisis. In response, the Countervailing Strategy placed even stronger emphasis on counterforce targeting (as opposed to the recovery economy), on targeting the Soviet leadership, and on being able to fight a prolonged nuclear war lasting perhaps weeks. The Soviets' belief in the possibility of a prolonged strategic conflict had therefore offered further opportunity for the Americans to attempt a limited nuclear strategy, while the value that the Soviets placed on military forces and the leadership offered targets that could be exploited in such a strategy.

The warfighting nature of this strategy was reflected in the new SIOP drawn up to accompany PD 59. SIOP 5D listed more than 40,000 potential targets, divided into four main categories: Soviet nuclear forces; other military targets; the military and political leadership; the war-supporting and war-recovery industries. Although all-out retaliation against a massive attack was not ruled out, the emphasis was clearly on warfighting as opposed to deterrence by punishment.[14]

Although the growing warfighting nature of American strategy was criticized not only for being unfeasible, but for having first strike connotations and for making nuclear war more 'thinkable', the emphasis has been maintained under the Reagan Administration. The key Reagan document on nuclear strategy, National Security Decision Directive (NSDD) 13, and SIOP 6 appeared to move away from denying the Soviets victory to attempting to secure American victory in a nuclear war – a Prevailing Strategy. When coupled with early Reaganite rhetoric on the possibility of limited nuclear war and of American victory in such a war, and with a resurgence in the belief that nuclear weapons could be used in a broader political context to bolster American diplomacy, nuclear strategy under Reagan appeared to be different in kind to that of his predecessors.

Criticism of these ideas, and the growing disillusionment with the prospects for controlling nuclear war, led to a retreat from more extreme statements on war-winning. More important, on 23 March 1983, President Reagan outlined his personal solution to the problems of nuclear war: the use of technology to provide a defence against nuclear attack. The Strategic Defense Initiative (SDI, or 'Star Wars') is technologically still far away, and its strategic desirability is far from certain (how would it deter a conventional attack on western Europe?). SDI, nevertheless, has become a major source of technical, political and strategic debate. Whether it will ever be incorporated into American nuclear strategy remains to be seen.

American nuclear strategy has been marked therefore, by a persistent dilemma: on the one hand, spasm responses such as Massive

Retaliation and MAD have been seen as undesirable; on the other hand, alternative warfighting strategies have been criticized as unworkable, with dangerously destabilizing first strike connotations. This dilemma emerged once the Soviet Union acquired its own nuclear capability, and became a central concern when it achieved parity with the United States at the strategic level. Ever more sophisticated theories of warfighting and war-winning do little to solve this dilemma, since at its heart is the essentially uncontrollable and immensely destructive nature of nuclear weapons.

Soviet nuclear strategy

In the 1960s and early 1970s, much of the thinking in the West about Soviet strategy concentrated on the idea of convergence: that the technology of nuclear weapons was such that the only possible response was that of MAD, and that therefore at some stage American and Soviet theories of deterrence would converge around this. The 1972 Anti-Ballistic Missile Treaty seemed to mark this convergence, with both sides agreeing to limit defences (and therefore the Soviets seeming to accept MAD). Developments in the 1970s and more recent research into Soviet strategy have emphasized that, far from following an American lead, the Soviets have their own distinctive approach to nuclear strategy, a product of their historical legacy, ideology and bureaucratic politics. Unlike abstract American theories of limitation and bargaining, the Soviet view of deterrence is very much a product of traditional military science and operational art. Contemptuous of 'metaphysical' American theories, Soviet strategy attempts to prevent war, but if war should occur then the policy is to fight it, to increase Soviet chances of survival and to secure victory if at all possible.[15]

In the aftermath of the Second World War, Soviet strategy ossified around Stalin's 'Permanently Operating Factors'. Formulated after the battle for Moscow, these principles emphasized size, quantity, and the destruction of enemy armies in a land war. Strategic bombing was peripheral, surprise a mere tactic, and no single weapon decisive. Despite this public rejection of atomic bombs as absolute weapons, Stalin nevertheless laid the foundations not only for the successful atomic and hydrogen bomb tests of 1949 and 1953 but also for the strategic bomber programmes of the 1950s. Acquiring a strategic arsenal was given high priority, and Stalin recognized at least some of the political and military implications of nuclear weapons. Given Western nuclear superiority, the small size of the Soviet stockpile, and Stalin's conservatism, however, nuclear weapons were far from the centre of Soviet doctrine.

With the death of Stalin in March 1953, Soviet strategy was released from the straitjacket of the Permanently Operating Factors. Surprise was recognized in the danger of an American first strike, and also in the benefits of pre-emption in limiting damage to the Soviet Union. The small size of the Soviet arsenal severely hindered the potential of this strategy, however, and victory was still seen in terms of the capture of western Europe by conventional forces.

In the early 1960s Kruschev began to challenge orthodox Soviet beliefs in the inevitability of war and its usefulness as a tool of policy, arguing instead for a minimum deterrent and reductions in conventional forces. If war was no longer inevitable, it could be deterred by the threat of nuclear retaliation. Moreover, if it was no longer a rational tool of policy, large armies to capture western Europe were not required. This was coolly received by the Soviet military, who countered that although war was not inevitable it might still occur, and therefore large armies would still be necessary to fight such a war. A compromise between the two positions was attempted in the publication in 1962 of Marshal Sokolovsky's *Military Strategy*. Arguing both the Kruschev line that the first phase of a war would be decisive, and the military's line that the eventual outcome would be dependent upon the surviving conventional forces, Sokolovsky's work was less a resolution of the controversy than an uneasy acceptance of the existence of both positions.[16]

The most visible development in Soviet nuclear policy, however, was not doctrinal but technological: the 1957 launch of Sputnik, and consequent American fears of a missile gap. Although the perception of a Soviet lead was used extensively by Kruschev for political capital, the reality was rather different. Problems with missile technology, and the embarrassment of the Cuban missile crisis, eventually punctured Soviet rhetoric. As the Americans began their massive build-up under Kennedy, and as McNamara began to emphasize ideas of limitation, so the Soviets' own missile programme faltered, and Kruschev was forced through Soviet weakness to scorn limitation.

With the fall of Kruschev in October 1964 the military gained an increased influence in the Kremlin, reflected in the growth of the

Soviet strategic arsenal. When this growth was added to statements from such leading figures as Major-General Talensk[17] that nuclear weapons could be used to achieve political ends and that victory was possible, hawks in the West feared that the Soviets were attempting to gain nuclear superiority and a war-winning capability. Other Soviet statements, however, emphasized the unprecedented disaster of a nuclear war. This difference could be a product of disinformation or propaganda, or could reflect splits on strategy within the Soviet leadership. It is more likely, however, that a contradiction does not exist, but is part of a strategy that attempts to prevent war partly by being able to fight it successfully. In this view, Soviet strategy attempts to prevent war, but, should it occur, seeks to fight and win it through pre-emption and damage limitation. Thus, although nuclear war would be political in that it would be the product of political differences, it would not be a useful tool of politics. Similarly, although Soviet ideology dictates the inevitable triumph of Socialism, the reality of nuclear destruction puts in question whether such a victory would have any value. Defensive measures and pre-emption might assist in the survival of the Soviet state, but cannot guarantee it. Therefore, a Soviet first strike can only be contemplated if an American attack is inevitable and imminent. Moreover, with the achievement of parity, escalation by either of the superpowers is a dangerous matter. As a result, Sokolovsky's emphasis on the inevitability of escalation has been rejected by more recent Soviet Chiefs of Staff (notably Ogarkov and Akhromeyev) as out of date, and the importance of conventional forces has increased owing to the penalties of escalation.

Thus, Soviet strategy is different in kind from that of the United States. Theories of bargaining and limitation have consistently been ignored in favour of war-fighting strategies, whose central aim has been the prevention rather than avoidance of war.

Strategies of other nuclear powers

Britain, the third state to acquire nuclear weapons, was the first to actively seek to develop them in 1941, prompted by the fear of a possible German project. In 1943, the small British project was incorporated into the larger and more advanced American project, thus establishing a close (and for Britain very profitable) nuclear partnership. At the end of the war co-operation was promptly curtailed by the Americans, leaving Attlee's Labour government with the difficult decision to continue atomic research independently at a time of national austerity. The decision to proceed with an independent project was made secretly in 1947 by a few senior Cabinet ministers, and reflected less a clearly thought out strategy than the political priorities of the day. As a great power, it seemed axiomatic that Britain should pursue this technology; moreover, only with a project of its own could Britain hope to re-establish its close nuclear relationship with the United States. Militarily, although nuclear weapons were portrayed as the 'great leveller', offsetting massive Soviet conventional superiority, the Labour government failed to provide a strategy for their use (only partly because Britain had yet to acquire these weapons).

Churchill's return to power in 1951 was followed the next year by the first successful British atomic test, and the first attempt to construct a strategy for the use of the bomb. Under the guiding influence of Air Force Chief of Staff Sir John Slessor, the Chiefs of Staff's Global Strategy Paper emphasized the massive retaliatory power of nuclear weapons in a strategy clearly foreshadowing that of Dulles's Massive Retaliation. Slessor moved away from ideas that there might be a period of 'broken backed warfare' where conventional military forces surviving a nuclear strike would decide a conflict, to emphasize simple punishment deterrence. In this there would be no realistic victor, and conventional forces would consequently play very much a secondary role.

As in the United States, so in Britain this strategy provoked a strong reaction. Whereas in the United States analysis used 'scientific' methods, such as systems analysis and game theory, British critics were rooted in a more 'classical' tradition of historical and philosophical method.[18] Nevertheless, critics such as Professor P. M. S. Blackett, Sir Basil Liddell Hart, and above all Sir Anthony Buzzard focused on much the same points as their American counterparts: the incredibility of such a response once the Soviet Union acquired nuclear weapons, and its moral implications. As an alternative strategy, Buzzard offered Graduated Deterrence, which attempted to provide distinctions between various categories of nuclear weapons (particularly tactical and strategic), which would allow the West to resort to the superior firepower of nuclear weapons without risking retaliation against cities.[19]

Official policy throughout the 1950s, however, remained committed to Massive Retaliation, although it was only with the Sandys review of 1957 that this was fully reflected in force structure. As late as 1955 Britain retained an army of 435,000, far in excess of the requirements of Massive Retaliation and a considerable strain upon the budget. The 1957 Defence White Paper therefore abandoned conscription and large conventional forces for a reliance on nuclear weapons and Massive Retaliation.[20] With the American nuclear guarantee to Europe, justifying the independent deterrent was not straightforward. With the growth in the American arsenal in particular, Britain could scarcely claim to provide a necessary numerical contribution to the West's deterrent. Justification, therefore, required concentrating upon the distinctive nature of the threat to Britain, and planners developed the argument that the independent deterrent was necessary to attack targets of low priority to the United States but of strategic significance to Britain (notably bases for medium-range bombers). Therefore, there seems to be some contradiction between public policy of Massive Retaliation and the counterforce rationale developed to justify the force's existence in the NATO framework. Less explicit, however, were doubts about the reliability of the American guarantee, particularly in the wake of Suez. The independent deterrent provided a hedge against possible American withdrawal, although for political reasons this could never be made explicit. Ironically, as doubts about the American guarantee grew, so Britain became increasingly dependent upon American technology in providing crucial parts for the Blue Streak missile, in agreeing in 1960 to sell Britain the Skybolt missile, and finally, in 1962, after cancelling Skybolt, in agreeing at the Nassau conference to supply Polaris.

Strategy, meanwhile, began to edge away from the extremes of Sandys. The 1962 Defence White Paper hinted at a more 'balanced' approach to deterrence, involving a greater role for conventional forces, while doubts about the American guarantee during Alex Douglas Home's premiership produced a drift towards a more Gaullist stance in the 1964 Defence White Paper.[21] This drift was stopped abruptly by the election of Harold Wilson's Labour government in 1964. Elected on a pledge to 'renegotiate' Nassau, it soon became clear that Wilson had no intention of abandoning the independent deterrent. Rather, his Defence Secretary Denis Healey concentrated on quashing ideas that Britain could 'go it alone', and on producing a rationale for the force within the NATO context. Healey's formulation of the 'second centre of decision-making' has remained official Government policy for more than two decades. This rationale states that, although the British government has every faith in the reliability of the US guarantee, the Soviets might question that guarantee. By having a second, specifically European centre of decision-making, not only is Soviet planning complicated, but the temptation to gamble on possible American hesitancy is reduced. As Lawrence Freedman has commented:

> The attraction of this approach lies as much in its diplomatic convenience as in the rigour of its strategic logic. It allows Britain to maintain an independent force, while insisting that this is for the greater good of the alliance.[22]

In addition to this official rationale, a number of other justifications have been offered for the retention of the British deterrent: that it is a weapon of last resort in deterring a Soviet nuclear attack; that it acts as a trigger for a possibly reluctant US use of nuclear weapons; that it adds to Britain's prestige, by buying a ticket to the top table. Alternatively, critics have argued that, given likely Soviet responses, the force could never realistically be used unless it was too late anyway; that it is an unnecessary drain on strained defence resources; that it adds little to Britain's prestige. What is remarkable about this is that very little actually concerns strategy. The arguments concentrate on the merits or otherwise of possession, rather than how the force might actually be used. At the most general level it appears that British planners, out of a lack of flexibility in force structure and strategic disinclination, pay little heed to American ideas of limitation and bargaining, rather being interested in punishment strikes against 'key aspects of Soviet state power' (usually interpreted as meaning Moscow). The Chevaline warhead modernization programme[23] of the 1970s can be explained as a development to overcome defences around Moscow, and the 1980 decision to buy the much more capable Trident missile had little or nothing to do with changes in strategy, being rather a straightforward replacement of the ageing Polaris force.

Like their British counterparts, French scientists were involved in wartime atomic research, but at a much lower level. Moreover, although France established an atomic energy commission (the CEA) as early as 1945, it was only in 1952 that this acquired a military dimension. By 1954, however, there were clear indications that a military programme was under way, prompted by fears of a resurgent

Germany, concern over the American guarantee to Europe, and desires
to re-establish French prestige (*grandeur*). In May 1957, Defence
Minister Bourges-Maunoury formally announced the establishment
of a military nuclear policy, independent of Britain and the USA,
to improve French standing within NATO, and on 11 April 1958
Prime Minister Felix Gaillard signed the official authorization for
the production of atomic bombs, effectively a ratification of a policy
already in existence.

With the Algerian Crisis and the fall of the Fourth Republic, the
wartime hero de Gaulle returned to power in France. De Gaulle's
defence policy was dominated by the mutually reinforcing ideas of
independence and *grandeur*. Alliances were not only incredible, given
the problems of extended deterrence (would an American President
risk the destruction of New York to save Paris?), but imposed
unacceptable limitations upon a state's freedom of action. Moreover,
given the deterrent power of French nuclear weapons, alliances such
as NATO offered little additional security. In addition, nuclear
weapons were politically important, not as tools of influence but
rather as symbols of French power and prestige. After the reverses of
Indo-china and Algeria, the development of nuclear weapons played
an important role in de Gaulle's attempt to place France back in the
centre of world politics.

Under the guise of 'Proportional Deterrence', French nuclear strategy closely resembled that of Massive Retaliation. Whereas American strategy emphasized a massive strike to paralyse the Soviet
Union, French strategy talked of a lesser response ('tearing an arm
off') proportionate to France's importance to the Soviet Union.
The centrality of nuclear weapons was reflected in the First Programme Law (1960), where funds for conventional forces suffered at
the hands of the nuclear programme. Although conventional forces
received greater emphasis in the Second Programme Law (1965),
this did little to erode the central position of nuclear weapons in
French strategy.

With France's withdrawal from NATO in 1967, French declaratory
strategy was altered to meet threats from any direction, including
the United States.[24] Although this doctrine of *tous azimuts* was
quickly reassessed in the wake of the 1968 Soviet intervention
in Czechoslovakia, it is important in indicating the independence
characteristic of Gaullist nuclear strategy, and reflected in the writings
of strategists such as Beaufre and Gallois.[25]

Pompidou's succession to de Gaulle in 1969 provided an opportunity to review defence policy. The review, undertaken by Michel Fourquet, identified the inflexibility of simple punishment retaliation, and the political and military isolation of *tous azimuts*. A more graduated deterrent strategy was therefore adopted, with the major threat clearly identified as coming from the East. This review was further refined in the 1972 defence white paper, which implicitly recognized two levels of conflict: a forward battle in West Germany (which might or might not include French conventional forces and tactical nuclear weapons) and, should this battle be lost and France invaded, a strategic nuclear exchange, with tactical nuclear weapons possibly being used as a warning shot. In this second battle, a single retaliatory blow was rejected in favour of a series of graduated responses, although the number of these would be few given the small size of both France and her strategic arsenal. Once again independent control was emphasized and, although co-operation with NATO was not totally excluded, the degree of such co-operation was restricted.

With the election of Giscard d'Estaing as President in 1974, defence policy was once again reviewed. Continuing concern over the inflexibility of French strategy led Giscard and Chief of Staff Guy Mery to increase the importance of conventional forces. Abandoning Fourquet's 'two battles', Mery announced in 1976 the doctrine of *sanctuarisation élargie* (enlarged sanctuarization) arguing that the defence of France could not be divorced from that of Western Europe as a whole, since the battle for West Germany would have a direct bearing on French security. French forces, therefore, would act as a second defensive line for NATO in West Germany, while tactical nuclear weapons would be used in battle rather than as warning shots preceding a strategic strike.

Despite official reassurances that this was little more than an evolutionary development, Gaullists criticized the doctrine as implicitly acknowledging reintegration into NATO and therefore reducing French independence. In addition, the emphasis on conventional forces was criticized as eroding deterrence by lessening the immediacy of the nuclear threat: if a war did not necessarily involve a strategic nuclear exchange it was once more a policy option. Against this onslaught Giscard was forced to retreat, at least in public, to the 'vague generalizations' of the 1960s.[26]

The election as President of socialist François Mitterand in 1981 failed to produce any significant change in emphasis away from nuclear weapons. Indeed, if anything, Mitterand appeared closer to de Gaulle than to Giscard. Although the creation of a rapid deployment force boosted French ability to support military action on the central front, reintegration into NATO was not seriously contemplated. The emphasis on independence through the possession of a strategic nuclear deterrent remained central to French defence policy, and was reflected in cuts in conventional forces to pay for the modernization of nuclear forces.

French nuclear policy, therefore, has been marked by a questioning of the credibility of extended deterrence, preferring the possession of an increasingly expensive independent capability to a reliance on the American guarantee. Although French strategy has moved away from initial Gaullist inflexibility, it still falls well short of American notions of limitation. A product of both the small size of the French arsenal and French national style in strategy, strategic nuclear options appear limited to strikes against cities, and the rungs on any ladder of escalation are few. In addition, a high premium is placed on the prestige acquired through the possession of nuclear weapons; their value is seen not in terms of direct political influence, but rather in providing a symbol of continuing great power status.

If a persistent feature of debates about the British and French deterrents is the reliability of their ally, the United States, then the origins of the Chinese deterrent lie in similar doubts about their one-time ally, the Soviet Union. Initial Chinese reaction to the atomic bomb was that it was little more than a 'paper tiger' that looked impressive but lacked substance. The decisive factor in war remained mobilization of the Chinese masses in a People's War, using weight of numbers and guerrilla tactics in place of a modern, professional army.[27] With the Soviet failure to fully support China against the United States in the Quemoy crisis of 1958, the Chinese began to question the reliability of their ally in a superpower confrontation involving the potential use of nuclear weapons. China thus began to argue for its own nuclear weapons, and as the Sino-Soviet split widened so the determination to acquire an independent capability matured, not as a weapon of military value, but rather as a political tool to prevent American nuclear blackmail and allow for better crisis management. Nuclear weapons also provided an important status symbol for China in Asia, and in its growing competition with the Soviets in the socialist camp. Ironically, just as the Chinese nuclear programme came to fruition in the mid-1960s, so the impact of the

Cultural Revolution produced an even more extreme emphasis on Maoist People's War doctrine.

Much as the death of Stalin allowed for greater flexibility in Soviet strategy, so the death of Mao in 1976 allowed for a movement away from the People's War doctrine, and the establishment of a more professional army with a greater emphasis on technology, including nuclear weapons.

Nevertheless, Chinese strategic concepts remain fundamentally different from those of both the West and the Soviet Union. Deterrence remains principally the task of conventional forces, using weight of numbers and size of territory to deny enemy invasion forces the ability to win. Nuclear forces are more directly concerned with lesser threats and crisis management. Chinese strategy may therefore be nearer to one of warfighting than punishment, but the legacy of People's War has produced a particular approach that does not readily fit into Western concepts of deterrence.[28]

Britain, France and China have therefore each produced distinctive national styles in nuclear strategy. Although all three share common features in the importance attached to independence, prestige, and doubts about the reliability of allies, as well as all experiencing financial and technical difficulties in maintaining credible forces, differences are equally apparent. The British force is incorporated into an Alliance framework, the French stand on the periphery of one, while the Chinese decisively split from the Soviet camp twenty years ago. Chinese strategy appears fundamentally different from Western concepts. Both Britain and France appear to reject American ideas of limitation and bargaining in favour of simple punishment deterrence. But it is not clear quite how the British force fits into NATO strategy, while the French appear to have moved away from the inflexibility of the Gaullist position.

Notes: Chapter 6

1 Bernard Brodie, *The Absolute Weapon* (New York: Harcourt Brace, 1946), p. 76.
2 Colin Gray has gone so far as to suggest that what the Soviet leaders value most is their ability to control the Soviet state, and that if the instruments of state control were threatened then this would be an effective deterrent. See Colin S. Gray, 'Nuclear strategy: the case for a theory of victory', *International Security*, vol. 4, no. 1 (1979), pp. 67–9.

3 Paul Bracken, *The Command and Control of Nuclear Forces* (New Haven, Conn., and London: Yale University Press, 1983).
4 Desmond Ball, *Targeting for Strategic Deterrence* (London: IISS, 1983), pp. 6–7.
5 David Alan Rosenberg, 'U.S. nuclear war planning, 1945–60', in Desmond Ball and Jeffrey Richelson (eds), *Strategic Nuclear Targeting* (New York: Cornell University Press, 1986), p. 43.
6 Quoted in Lawrence Freedman, *The Evolution of Nuclear Strategy* (London: Macmillan, 1981), p. 85.
7 John Foster Dulles, 'Policy for security and peace', *Foreign Affairs*, vol. 33, no. 3 (1954).
8 Rosenberg, pp. 44–6; Fred Kaplan, *The Wizards of Armageddon* (New York: Simon & Schuster, 1983), p. 134.
9 Rosenberg, pp. 50–1.
10 Freedman, pp. 245–9.
11 Quoted by Ball, p. 18.
12 Aaron L. Friedburg, 'The evolution of U.S. strategic doctrine, 1945–1980', in Samuel P. Huntington (ed.), *The Strategic Imperative: New Policies for American Security* (Cambridge, Mass.: Ballinger, 1982), pp. 76–80.
13 Address by US Secretary of Defense Harold Brown, 20 August 1980, *Survival*, vol. 22, no. 6 (1980), p. 268.
14 Ball, p. 23; Brown, pp. 268–9.
16 Robert Levgold, 'Strategic "doctrine" and SALT: Soviet and American views', *Survival*, vol. 20, no. 1 (1979), p. 9; Dennis Ross, 'Rethinking Soviet strategic policy: inputs and implications', *Journal of Strategic Studies*, vol. 1, no. 1 (May 1978), pp. 5–6.
16 Marshal V. D. Sokolovsky, *Soviet Military Strategy*, 1st edn, edited by Herbert Dinerstein, Leon Goure and Thomas Wolfe (Englewood Cliffs, NJ: Prentice-Hall, 1963); Freedman, pp. 263–4.
17 Raymond L. Garthoff, 'Mutual deterrence and strategic arms limitation in Soviet policy', *International Security*, vol. 3, no. 1 (1978), p. 115.
18 John Garnett, 'British strategic thought', in John Baylis (ed.), *British Defence Policy in a Changing World* (London: Croom Helm, 1977), p. 163.
19 For the debate between Massive Retaliation and Graduated Deterrence, see A. J. R. Groom, *British Thinking about Nuclear Weapons* (London: Frances Pinter, 1974).
20 *Defence: Outline of Future Policy: 1957*, Cmnd 124 (London: HMSO, 1957).
21 *Statement on Defence 1962: The Next Five Years*, Cmnd 1639 (London: HMSO, 1962); *Statement on Defence 1964*, Cmnd 2270 (London: HMSO, 1964).
22 Lawrence Freedman, *Britain and Nuclear Weapons* (London: Macmillan, 1980), p. 129.
23 The Chevaline programme was an independent UK venture to improve the penetrative capability of Polaris by installing decoys and other

penetration aids. For details see C. J. McInnes, *Trident: The Only Option?* (London: Brassey's, 1986), pp. 4–10.
24 See General Ailleret, 'Directed defence', *Survival*, vol. 10, no. 1 (February 1968), pp. 38–43.
25 André Beaufre, *Deterrence and Strategy* (London: Faber & Faber, 1965); Pierre Gallois, *The Balance of Terror: Strategy for the Nuclear Age*, trans. Richard Howard (Boston: Houghton Mifflin, 1961).
26 David S. Yost, *France's Deterrent Posture and Security in Europe: Part 1: Capabilities and Doctrine* (London: IISS, 1984), pp. 7–9.
27 Freedman, *The Evolution of Nuclear Strategy*, pp. 274–6.
28 ibid., p. 282.

Further reading: Chapter 6

Ball, Desmond, and Richelson, Jeffrey, eds, *Strategic Nuclear Targeting* (Ithaca NY: Cornell University Press, 1986).
Brodie, Bernard, *Strategy in the Missile Age* (Princeton, NJ: Princeton University Press, 1959).
Freedman, Lawrence, *The Evolution of Nuclear Strategy* (London: Macmillan, 1982).
Freedman, Lawrence, *Britain and Nuclear Weapons* (London: Macmillan, 1980).
Gray, Colin S., *Strategic Studies and Public Policy: The American Experience* (Lexington, Ky: University Press of Kentucky, 1982).
Gray, Colin S., *Nuclear Strategy and National Style* (London: Hamilton, 1986).
Jervis, Robert, *The Illogic of American Nuclear Strategy* (Ithaca NY: Cornell University Press, 1984).
Kaplan, Fred, *The Wizards of Armageddon* (New York: Simon & Schuster, 1983).
Kahn, Herman, *On Thermonuclear War* (Princeton, NJ: Princeton University Press, 1960).
Snyder, Glenn, *Deterrence and Defence* (Princeton, NJ: Princeton University Press, 1961).
Sokolovsky, V. D., *Soviet Military Strategy*, 3rd edn, ed. by Harriet F. Scott (London: Macdonald and Jane's, 1975).

7

Limited War

ROBIN BROWN

The nuclear bomb created for the first time the real possibility of global devastation as a result of warfare. This, it was argued, had made war impossible – creating a revolution in the nature of international politics. But within a few years it became obvious that the 'revolution' was less revolutionary than some had suggested. The traditional pattern of international relations, aggression and war, reasserted itself. If nuclear weapons had made war too devastating to be an instrument of policy though, how could the challenge of war be met? The objective of limited war was to meet this challenge, to find ways in which force could be used to meet aggression without threatening global devastation. In this original form 'limited war' has now lost its meaning, but the needs that it addressed – the limitation of conflict and the risks and uses of escalation – remain central to strategic studies. The evolution and application of these ideas form the core of this chapter. Our focus will be on the American theory of limited war, since the concepts developed in the United States formed a unique and original approach to international conflict, one that continues to shape most Western thinking on strategic issues, indeed shapes our perception of many important problems.

War and limited war

The form that war takes depends on the form of the states waging it. The French revolution and the industrial revolution brought vast increases in the size of armies and the destructiveness of their weapons over those of the eighteenth century. The culmination of these events were the World Wars, when the combatants sought to mobilize their entire human and economic resources to destroy the opponent, creating massive suffering. In retrospect, the dynastic wars of the eighteenth century appeared to many as models of civilization, but, as Clausewitz argued, it is impossible to turn back the clock. The scope of the wars of the *ancien régime* was restricted by the means available to rulers.[1] Limited tax bases and the need for professional armies restricted the size of forces and the duration of campaigns. The aftermath of the French revolution turned war from the business of kings to the business of peoples, bringing about an expansion in scope and destructiveness. Once this had occurred it was impossible that wars would resemble those in the past, since a state that clung to the methods of the past would be quickly overcome by one that adopted the new methods. The addition of the industrial revolution led to the slaughter of the First World War.

In the wake of this struggle military thinkers sought to avoid a repetition of the stalemate. This was not only an attempt to find a better way of winning, but in the case of thinkers such as Fuller and Liddell Hart, to find ways in which total war could be avoided. For them, machine warfare was seen in the interwar period as being an antidote to total war. Small professional armoured forces could decide wars without involving the mass of the population.[2] But the Second World War demonstrated that machine warfare was the apotheosis of total war rather than its negation. The allied states were unwilling to accept the verdict of Hitler's *Blitzkrieg* victories and mobilized their resources to reverse them. Even before the explosion of the first atomic bomb Liddell Hart was again demanding a return to civilized warfare. Thus postwar limited war thinking was an answer to the same question that Liddell Hart had already been addressing, asked with new force by nuclear weapons: Is it possible for states to wage war without resorting to their full range of weapons?[3]

Clausewitz argued that the nature of any war is determined by the nature of the combatants, the quality of the armies and commanders that they fielded and their objectives. The nature of the objectives was in part a function of the other two. A war aimed at the total defeat of the opponent would result in maximum resistance; thus maximum effort was required.[4] In the nuclear age this reasoning faces a problem. A world exists in which there are two blocs, one of which is pledged to destroy the other. Destroying the enemy militarily will only result in self-destruction. Total objectives will lead to total means, but total means have become self-defeating. How can conflict be waged between nuclear-armed adversaries without leading to mutual destruction? Limited war theory attempts to provide a framework for the conduct of conflict where the normal relationship between means and ends is doubtful. Thus 'limited war' relates to conflict between nuclear-armed states. The development of limited war thinking has to be understood in this context. Indiscriminate use of the term to indicate any war short of all-out nuclear war simply confuses the issue. Thus, although some commentators have described the Gulf War as a 'limited war', in terms of objectives, degree of mobilization and methods relative to the means available, it seems more sensible to regard the conflict as simply a 'war' rather than as a 'limited war'.

Expectations of the Third World War

Until the Korean War broke out in June 1950 the basic case for American defence planning was Soviet aggression against Europe and the Middle East. This would be regarded as the opening of the Third World War. The American response would be an air offensive, using atomic and conventional bombs. The shortage of nuclear weapons prevented a decisive blow. A conflict on the pattern of the Second World War would follow, the United States mobilizing its industrial base for a protracted conflict. Limited war was not considered, and the 'nuclear revolution' had yet to make a serious impact on military thinking. Defence resources had yet to be concentrated on strategic air power with the aim of deterring this ultimate conflict.[5]

In the early part of 1950 the exclusive concern with the danger of general war was questioned in a high-level governmental study entitled *United States Objectives and Programs for National Security*, better known as NSC-68. This argued that growing Soviet military capabilities, in particular the atomic bomb, could result in a series of limited aggressions, each too small to warrant war. Because possession of the atomic bomb could not deter all challenges to the free world it was necessary to develop forces that could meet these lesser challenges and defeat them.[6] This question of what nuclear weapons can and cannot deter remains central to many controversies today.

Korea

The North Korean invasion of the South occurred as President Truman was considering NSC-68. On the face of it, Korea provided justification for the document's arguments. Korea was the prototype limited war, and since much of the writing of the 1950s is generalization based on the Korean experience, an understanding of the way in which that conflict was perceived is crucial to the understanding of these writings.

The North Korean invasion seems to have been initiated by Kim Il Sung as a way of reuniting his country with the knowledge and support of Stalin. Both Stalin and Mao calculated that there was little risk of American intervention. The conflict was an internal affair and the South was thought to be so weak that it would collapse rapidly, creating a *fait accompli*.[7] The reaction of the United States and its allies to the invasion was shaped by two factors: first, the political context and the resulting costs of doing nothing and, secondly, the military weakness of the West.

In 1950 the Korean invasion was seen in the West as a deliberate act of aggression carried out with the full approval and support of the Soviet Union as part of the global strategy of the Soviet bloc. Truman was caught in a dilemma. On the one hand, failure to act would have devastating consequences. The proximity of Korea to Japan might mean a swing away from the West as American impotence was demonstrated. Moreover, the recently concluded North Atlantic Treaty was regarded as a psychological prop for European reconstruction. Inaction in the face of communist aggression would destroy whatever confidence it had generated. Failure to act would also demonstrate the weakness of the United Nations and could be the start of a new series of aggressions that would end in world war in the same way as the events of the 1930s. Decisive action could prevent these consequences.[8] But against these considerations in favour of intervention was the realization that Korea was a secondary theatre. What if the attack were merely a strategic feint to divert attention and draw troops to east Asia as the decisive offensive in Europe was prepared? The problem was exacerbated by the weakness of the American armed forces, both nuclear and conventional. Commitment to Korea could leave Europe undefended. This was the basic constraint on Western policy in Korea. Doing nothing was dangerous, but so was doing too much.

The scope of the American response was therefore limited by the shortage of troops, equipment, aircraft and nuclear weapons. Attrition in Korea could diminish the ability to deter or wage a Third World War in Europe. Atomic weapons were too scarce to be wasted on unsuitable targets in a secondary theatre, while the air campaign was constrained by the fact that bombers being risked over North Korea would be needed to carry bombs against China if the war should spread.[9]

The collapse of the North Korean armed forces after the UN American landings at Inchon, and the possibility of reunifying the country on the South's terms led to concern about the danger of Chinese interventions. To prevent this, MacArthur was not to use non-Korean forces in the provinces along the Yalu River, the border between Korea and the Peoples Republic.[10] These instructions were ignored, but compared with the fundamental failure to realize that the Chinese perceived the advancing UN forces as a threat this was a minor factor. The intervention of Chinese 'volunteers' caught the UN off balance in an untenable strategic position at the end of the tenuous supply lines, resulting in a precipitous retreat. Evacuation of the peninsula again appeared a possibility, but the advance of the Chinese exposed their own supply lines while shortening those of the UN forces, allowing an equilibrium to be established. Without additional forces a UN advance could find itself once more overstretched, with weak logistics. For the Chinese the achievement of their defensive objective and the firepower of the entrenched UN troops militated against further advance. Thus a stalemate was reached.

Although the front had stabilized (new offensives were aimed at securing better defensive positions rather than shattering the opponent), the war continued for another two years as armistice negotiations dragged on. Although the fear of a Soviet attack in Europe receded and the military position of the West improved, there was reluctance to expand the war into China in order to bring about a speedier end. The conflict had become a struggle over the terms of the armistice, which was only resolved by Eisenhower's determination to end the conflict, if necessary by expanding the war into China and using atomic weapons.[11]

The lessons of Korea

Korea indicated the importance of the military aspects of the conflict with the Eastern bloc, and that the danger of being 'nibbled to death' was real. It demonstrated that the free world was engaged in a long-term struggle against an aggressive alliance. Korea was seen as the first of a series of challenges in the 'grey areas' of the Third World.

Although the threat was clear, how to manage it was the subject of a prolonged and acrimonious debate. The intervention in Korea was initially popular, but public support waned as the war continued, and was one of the reasons for the defeat of the Democrats in the 1952 US presidential election. Ideas of limiting military spending in order to ensure economic stability for the protracted struggle, and the futility of conventional combat against the manpower of Asia pushed the new Republican President, Dwight D. Eisenhower, towards the 'New Look' in defence policy. This emphasized strategic nuclear air power and the reorganization of the army for the nuclear battlefield. In the case of a limited challenge, like Korea, the United States would support local resistance with atomic weapons. Administration directives stated that nuclear weapons were like any other weapons. If American troops went into combat they could expect to use tactical nuclear weapons. The New Look sought to replace manpower with nuclear firepower and to avoid another Korean stalemate by stressing that there would be no hesitation in using nuclear weapons – hoping to deter or if necessary win such a conflict.[12]

The combination of limited defence budgets and the emphasis on the strategic forces meant financial pressure on the other services, especially the army. Throughout the Eisenhower years army officers and civilian strategists campaigned in favour of 'limited war forces', arguing on the lines of NSC-68 that it was incredible to threaten to use nuclear weapons in response to a small attack. Deterring and, if necessary, defeating such attacks required ground, air and naval forces capable of rapid intervention. This argument was aided by the caricature of the New Look as 'Massive Retaliation', whereby any aggression of whatever scale would result in the bombing of Moscow – a threat that lacked credibility. The limited war advocates saw Korea as a success: it showed that limited attacks could be defeated. There was no alternative to being prepared to fight such attacks if they were to be deterred, but Eisenhower's priority for strategic forces was threatening the ability to meet these threats.

The limited war theorists

Although there were differences among advocates of limited war strategies such as Robert Osgood, William Kaufmann and Henry Kissinger among the civilians, and Maxwell Taylor, Mathew Ridgway and James Gavin from the military, there were also common themes.[13] Their work was prescriptive. They sought to persuade the United States government to adopt their ideas, which they believed formed an approach by which conflict could be carried on in the nuclear age without total war with all its dangers. States had to *choose* to restrain their conduct; limitation of conflict was not automatic, and if either side did not make this choice then total war would be the outcome. Thus, their analysis of conflict could not have universal validity and, while it might apply to the situation of the 1950s, changing circumstances might make it irrelevant later. This historical context is important in assessing the continuing influence of limited war thinking. Are current ideas shaped by concepts that have lost their relevance with the passage of time?

Central to the thinking on limited war was the idea of protracted conflict between nuclear-armed blocs: that the conflict between communism and the free world was irreconcilable and would continue. In this conflict, the most likely area of struggle was the periphery of the Soviet bloc in Asia. If the West was not adequately prepared, the cold war could become hot as opportunities for limited gains were seized by the opponent. Adequate forces for meeting these challenges were essential, if the choice between nibbling and general war was to be avoided.

One point of disagreement was whether these forces should be armed with conventional or nuclear weapons. Kaufmann argued for the former, Kissinger for the latter.[14] Tactical nuclear weapons provided a cheap way of offsetting the superior manpower of the enemy and allowed exploitation of Western technical superiority. On the other hand, improving Soviet nuclear capabilities would reduce the credibility of the threat: who would want to be defended if nuclear devastation of their country was a probable outcome? Moreover, what would be the political impact of the West's being the first to use nuclear weapons? By 1960, therefore, a consensus had emerged in favour of a conventional option.[15]

What should be the objectives of limited wars also presented a problem. If the blocs were engaged in combat while using only a fraction of their military potential, an expansion of the conflict was always possible. Thus, restraint in the choice of objectives was necessary. A decisive defeat could cause one side or the other to escalate the conflict. If limited wars were part of a long-term struggle, in which the Soviet bloc attempted to weaken the West by gradual attrition rather than decisive defeat, individual conflicts would therefore only be important to the extent that they furthered this aim. The marginal significance of the prize meant that the willingness to escalate was limited, so the war could be 'won' by imposing costs on the opponent that exceeded the gains that could be expected from continuing the conflict.[16] If the war was weakening the East more than the West, it would be sensible for the Soviets to desist from their aggression. Thus, victory was achieved by imposing a favourable rate of attrition rather than by inflicting decisive defeats on the opponent.

The dangers of escalation with the consequent emphasis on attrition created problems with the military aspects of the conflict. Traditional military thinking emphasizes surprise, secrecy, offensive action and decision. MacArthur's push for more violent action against the Chinese had shown the dangers of such a mind set in the conduct of a limited war. Pushing too hard might lead to escalation.[17] Therefore, tight controls must be placed on the military. Limits must be placed on the type of targets that could be struck, weapons that could be used and the geographical extent of the conflict. Clearly enunciated, these would signal the willingness of the West to limit the conflict. Here theorists and advocates could point to Korea where, it was argued, both sides had reciprocally observed restraints. The UN forces had not struck targets in China, even though China provided both the bulk of the troops locked in combat with the UN and the bases for the MiGs that daily tangled with the American Sabres over North Korea. The granting of 'sanctuary' to Chinese territory, it was suggested, had its counterpart in the immunity granted to the UN logistic bases in Korea and Japan and the sea lanes between them.[18] This showed that the communist bloc was willing to accept reciprocal limitations on the conduct of wars, and that such limitations were feasible.

This interpretation can be challenged, however. What restrained the two sides was not commitment to a set of rules but an assessment of the military options open to the other. On the UN side, although expanding the war was seen as one way of bringing about its termination, the risk of Soviet intervention and attacks on Hong Kong and Taiwan acted as a restraining counterbalance. Moreover, expansion of the war could only weaken the forces available for the defence of Europe and complicate the termination of the war. The Chinese ability to expand the war was restrained by concern about what the response of the UN command might be, and the basically defensive objectives of Chinese involvement. Therefore, the situation was one of mutual deterrence, produced by a unique military and political context, which would be different in other conflicts.[19]

The crucial assumption behind limited war was that each outbreak of fighting was only a part of a larger whole and had to be waged as such. For this reason, limited war thinking was initially applied to Third World contingencies, not to Europe. If war occurred in Europe it would indicate a Soviet decision for a showdown, which would be met by the unleashing of Strategic Air Command against the Soviet bloc with the simple objective of causing maximum death and destruction. War in Europe would not be part of a larger war of attrition but one of the major objectives of the basic conflict.[20]

With the growth of Soviet nuclear forces, however, doubts about the American guarantee were created and, as a result, elements of limited war thinking began to be applied to Europe. In Britain this resulted in a debate between advocates of 'Graduated Deterrence' and Massive Retaliation. The former argued that the initial response to an attack should be to use tactical nuclear weapons against a range of military targets within a certain range of the battlefield. Only if this failed to contain the aggression would the strategic attacks be carried out. It was argued that the growth of Soviet nuclear capability made the threat of an immediate strategic attack incredible. The opponents of this view countered that the unwillingness to carry out strategic attacks would weaken deterrence by showing a lack of resolve.[21] Variations on this debate took place throughout NATO, reaching a peak with Robert McNamara's proposal for a new strategy of 'Flexible Response'.

Escalation and coercive diplomacy

The concept of Flexible Response must be related to the second wave of limited war thinking, a wave dominated by the ideas of Thomas Schelling and Herman Kahn, which continues to exert a powerful influence on Western strategic thinking today. The definitive works are Schelling's *Arms and Influence*, published in 1966, and Kahn's *On Escalation*, published a year earlier, which systematize ideas that had gained currency during the early 1960s.

During the 1950s war came in two types: limited and general. In official American usage a general war was any war involving Soviet and American troops, in which nuclear weapons would be used from the outset. A limited war was any conflict in which American troops were involved. Nuclear weapons might be used.[22] Although the possibility of a limited war expanding to a general war was recognized, the relationship between the two was not subject to detailed examination. A major part of the second wave of limited war thinking was the advocacy of a new approach to conflict that integrated limited and general war strategy into parts of a whole. The links between the two were provided by applying limited war thinking to Europe and by the discussion of counterforce concepts for general war. The result was the 'escalation ladder' or the 'spectrum of conflict'.

In its most fully developed form the ladder of escalation consisted of 44 'rungs' or levels of conflict, arranged in order of violence. At the bottom were 'Cold War', 'ostensible crisis' and 'political, economic, and diplomatic gestures'; at the top were 'civilian devastation attack', 'some other kinds of controlled general war', and at the very top 'spasm or insensate war'.[23] These rungs were collected into groups such as 'traditional crises', 'bizarre crises' and 'military central wars'. These groups were divided from each other by 'thresholds' or 'firebreaks' such as the 'nuclear war is unthinkable threshold', the 'no-nuclear use threshold' and the 'city targeting threshold'. At all except the level of 'spasm war' it was possible to argue that the conflict was limited in some way. Limited war was no longer a discrete phenomenon but part of a wider whole. Making these linkages explicit opened up new approaches to the conduct of the East–West struggle.

Limited war was conceived in the 1950s as a military contest of restricted scope. The outcome would be determined by the ability of one side to inflict unacceptable costs on the other. The new thinking, however, had the effect of downgrading the military aspects. Kahn argued that, as the level of violence became greater and greater, control became more difficult. Thus, as a conflict moved up the ladder of escalation there was an increasing danger of 'eruption' to the highest levels. This is obviously highly undesirable to both sides. Therefore, if one side is willing to escalate to a higher level than the other, it will win – if control doesn't break down and 'eruption' occur.[24] Military capability then becomes secondary to willingness to tolerate risk, what is termed 'resolve'. Victory will go to the side less willing to back down (an idea of conflict as a competition in risk-taking, which was most highly developed in the work of Schelling). Kahn argued that both sides possessed differing arrays of capabilities, which might give advantages at different levels on the ladder. This created opportunities for each side to attempt to wage the conflict at the level at which it enjoyed an advantage. Given that neither side would be very keen to go to the upper rungs of the ladder, a state that had an advantage at the lower rungs might be able to use its advantage to good effect if the absolute costs of escalating the conflict were unacceptable to the other side. Conversely, a state that had an advantage at higher levels had no need to match the capabilities of the opponent at lower levels, provided there was a willingness to escalate. The ability to use relative advantages to control the level of the conflict was termed 'escalation dominance' by Kahn.[25] The notion of escalation dominance is central to the analysis of NATO strategy, which will be discussed later in this chapter.

Kahn's escalation ladder, although undermining the distinctiveness of limited war, still showed that in some circumstances conflicts would be decided by combat. Schelling's ideas marked an even more radical break with the past. His first book on strategic issues, *The Strategy of Conflict*, had dealt with what he termed 'tacit bargaining'.[26] In a limited war, how were the limits determined if there was no direct communication between the opponents? As it was essential that both sides agreed on limits if disaster were to be avoided, both would be looking for limits. Schelling argued that some potential limits would be obvious to both sides. Examples of these 'saliencies' were 'no nuclear weapons', or political or geographical features such as borders or rivers. Although there was an infinite number of potential limits, it would be much easier to arrive at limits such as 'no chemical weapons' than 'no more than x quantity of chemical weapons' in the absence of communication. The willingness to observe certain limits could be made clear by statements and deployments of troops and by the conduct of operations 'signalling' intentions. Because of the overriding need to reach some agreement on limits, it might be possible to propose unilaterally some limits, which the opponent might be compelled to accept simply because of the lack of alternatives. In the *Strategy of Conflict*, tacit bargaining was a way of determining the scope of a limited war; by the time *Arms and Influence* was published, it had come to supplant it.

Schelling took a stage further Kaufmann's idea that the objective of limited war was to impose unacceptable cost on the enemy. Why do it by inflicting casualties on his armed forces? Surely it was easier to identify what he held dear and *threaten* that. In the past this had only been possible by defeating the enemy's armed forces, but in the air-age this was no longer necessary. Schelling advocated a strategy of 'coercive diplomacy'. A state would initiate an action that was regarded as unacceptable. The initial response would be a diplomatic protest and a warning of the consequences if it were ignored. This would be followed by a demonstration of force 'to show resolve'. If this still proved inadequate, a target or group of targets that were valued by the enemy could be attacked. If necessary, more and more of these targets could be struck, but the intended effect of these attacks was not so much in the destruction caused as in the indication of resolve they gave. If the objectionable action was not stopped, more destruction would be forthcoming. Each attack was a *threat* of more to come. Eventually, the expected costs of continuing the aggression would come to exceed the expected benefits.[27]

The idea of coercive diplomacy had major advantages for decision-makers. The experience of Korea and the dismissal of MacArthur had shown up the difficulty of maintaining close control over military operations, and it was feared that in a complex and sensitive situation military forces could inadvertently trigger escalation. Coercive diplomacy allowed military operations to be broken up into a series of discrete actions that could be subject to close political control, minimizing the risk of unintentional escalation. These ideas fitted in with the interest in the techniques of crisis management that were becoming fashionable in the wake of the Cuban Missile Crisis, in the aftermath of which it had become apparent that the armed forces had been acting in ways that could have led to clashes with Soviet forces without the knowledge of top decision-makers.[28] Coercive diplomacy's combination of gradually increasing pressure, signalling, and strict control appeared an ideal way to manage conflict in the nuclear age.

Although the new thinking incorporated some of the ideas of the original limited war thinking it was very different in general approach.[29] Limited war in its original conception was a military conflict that would be conducted within defined boundaries, and whose outcome would be determined by the relative willingness to endure the costs inflicted. If one side felt that it could gain an advantage by expanding the conflict, or if it believed that the stake was too important to be settled in such a constrained conflict, then it might choose to escalate. If the limits were not clearly defined, escalation might occur as a result of an unintentional transgression. The new thinking had a much more abstract character in which conflicts were to be determined not by casualties but by persuading the other side that you were more willing to risk nuclear devastation than they were. Armed forces were primarily threats, more useful held in reserve than in combat. Although this abstraction held the advantage of providing an approach that could be applied to any confrontation from a trade dispute to an attack on Europe, the disadvantage was a gap between the theory and its practical application. In any particular conflict, how could the level of pain to be inflicted be identified in advance? What strategy was the optimum one for inflicting it? How could an opponent's tolerance of risk be measured? What were the risks of any particular step? The overall effect was to decrease sensitivity to the nuance of particular conflicts and increase the sensitivity to some general factors – in other words to treat all conflicts the same. As symbolic actions were stressed, meanings could be read into troop deployments that were not intended. During the Vietnam war, for example, at least one American official was unable to believe that the North Vietnamese intended to use their new surface-to-air missiles against American planes, insisting instead that they were an indication of Soviet support and a threat, not a real military factor.[30] In practice, it was difficult to assess the risks of escalation attached to any action, the test of wills being independent of political interests. Thus, the theory lacked a way to measure risk, with the result that the danger of escalation was cited as an obstacle to practically any action.

The abstraction of escalation theory from political context is the fundamental motivation behind Soviet rejection of many aspects of limited war theory. This is crucial, because if a war is to be limited in scope through deliberate restraint on the part of the combatants rather than lack of means, that restraint will have to be mutual (unless one side is so superior that it can defeat the enemy while unilaterally observing restraints). Although the Soviet position on the feasibility of limited war has evolved, there is no willingness to accept the idea of war as 'a competition in risk taking' rather than a test of arms. Soviet scepticism was based on doubts about the feasibility of such a competition, both for technical reasons (were command and control systems up to such a demanding task?) and for basic sociopolitical reasons. If the two fundamentally opposed social systems, capitalism and socialism, were to engage in a life-or-death struggle, it was inconceivable that either side would accept its total destruction without using every weapon at its disposal. Total objectives would lead to total means. Given the impracticability of limitation, dependent on the restraint of the capitalists as it would be, a better way of protecting the socialist countries was simply to use all available means to attack the opponents weapons in order to limit the damage that could be inflicted, regardless of the intentions or willingness to exercise restraint or not.

During the 1960s Soviet writings emphasized that war between the superpowers would be global and nuclear. To some extent this belief was encouraged for purposes of deterrence. The United States possessed capabilities for limited warfare, especially nuclear, that were far superior to those of the Soviet Union. This could mean that it would be the Soviet Union not the United States that would face the choice between suicide and surrender. Thus, by emphasizing the inevitability of escalation and Soviet determination to act on this basis, the United States would be deterred from making use of its capacity for controlled conflict. Soviet thinking has evolved as their capabilities for fighting limited conflicts have improved, towards views that resemble the original concept of limited war: military conflicts waged within identifiable limits for limited objectives. The implication of this for Western security will be discussed later in this chapter.[31]

The early 1960s, therefore, saw the development of the ideas of coercive diplomacy, escalation ladders and escalation dominance that remain central to today's strategic thinking. Limited war lost its sharply defined boundaries as the 'spectrum of conflict' integrated all levels of conflict, including controlled strategic war and war in Europe. The early 1960s also marked the beginning of the conflict that was to be a test bed for limited war thinking.

Vietnam: limited war in action

Limited war thinking was stimulated by the Korean conflict, and its theses were based on generalizations drawn from it. Vietnam saw the application of many of these ideas. Whether or not the Americans were consciously applying limited war theory, many of the concepts underlying and shaping their policy were the same as those shaping limited war theory.

Vietnam was not a limited war in the way that we have defined one, a conflict between nuclear-armed adversaries. To the extent that North and South Vietnam possessed different social systems it was a war between blocs, but like Korea the impetus for the conflict came from the local communist protagonist rather than from Moscow or Beijing. Thus, there was a fundamental difference of magnitude in the costs that North Vietnam and the United States were willing to pay to continue the conflict. If the adversary had been the Soviet Union the value to be gained from incorporating South Vietnam into the Soviet bloc would be limited and the acceptable costs equally so. For North Vietnam's leadership there was a much greater willingness to pay in blood than the United States could have ever hoped to muster.

This difference was basic to the outcome of the war. North Vietnam was fighting a total war, a natural consequence of total aims – the elimination of the South Vietnamese state. The United States was fighting a limited war, both in the way that the conduct of the conflict was shaped by limited war concepts and in basic fact that victory in Vietnam was only one of the nations priorities. The war did not have an unconditional right to demand the resources needed to win it but had to operate under constraints that other priorities imposed. For the Johnson administration the war was a threat to the 'Great Society'. Steps to put the nation on a war footing, for instance by mobilizing the reserves, would lead to calls for domestic spending to be slashed to finance the war, effectively killing the new social programmes. Johnson was not simply faced with anti-war protesters on the left but also with the possibility that pressure would emerge from the right for an expansion of the war in order to win it. Such an expansion would threaten the Great Society.[32] Thus, the administration was searching for a compromise that would satisfy both. The result was what has been termed 'the minimum necessary and the maximum feasible'. Before 1965 American presidents sought to do just enough to prevent the collapse of the South, but once large numbers of troops had been committed the aim was to do as much as possible to win the war, subject to minimizing the domestic disruption.[33] Both strategies had more to do with domestic politics in the United States than with what was needed to defeat the North.

The gradual increase in American involvement was motivated by defensive factors, centring around the unwillingness to accept the consequences of a communist victory. As enemy capabilities grew, American commitment also grew. Incrementalism of this kind worked against the development of a coherent picture of the situation and the creation of a 'theory of victory' – an idea of just how the political objectives were to be achieved or a clear understanding of what those objectives were, or even if they were achievable.[34]

For the United States the costs of defeat were seen as being relatively clear cut. The value of South Vietnam and its people were seen as being secondary to the more generalized consequences. Communist victory would threaten the whole of south-east Asia: besides Laos and Cambodia, Thailand, Malaysia, Burma, Indonesia and beyond could be affected. Given that the 1960s were a period of considerable instability throughout the region, the shock of the collapse of the Saigon regime might have had a greater impact than it did when it finally occurred. On a global basis, it was feared that failure to defend South Vietnam would destroy confidence in American guarantees throughout the world and, by demonstrating lack of resolve, would encourage Soviet expansionism. This was an argument that was to recur until the final collapse of the South,[35] and was an argument that had found favour with the limited war theorists. In a protracted struggle in which each limited war was merely an episode, failure in one case to respond would reduce the credibility of the security guarantee to other states on the periphery of the Soviet bloc and encourage aggression. Successfully defeating an attack would reduce the future incidence. This was an argument that Kennedy found persuasive – South Vietnam was an opportunity to show that the United States was willing and able to defeat 'wars of national liberation'.[36] The Secretary of Defense Robert McNamara, among others, held the opinion that Vietnam was just the first of a series of limited challenges that would have to be met during the 1960s.[37] This belief contributed to the desire to avoid too great a level of mobilization. Osgood, among others, had argued that limited war was alien to the American people, and that once roused they would demand nothing less than total victory, an objective that was too dangerous to pursue in the nuclear age. Thus the American people had to be educated to accept limited war as a normal state of affairs.[38] As the war progressed, the American leadership was trapped between its desire to avoid pressure to escalate the war and its desire to wage it.

Although the war in Vietnam was believed to be necessary, it was also necessary to show restraint in its conduct. There was concern in some quarters that China or the Soviet Union could intervene in response to American actions, thus necessitating strict restraints on the conduct of the war. There is considerable doubt about how real this fear was, in official circles at least. Intelligence estimates discounted the possibility, but both hawks and doves had reasons for advancing the argument, anyway. For the hawks, the possibility of Chinese intervention justified demands for more troops to be made available; for the doves, it was an all-purpose argument against demands for more to be done to win the war. The Johnson administration purposely built up limits to the conflict to ward off the hawks, but were then assailed by the doves when a deteriorating situation forced them to break the self-imposed limits.[39]

At the political level, American policy was driven by contradictory impulses, resulting in a lack of clear objectives in one of the most complex wars of the postwar period. The United States' basic aim was to bring about the consolidation of a viable South Vietnamese state, which would enjoy sufficient support to resist insurgency or attack from the North. The military instrument could not create a state; rather, it had to bring about the conditions for this to be possible. The threat was complex, consisting firstly of an internal guerrilla movement, the National Liberation Front (NLF) or Viet Cong (VC), which enjoyed external support. Although originally made of cadres from the South, attrition resulted in its losing its indigenous nature as casualties were replaced by Northerners.[40] The VC problem was compounded by the infiltration of regular North Vietnamese Army (NVA) units into the South after 1964. It was hoped that by inflicting defeats on South Vietnamese and American forces and by capturing territory Southern morale would be shattered, creating the conditions for a general uprising against the Saigon regime. Thus the American response had the single aim of the creation of conditions for the stabilization of the South Vietnamese state, which was pursued in three ways: first, the building of political conditions favourable to this; stemming from this, the need to prevent the military defeat of the South; finally, this would be made much easier by halting North Vietnamese support for the Viet Cong and direct military participation.

Large-scale intervention in South Vietnam was triggered by the need to avoid defeat. The intervention of units of the North Vietnamese Army (NVA) had created a rapidly deteriorating situation, which US involvement reversed. The scope of US action was limited by the need to create a logistical infrastructure adequate to support a modern army with its home on the other side of the Pacific. The military objective was to impose an unfavourable rate of attrition on the NVA forces, resulting in a decision to desist – the classic limited war objective.[41]

In military terms this strategy proved to be effective. The presence of the American forces allowed the stabilization of the South and the gradual destruction of the VC cadres, as well as allowing the defeat of NVA–VC military moves. The communist campaign that culminated in the 1968 Tet offensive, the Winter–Spring Campaign, was motivated by a deteriorating military situation as viewed from Hanoi.[42] The result of the offensive for the North was an unmitigated disaster militarily, but politically a triumph. In the United States the fact that such a large-scale attack could occur after three years of full-scale American involvement was seen as discrediting the administration's policy and strategy as well as the leadership.[43]

The initiation of the build up of American ground forces in 1965 was not seen as being likely to bring about rapid results. Although it would stave off defeat it would not persuade the North to desist. This latter aim was to be achieved by 'Rolling Thunder', a campaign of air attacks following the principles of coercive diplomacy.[44] The initial targets were military and confined to the area just above the De-Militarized Zone (DMZ), the border separating North and South. The target list, geographical scope and intensity were all gradually increased. The rationale was that carrying out the bombing would signal American resolve, while the increasing scope would convey a threat of the consequences if action against the South were not halted. It was believed that the North Vietnamese leadership would be open to 'compellence', as Schelling termed it, through the threat to their industrial base.

Rolling Thunder was controversial from the start. The military leadership, for example, favoured an immediate air offensive against all significant targets, with the dual aim of breaking Hanoi's will and stopping the infiltration of men and supplies into the South. (Whether this would have been any more successful is open to question: the Northern leadership may have been unmoved, while by refusing combat, Communist forces in the South could control the rate at which they consumed supplies, thus limiting the effect of an air interdiction campaign.) Rolling Thunder, moreover, demonstrated the difficulty of applying coercive diplomacy. In Schelling's original conception the fear of uncontrolled escalation would be hanging over the combatants. In Vietnam this was not the case, and the Americans had no idea of what would be required to make the North desist. The graduated build up of attacks allowed the development of a sophisticated and effective air defence system in the North, counter-measures to which were constrained by the careful calibration of the offensive. Since the campaign was regarded as a delicate mechanism of diplomatic signalling, tight constraints were placed on air operations: to minimize collateral damage maximum precision in bombing was required even if the attacking aircraft were in greater danger as a result; attacks on air defence sites were only permitted if the sites concerned were actually firing; attacks on dikes were prohibited, allowing anti-aircraft weapons to be placed on them; attacks on built up areas were normally restricted, with the result that supplies were stored in the streets; attacks on Haiphong port were prohibited if 'third-party' ships were alongside; attacks on communication links with China were restricted; enemy aircraft could only be engaged after visual identification, forfeiting the advantage of radar-guided air-to-air missiles. Whether the absence of these constraints would have made any difference to the success of the bombing is debatable, but they reduced the impact and increased the cost of the strategy.[45]

In its original formulation the idea of coercive diplomacy amounted to the proposition that a state will stop doing something when the expected costs are greater than the expected gains. In Vietnam it proved impossible to achieve the necessary expectation of cost on the part of the communists. If an opponent is committed enough to his cause, the level of cost required may be indistinguishable from inflicting a decisive military defeat. In Vietnam that was something that could only be achieved by increased forces or by the willingness to continue large-scale American involvement for an indefinite period. In the wake of the shock inflicted by the Tet offensive neither of these options were seen as being practicable.

For Nixon and Kissinger peace in Vietnam was a priority, but, like Johnson and Kennedy, they were unwilling to countenance defeat because of its international implications.[46] Defeat would destroy America's credibility as they attempted to negotiate the deals that would create détente, but their commitment to Vietnam was not unlimited. Although anti-war sentiment peaked as troop withdrawals continued, Nixon was far more willing than Johnson had been to take some of the actions advocated by the hawks, such as taking the war into the communist sanctuaries in Cambodia and Laos, and launching new air offensives against the North. The 1972 Linebacker I and Linebacker II bombing campaigns dispensed with many of the restraints imposed on Rolling Thunder. Against the background of American withdrawal and diminishing domestic support, however, the impact of these moves on the North were limited. With the 1972 Christmas air offensive (Linebacker II), Hanoi found itself at the mercy of American air power, its supplies of surface-to-air missiles exhausted. But the concessions that it made to return to the negotiating table and agree to the Paris Accords were negligible: it was unlikely that the Americans would step in to defeat a new onslaught against the South.

Limited war theory had been built on the assumption that the opponent was cautious and value-maximizing, not a 'fanatically determined individual who will battle on until the weapons are dashed from his hands'. As Kaufmann observed, 'it is not a stereotype from which it becomes possible to construct a working model of limited war'.[47] Unfortunately for the people of South Vietnam and the United States, the determination of the North was such as to render attempts at coercion fruitless. Neither Johnson nor Nixon was prepared to adopt 'win' strategies – for instance, to mount sustained large-scale operations into Cambodia, Laos and the DMZ to cut off infiltration. Fundamentally, the conflict was 'asymmetric': the communists were more willing to 'pay any price, bear any burden', and the United States was not willing to make the sacrifices necessary for victory. Limited war theory was based on a fundamental symmetry of commitment to local conflicts by East and West.[48] The intrinsic significance of the prize was limited, and the willingness to bear costs and risks similarly so on both sides. Because the West possessed greater resources and better technology it would be possible to ensure that the costs to the opposition reached an unacceptable level first. In Vietnam, the United States was neither prepared to win through defeating the North, nor to pay the price needed to sustain the conflict over the period needed for 'Vietnamization' to pay off. Fundamentally, limited war thinking was irrelevant to the political realities of the conflict, but when superimposed on those realities it obscured the complexities of the situation, exaggerated the need for restraint, and gave false (if admittedly limited) hopes of defeating the opponent.

For the United States the world of the early 1970s was very different from that of the early 1960s. Nixon and Kissinger no longer assumed that the United States would be faced with a series of limited conflicts in the Third World. Although competition would continue, they did not believe that American troops would be committed in large numbers. The original concept of limited war had been rendered obsolete by changing political circumstances. Nevertheless, the concepts of limitation and escalation continued to shape thinking about East–West conflict.

The debate on NATO strategy

The issues of limited war and escalation are central to the continuing debate on NATO strategy, a debate that in essence has been conducted for at least thirty years. The crucial issue has been the relative weight that should be attached to nuclear and conventional weapons in NATO's defence posture. The positions held by governments are shaped by political factors that cannot be considered here, but it is worthwhile to trace the outlines of the alternative positions.[49]

During the 1950s NATO's strategy was based on American strategic superiority. It was unlikely that NATO could stop a Soviet attack on Western Europe, so the main response would be strategic counter-attacks on the USSR. Soviet retaliation on the United States was not considered to be significant enough to deter the execution of the attack. Thus US strategic superiority allowed the United States to threaten the Soviet Union with the immediate and massive escalation of any conflict.

The emergence of Soviet strategic forces and the work of the limited war theorists raised questions about the credibility of this strategy. If the Soviet Union could absorb an American attack and still retaliate, would the United States still be willing to carry out its threat to launch nuclear attacks on the Soviet Union in response to an attack on Europe? Strategic theorists attacked the problem on several levels. The first aimed at reducing the costs of escalation to the strategic level. If the United States had the ability to limit the consequences of a strategic attack on itself, then it would be more likely to carry out its guarantee to Europe; hence the threat was more credible. Initially the Kennedy administration followed this line (advocating, among other things, a massive shelter programme), but by the mid-1960s it had come to be regarded as a recipe for an open-ended military build up, and McNammmara turned to arms control and the idea of Assured Destruction. This approach meant that an attack on Europe would be deterred by the threat of deliberate escalation to the upper rungs of the escalation ladder.

The second approach to the problem was also pursued by McNamara. This formed the core of his proposal that NATO should adopt a policy of 'Flexible Response'. A re-analysis of intelligence data showed that Soviet forces in Europe were much less capable than had been thought. It was thus feasible for NATO to develop the ability to halt an attack without having to resort to nuclear weapons. If NATO possessed this capability, then the credibility of NATO's threat to use nuclear weapons against a conventional attack became irrelevant. There was little doubt that NATO would use nuclear weapons in retaliation for a nuclear attack. Since the Soviet Union would not launch a purely conventional attack because it could be defeated, it was then faced with the question of whether to use nuclear weapons. But, as NATO would then retaliate, the Soviet Union would be deterred from any military action. In terms of the ladder of escalation, the idea was to have sufficient capability to deter the Soviets at any level of conflict. Instead of deliberately escalating the conflict, NATO would seek to limit it, leaving the other side with the difficult decision to escalate. Although American strategic superiority meant that the relative costs of escalation would be greater for the Soviet Union than for the United States, the absolute toll of nuclear war was (and is) a powerful deterrent to the execution of escalatory threats. These two answers to NATO's problem can be characterized as nuclear superiority versus across-the-board parity. Of the two, the second option had the important advantage that strategic arms control became more feasible, because the United States was not committed to a full-blown policy of maintaining an unmistakable superiority.

McNamara's version of 'Flexible Response' was coolly received in Europe. In the past, Soviet conventional aggression would have resulted in the thermonuclear devastation of the USSR; under McNamara's proposal, all that would be threatened would be conventional resistance. This was seen as weakening deterrence and the American commitment to Europe, while conventional war was seen as being as devastating for Europe as a nuclear one.

If the two American positions resembled the ideas of Kahn, the preferred European position resembles some put forward by Schelling, who suggested ways in which threats that were irrational to carry out (such as the threat to blow oneself up along with the victim) could still serve as credible deterrents.[50] The *possibility* that the threat might be carried out served to deter. Although the Europeans accepted that it was incredible to threaten an immediate nuclear response to any attack, however limited its scope, they argued that it was important to convince the Soviet Union that any conflict would go nuclear, with a danger of uncontrolled or even deliberate escalation to involve Soviet territory. Possessing conventional forces that were inadequate for a full-scale defence would make it clear that NATO had no alternative to deliberately escalating the conflict. By the mid-1960s American involvement in Vietnam and European opposition had made the creation of a conventional defence impracticable, and in 1967 NATO adopted 'Flexible Response' as policy. McNamara had sought to avoid nuclear use, the NATO document did not. A conventional attack would be met with conventional weapons until they proved inadequate, at which point NATO would use tactical nuclear weapons. If these were not sufficient to cause the Soviet Union to desist, then American strategic weapons would be used. Nuclear war would be devastating for Europe and could not be seen as a rational action, but threatening it provided a great deal of deterrence without the expense of the conventional forces required by McNamara's version of Flexible Response. NATO's strategy, therefore, represents a compromise between the needs of deterrence (the nuclear threat) and of defence if deterrence fails (conventional forces). The result is open to severe criticism as it fully encapsulates none of the strategies. Supporters of the NATO orthodoxy challenge the critics by pointing to the deterrent effect of the nuclear threat and the likelihood that any conflict in Europe will rapidly become nuclear. But the critics, in their turn, point to the growing incredibility of the threat to go nuclear in the face of Soviet nuclear parity or superiority, and Soviet conventional capabilities.

During the past two decades Soviet nuclear thinking has been evolving away from the belief that any East–West conflict will automatically become global and nuclear. Improving conventional and theatre nuclear forces have allowed new options. In particular, it appears that the Soviet Union would seek to keep a war conventional, hence the declaration that the Soviet Union will not be the first to use nuclear weapons (though this would not inhibit them from attempting to pre-empt NATO nuclear use). Even in a conventional conflict, destruction of the West's nuclear weapons and their supporting infrastructure would be a primary objective of all Soviet military operations. If a conflict did go nuclear it appears that the Soviet Union might refrain from attacking the United States provided that

Soviet territory did not come under attack. Soviet military thinking
seems to have turned through 180 degrees from the belief in the
1960s that nuclear conditions would permit a very rapid advance for
ground forces, to the fear that nuclear use would lead to an offensive
becoming bogged down and, as a result, is to be avoided.[51]

Unless fatally disrupted by Soviet pre-emption, a NATO nuclear
response to nuclear attack is to be expected, so Soviet nuclear reliance
in the 1960s had the effect of masking some of the ambiguities
in NATO strategy. If the Warsaw Pact was likely to use nuclear
weapons anyway, the credibility of NATO's threat to use nuclear
arms against conventional attack was irrelevant. But as the Soviet
strategy and posture evolved the problems become clearer. This can
be seen in three controversies that have erupted about NATO strategy
in the past decade.

During the 1970s there was a resurgence of interest in battlefield
nuclear weapons.[52] A new generation of weapons, including those
with very low yields and those with enhanced radiation and reduced
blast (the neutron bomb) were available. Deploying these in Europe
would enhance deterrence because they would be less devastating to
the environment than existing types, making the threat to use them
on German territory more credible. Indeed it might be possible to use
them very early in a conflict in a coherent strategy to defeat Soviet
armoured forces, with low yield reducing the dangers of unintended
escalation. Objections were raised that this was making the nuclear
threshold unacceptably low, although it would arguably reduce the
risk of war by decreasing the absolute cost of going nuclear for NATO.
In response, others argued that once the nuclear threshold was crossed
then any further attempts at limitation are unlikely to succeed.

The second recent controversy about escalation in Europe stemmed
from the 1979 decision to deploy new intermediate-range nuclear
forces (INF) in Europe. The arguments for and against the deployments clearly demonstrated differing perspectives on escalation. The
problem that INF were meant to address arose from the state of parity
at the strategic level of armaments. If the United States lacked an
advantage in strategic forces over the Soviet Union, its threat to use
strategic nuclear weapons against the Soviet homeland in retaliation
for an attack on Europe would be irrational and become increasingly
incredible. This would leave Europe at the mercy of Soviet theatre
forces. The solution was to deploy American weapons in Europe which
could strike the Soviet Union. The rationale was that they were likely

to become so caught up in any conflict and the pressure to 'use them or lose them' that they would indeed be used against the Soviet Union, crossing the 'homelands' threshold' and triggering a strategic exchange between the superpowers as the Soviet Union retaliated against the United States. This would strengthen the 'coupling' between America and Europe, making it clear to the Soviet Union that any attack on Europe would lead to nuclear attacks against Soviet targets by the USA, aiding deterrence. Sceptical Americans pointed out that, because the consequences of using INF against the Soviet Union would be identical to using strategic forces, the use of INF would be no more likely. The argument was, in effect, between those who wanted to use the risk of escalation as a deterrent threat and who saw INF as a way of increasing this risk, and those who argued that the irrationality of inviting self-destruction would undermine the credibility of the strategy. Despite widespread doubts about the military value of the deployments, they proceeded for political reasons, meeting strong popular opposition.[53]

In an attempt to allay public fears about nuclear war a third controversy was triggered. Robert McNamara and others suggested that NATO should, in effect, implement the original conception of Flexible Response. It should build up its conventional forces and declare that it would not be the first to use nuclear weapons. The controversy followed many of the lines of the original debate on Flexible Response, the supporters of the current policy arguing that the nuclear threat should not be pushed too far into the background.[54]

The controversies about European security revolve around a recurrent set of linked questions: What is the threat? What deters? How likely is escalation? Should we attempt to maximize or minimize the risks of escalation? These questions were at the heart of limited war thinking as much as they are the heart of today's debates. The difference is that a changing political situation has meant that there is less emphasis on limited war as a component of a continuing confrontation and more on specific scenarios and policies. It has become clear that there is a growing reluctance on both sides of the Iron Curtain to contemplate the use of nuclear weapons, but at the same time the armed forces involved possess a growing array of nuclear capable systems. This has focused attention on the possibility of conventional conflict and on the stability of the threshold between conventional and nuclear conflict both in Europe and in other areas such as the Gulf. Various issues have been raised.

Some have pointed to the danger of conventional attacks on Soviet forces or territory being mistaken for nuclear attacks and triggering a nuclear response. Others have pointed out the simple problem that, if the West had conventional forces powerful enough to defeat Soviet attacks, the Soviet Union would still retain the option of escalation. The new emphasis on conventional warfare has also raised questions about political control of conflict. If the threat of escalation has lost credibility, then the outcomes of combat at the conventional level become more important, leading to a renewed emphasis on military aspects. The corollary is a new emphasis on virtues such as aggressiveness, surprise and seizing the initiative, characteristics that have always caused concern among limited war thinkers because of the fear that military actions might negate attempts by politicians to manage a crisis or restrain escalation.

Many of these problems are overstated, but their consideration is a serious attempt to come to grips with the problems of limitation and escalation[55] that created limited war. The classic American theorizing is one approach to these problems, one that was flawed by its fundamental assumption about the nature of the cold war. In its attempt to provide a generalized set of strategic prescriptions it obscured the particular elements of conflicts. Yet, despite this, many elements of limited war thinking remain part of the strategic debate and of national policy.

Notes: Chapter 7

1 Carl Von Clausewitz, *On War*, trans. and ed. Michael Howard and Peter Paret (Princeton, NJ: Princeton University Press, 1976), Book 8, chap. 8B.
2 Hew Strachan, *European Armies and the Conduct of War* (London: Allen & Unwin, 1983), pp. 153–6.
3 Brian Bond, *Liddell Hart: A Study of his Military Thought* (London: Cassell, 1977), p. 173.
4 Clausewitz, *On War*, Book 1, chap. 1.
5 Thomas H. Etzold and John Lewis Gaddis (eds), *Containment: Documents on American Policy and Strategy, 1945–50* (New York: Columbia University Press, 1978), pp. 302–38.
6 Reprinted in Etzold and Gaddis, *Containment*, pp. 385–442.
7 Nikita S. Khrushchev, *Khruschev Remembers*, trans. and ed. Strobe Talbott (London: Sphere, 1971), p. 333.

8   Ernest R. May, '*Lessons*' *of the Past: The Use and Misuse of History
     in American Foreign Policy* (New York: Oxford University Press, 1973),
     chap. 3; Rosemary Foot, *The Wrong War: American Policy and the
     Dimensions of the Korean Conflict, 1950–1953* (Ithaca, NY: Cornell
     University Press, 1985), pp. 59–60.
9   Omar N. Bradley and Clay Blair, *A General's Life* (London: Sidgwick
     and Jackson, 1983), pp. 649–50; David Alan Rosenberg, 'US nuclear
     stockpile, 1945 to 1950', *Bulletin of the Atomic Scientists*, vol. XXXVIII,
     no. 5 (May 1982), pp. 25–30; M. J. Armitage and R. A. Mason, *Air Power
     in the Nuclear Age, 1945–82: Theory and Practice* (London: Macmillan,
     1983), pp. 33–4; James F. Schnabel, *Policy and Direction: The First
     Year* (Washington, DC: Office of the Chief of Military History, United
     States Army, 1972).
10   Schnabel, *Policy and Direction*, pp. 182, 218.
11   On the course of the conflict and American policy, see David Rees, *Korea:
     The Limited War* (London: Macmillan, 1964); Foot, *The Wrong War*.
12   Samuel F. Wells, 'The origins of massive retaliation', *Political Science
     Quarterly*, vol. XCIV, no. 1 (Spring 1981), pp. 31–52; Samuel P.
     Huntington, *The Common Defense: Strategic Programs in National
     Politics* (New York: Columbia University Press, 1961), pp. 64–88.
13   Robert E. Osgood, *Limited War: The Challenge to American Strat-
     egy* (Chicago: Chicago University Press, 1957); William W. Kaufmann
     (ed.), *Military Policy and National Security* (Princeton, NJ: Princeton
     University Press 1956); Henry A. Kissinger, *Nuclear Weapons and For-
     eign Policy* (New York: Harper, 1957); Maxwell D. Taylor, *The Uncer-
     tain Trumpet* (New York: Harper, 1959); Mathew B. Ridgway, *Soldier:
     The Memoirs of Mathew B. Ridgway* (New York: Harper, 1956); James
     M. Gavin, *War and Peace in the Space Age* (New York: Harper, 1958).
14   Kissinger, *Nuclear Weapons*, chap. 6; Kaufmann, 'Limited war' in
     Kaufmann (ed.), *Military Policy*, pp. 102–36, specifically on p. 121.
15   Kissinger revised his views: see Henry A. Kissinger, *The Necessity for
     Choice: Prospects for American Foreign Policy* (New York: Harper,
     1961), chap. 3.
16   Kaufmann, 'Limited war', p. 113.
17   Osgood, *Limited War*, pp. 135, 241.
18   Bernard Brodie, *Strategy in the Missile Age* (Princeton, NJ: Princeton
     University Press, 1959; paperback edn, 1965), p. 328.
19   Morton Halperin, *Limited War in the Nuclear Age* (New York: Wiley,
     1963), chap. 4.
20   This was true of the limited war advocates and official policy, e.g.
     Kaufmann, 'Limited war', p. 132; David Alan Rosenberg, 'The origins
     of overkill: nuclear weapons and American strategy, 1945–1960', in
     Steven E. Miller (ed.), *Strategy and Nuclear Deterrence* (Princeton, NJ:
     Princeton University Press, 1984), pp. 113–81, specifically on p. 152.
21   Compare Anthony Buzzard, 'Massive retaliation and graduated deter-
     rence', *World Politics*, vol. VIII, no. 2 (January 1956), pp. 228–37 and
     John Slessor, *The Great Deterrent* (London: Cassell, 1957).
22   Taylor, *The Uncertain Trumpet*, pp. 7–8.

23   Herman Kahn, *On Escalation: Metaphors and Scenarios* (London: Pall Mall, 1965), p. 39.
24   Kahn, *On Escalation*, p. 8.
25   Kahn, *On Escalation*, pp. 23–4, 290.
26   Thomas C. Schelling, *The Strategy of Conflict* (Cambridge, Mass.: Harvard University Press, 1960), chap. 3 and appendix A.
27   Thomas C. Schelling, *Arms and Influence* (New Haven, Conn.: Yale University Press, 1966), pp. 2–5, 172.
28   Graham T. Allison, *The Essence of Decision: Explaining the Cuban Missile Crisis* (Boston, Mass.: Little, Brown, 1971), pp. 127–32, 138, 140–1.
29   Schelling, *Arms and Influence*, p. 166.
30   William C. Westmoreland, *A Soldier Reports* (New York: Dell, 1980), pp. 153–4.
31   On Soviet views of limited war thinking, see Roman Kolkowicz, 'US and Soviet approaches to military strategy: theory vs. experience', *Orbis*, vol. XXV, no. 3 (Summer 1981), pp. 302–29; Peter H. Vigor, *The Soviet View of War, Peace and Neutrality* (London: Routledge and Kegan Paul, 1975); James M. McConnell, 'Shifts in Soviet views on the proper focus of military development', *World Politics*, vol. XXXVII, no. 3 (April 1985), pp. 318–43.
32   Leslie H. Gelb with Richard K. Betts, *The Irony of Vietnam: The System Worked* (Washington, DC: Brookings, 1979), pp. 223, 266–7.
33   Gelb with Betts, *Irony of Vietnam*, pp. 278–81.
34   The term is Kahn's. Herman Kahn, 'Issues of thermonuclear war termination', *The Annals*, vol. CCCXCII (November 1970), pp. 133–72, specifically pp. 164–5.
35   Gelb with Betts, *Irony of Vietnam*, pp. 240–5.
36   Russell F. Weigley, *The American Way of War: A History of United States Military Strategy and Policy* (Bloomington, Ind.: Indiana University Press, 1977), p. 460.
37   Robert E. Osgood, 'The reappraisal of limited war', in Alastair Buchan (ed.), *Problems of Modern Strategy* (London: Chatto & Windus/ISS, 1970), pp. 92–120, specifically on pp. 99–100, fn. 3.
38   Osgood, *Limited War*, pp. 35–6.
39   Gelb with Betts, *Irony of Vietnam*, pp. 264–5, 267–71.
40   Douglas Pike, *Viet Cong: The Organization and Techniques of the National Liberation Front of South Vietnam* (Cambridge, Mass.: MIT, 1966), p. 324; Douglas Pike, *War, Peace and the Viet Cong* (Cambridge, Mass.: MIT, 1969), pp. 9–10, 55, 96.
41   For the military aspects of the conflict, see Dave Richard Palmer, *The Summons of the Trumpet: A History of the Vietnam War from a Military Man's Viewpoint* (New York: Ballantine, 1984); Westmoreland, *A Soldier Reports*; Robert Thomson, *No Exit from Vietnam* (London: Chatto & Windus, 1969).
42   Pike, *War, Peace and the Viet Cong*, pp. 122–31.
43   On the impact of Tet, see Herbert Y. Schandler, *Lyndon Johnson and Vietnam: The Unmaking of a President* (Princeton, NJ: Princeton University Press, 1977).

44   See Wallace J. Thies, *When Governments Collide: Coercion and Diplomacy in the Vietnam Conflict* (Berkeley, Calif.: California University Press, 1980).
45   William W. Mommyer, *Air Power in Three Wars* (*World War II, Korea, Vietnam*) (n.p.: Department of the Air Force, 1978); Armitage and Mason, *Air Power in the Nuclear Age*, chap. 4.
46   Henry A. Kissinger, *The White House Years* (London: Weidenfeld & Nicolson, 1979).
47   Kaufmann, 'Limited war', p. 117.
48   Andrew Mack, 'Why big nations lose small wars: the politics of asymmetric conflict', in Klaus Knorr (ed.), *Power, Strategy and Security* (Princeton, NJ: Princeton University Press 1983), pp. 126–51.
49   For an introduction to the issues, see David N. Schwartz, *NATO's Nuclear Dilemmas* (Washington, DC: Brooking's, 1983).
50   Schelling, *Arms and Influence*, chap. 2.
51   For the evolution of Soviet thinking, see Dennis M. Gormley and Douglas M. Hart, 'Soviet views on escalation', *Washington Quarterly*, vol. VII, no. 4 (Autumn 1984), pp. 71–84; Steven M. Meyer, *Soviet Theatre Nuclear Forces, Part I: Development of Doctrine and Objectives*, Adelphi Papers No. 187 (London: IISS, 1984); Christopher Donnelly, *Heirs of Clausewitz: Change and Continuity in the Soviet War Machine*, Occasional Paper 16 (London: IEDSS/Alliance, 1985).
52   For instance, William R. Van Cleave and S. T. Cohen, *Tactical Nuclear Weapons: An Examination of the Issues* (London: Macdonald & Jane's, 1978)
53   On INF, see Strobe Talbott, *Deadly Gambits* (London: Pan Books, 1985), part 1; Schwartz, *Nuclear Dilemmas*, chap. 7.
54   On the 'no first use' controversy, see Frank Blackaby *et al.* (eds), *No First Use* (London: Taylor and Francis/SIPRI, 1984); John D. Steinbruner and Leon V. Sigal (eds), *Alliance Security: NATO and the No First Use Question* (Washington, DC: Brookings, 1983).
55   For instance, Barry R. Posen, 'Inadvertent nuclear war?: Escalation and NATO's northern flank', *International Security*, vol. VII, no. 2 (Fall 1982), pp. 28–54; Graham T. Allison *et al.* (eds), *Hawks, Doves and Owls: An Agenda for Avoiding Nuclear War* (New York: Norton, 1985); Joshua M. Epstein, *Strategy and Force Planning: The Case of the Persian Gulf* (Washington, DC: Brookings, 1987); Gormley and Hart, 'Soviet views'.

Further reading: Chapter 7

Blackaby, Frank *et al.* (eds), *No First Use* (London: Taylor & Francis/SIPRI, 1984).
Clark, Ian, *Limited Nuclear War: Political Theory and War Conventions* (Oxford: Martin Robertson, 1982).
Foot, Rosemary, *The Wrong War: American Policy and the Dimensions of the Korean Conflict, 1950–53* (Ithaca, NY: Cornell University Press, 1985).

Kahn, Herman, *On Escalation: Metaphors and Scenarios* (London: Pall Mall, 1965).

Kaufmann, William W. (ed.), *Military Policy and National Security* (Princeton, NJ: Princeton University Press, 1956).

Kissinger, Henry A., *Nuclear Weapons and Foreign Policy* (New York: Harper & Row, 1957).

Kissinger, Henry A., *The Necessity for Choice: Prospects of American Foreign Policy* (New York: Harper & Row, 1961).

Osgood, Robert E., *Limited War: The Challenge to American Strategy* (Chicago, Ill.: Chicago University Press, 1957).

Osgood, Robert E., *Limited War Revisited* (Boulder, Colo: Westview, 1979).

Schelling, Thomas C., *The Strategy of Conflict* (Cambridge, Mass.: Harvard University Press, 1960).

Schelling, Thomas C., *Arms and Influence* (New Haven, Conn.: Yale University Press, 1966).

Summers, Harry G., *On Strategy: A Critical Analysis of the Vietnam War* (Novato, Calif.: Praesidio, 1982).

Thies, Wallace J., *When Nations Collide: Coercion and Diplomacy in the Vietnam Conflict, 1964–1968* (Berkeley, Calif.: California University Press, 1980).

Rosen, Stephen Peter, 'Vietnam and the American theory of limited war', *International Security*, vol. VII, no. 2 (Fall 1982), pp. 83–113.

8

Guerrilla Warfare: Insurgency and Counter-insurgency Since 1945

IAN F. W. BECKETT

Prior to the twentieth century, guerrilla warfare was generally understood as a purely military form of conflict. The classic tactics of 'hit and run' might be employed by indigenous groups in opposition to foreign or colonial occupation, either where a conventional army had been defeated or had never existed. Alternatively, guerrilla warfare was also a term applied to the role of irregular troops acting as partisans in support of conventional military operations. Rarely did the primarily unsophisticated practitioners of guerrilla warfare in past centuries display any wider comprehension of the potential of irregular modes of conflict in the way that has become commonplace in the modern world. Indeed, it was only in the 1930s and 1940s that guerrilla warfare became revolutionary in intent and practice, with social, economic, psychological and, especially, political elements grafted on to traditional irregular military tactics. More properly, modern revolutionary guerrilla warfare might be better termed insurgency.

Insurgency and terrorism have become the most prevalent form of conflict since 1945. Indeed, in 1983, a directory of the guerrilla and terrorist organizations in existence since 1945 catalogued 147 groups existing or having existed in Europe, 115 in Asia and Oceania, 114 in the Americas, 109 in the Middle East, and 84 in Africa: a staggering total of 569 groups.[1] Of course, many of these groups were small and obscure and of little account in either national or international politics. Yet, the proliferation of organizations of this kind since the Second World War does suggest that the use of guerrilla and terrorist tactics is perceived widely as an effective means either of achieving power and influence or of bringing a cause to the notice of the national or international community.

The nature of these groups has been immensely varied, with ideologies ranging from the extreme left to the extreme right of the political spectrum. Communism in one form or another has often motivated revolutionary guerrilla warfare, but groups have also fought in the name of nationalism, separatism, tribalism or a combination of all these. Although many guerrilla campaigns have continued to take the form of traditional rural action, with the insurgents operating from refuges in mountains, forests, jungles and swamps, a feature of the post-1945 conflicts has been the growth of urban guerrilla warfare and, of course, that of international terrorism.

The guerrilla in history

There is nothing particularly modern about guerrilla warfare – the first documented reference to a conflict that could be described as illustrating the characteristics of irregular warfare occurs in a Hittite parchment dating from the fifteenth century BC. Similarly, one of the first military theorists to make relevant observations on the conduct of irregular warfare was the ancient Chinese author, Sun Tzu, writing in about the fifth century BC. The Bible provides many illustrations of guerrilla warfare, as do contemporary historians of Rome's imperial expansion. Examples also abound in the Middle Ages and more modern times. During the American War of Independence (1774–83), for example, a number of talented guerrilla tacticians emerged on both sides, including the American, 'Swamp Fox' Marion, and the British light cavalryman, Banastre Tarleton. The French Revolutionary and Napoleonic Wars (1792–1815) saw a series of bitterly fought campaigns waged by irregulars against French armies, such as that of Toussaint L'Ouverture on Haiti (1791–97), royalists in the Vendée (1793–96) and the Tyrolean nationalist, Andreas Hofer (1809). Of course, it was the struggle of Spanish irregulars against the French between 1808 and 1814 that provided the word *guerrilla* itself. Meaning literally 'little war', it was coined to describe the tactics of the Spanish *partides*, but came to be applied to the practitioners themselves. The remainder of the nineteenth century was not entirely devoid of examples of irregular warfare in western Europe. The struggle for the unification of Italy was marked by guerrilla conflict and, after the defeat of the main French field armies at the beginning of the Franco-Prussian War (1870–71), resistance was continued by so-called *francs tireurs*. Moreover, all the major powers fought virtually continuous campaigns against assorted native opponents in their expanding colonies, such campaigns continuing well into the twentieth century.

Not surprisingly, irregular tactics were thus the subject of a number of theoretical works written long before the twentieth century. Major military theorists in the eighteenth and nineteenth centuries, such as de Saxe and Jomini, devoted at least passing attention to irregular warfare, but, increasingly, books were devoted solely to the subject. Some of the earliest of these texts were written by the Frenchmen, Grandmaison (1756) and de Jeney (1759),[2] and two Hessians, Emmerich (1789) and Ewald (1796),[3] distilled some of the lessons of irregular warfare in the New World. However, it was the experience of the French Revolutionary and Napoleonic Wars and the subsequent social, political and economic unrest, that did most to advance theoretical writing on guerrilla war. Authors included the Prussian, von Decker (1822); the Frenchman, de Corvey (1823), and the Poles, Chrzanowski (1835) and Stolzman (1844).[4] But what marked most of these works was a concern with the likely contribution of irregulars acting as partisans on the flanks and rear of an opposing army in support of conventional operations. Indeed, such partisans were mostly envisaged as detached regular troops.

The concept of a 'people's war', familiar to twentieth century exponents of guerrilla warfare, was hardly distinguishable in any of the earlier writing on the subject. Although Karl von Clausewitz (1788–1831) was also primarily interested in guerrilla warfare as an operational strategy within a conventional military framework, his classic, *On War* (1832–44), did at least allude briefly to the political implications of national resistance to an invader.[5] However, he did not interpret guerrilla warfare as a means of popular revolution. Equally, later theorists of revolution such as Marx and Lenin undoubtedly inspired innumerable subsequent movements that practised guerrilla warfare as a revolutionary tactic, but neither actually contributed much to the theory of guerrilla warfare itself. Marx and his collaborator, Engels, believed that there was little scope for people's war in industrialized Europe and that the revolution would depend upon a moral rather than a military collapse of capitalist authority at an appropriate moment in the future. Like Engels, Lenin was something of a student of military affairs, but it is difficult to find any real statement of significance on guerrilla warfare in his many volumes of collected writings. Indeed, Lenin dismissed guerrilla warfare as 'left adventurism' and regarded it merely as one of a number of tools that might be employed by the revolutionary as a substitute for adequate conventional military strength. His actual contribution to guerrilla warfare derived much more from the organizational weapon of a communist party capable of organizing the proletariat as an instrument of revolution. Significantly, Trotsky, who became the first People's Commissar for War and Chairman of the Supreme Military Soviet in March 1918, moved swiftly to eliminate what was termed *partizanshchina* ('partisan spirit' or 'guerrilla-ism') in the newly established Red Army in the belief that it represented a weapon of the weak rather than the strong, and that it encouraged attitudes subversive of centralized party authority. During the Second World War, Soviet partisans engaged in guerrilla warfare against occupying German forces were invariably detached regular troops acting in support of conventional operations and under the strictest party control.

In fact, the only writers before the twentieth century who seem to have made any real direct connection between guerrilla warfare and revolution were Carlo Bianco and Johannes Most.[6] An Italian who had fought in the Carlist War in Spain, Bianco published a two-volume work in 1830 that offered 'people's war' as a means of freeing Italy itself from foreign domination. Most, a German Social Democrat who eventually settled in the United States, can be regarded in some respects as a pioneer of both modern urban guerrilla warfare and international terrorism through his emphasis, in a work of 1884, on the systematic use of terror by a small group of activists utilizing the most modern technology available in pursuit of 'propaganda of the deed'.

In practice, however, guerrilla warfare continued to be waged along traditional lines for much of the first half of the twentieth century, although there were some groups and individuals who were beginning to harness guerrilla or terrorist tactics to the pursuit of overtly political ends. Between the 1880s and the 1930s, the Internal Macedonian Revolutionary Organisation (IMRO) devoted considerable attention to building an integrated military and political organization in its struggle against Turkish and, later, Bulgarian domination. Similarly, the Irish Republican Army (IRA) was a true forerunner of modern revolutionary groups in terms of its politically inspired campaign against the British authorities in Ireland between 1919 and 1921. Supposedly, it inspired the founders of the British Special Operations Executive (SOE) during the Second World War.[7] The Ukrainian anarchist, Nestor Makhno, who fought against the Bolsheviks in the latter stages of the Russian Civil War, was one individual guerrilla leader who displayed a thoroughly modern understanding of the political and socioeconomic potential of insurgency. Another was the Nicaraguan radical, Augusto Sandino, who waged a campaign against the Nicaraguan National Guard and its United States Marine allies between 1927 and 1933. Ironically, however, one of the most influential guerrilla theorists of the early twentieth century, T. E. Lawrence (1888–1935), was not a revolutionary at all.

Lawrence's precise role in the 'Arab Revolt' against the Turks during the First World War remains a matter of some controversy, and there is little doubt that his achievements were exaggerated not only by his own hand but also by that of the British military writer, Basil Liddell Hart, who saw Lawrence's theories and methods as ideally complementary to his own concept of the 'indirect approach'. Nevertheless, Lawrence's writings on guerrilla warfare,[8] notably his article for the *Encyclopaedia Britannica* in 1927, represented a classic and elegant exposition of the possibilities of guerrilla warfare, based on a sound assessment of the political implications for Arab nationalism. In common with many other writers, Lawrence expounded on the military aspects of guerrilla warfare, stressing the importance of secure base areas and the exploitation of space by small and highly mobile forces furnished with good intelligence. But, above all, Lawrence perceived the importance of popular support, claiming that a successful rebellion could be accomplished with only 2 per cent active support among the population, provided the remining 98 per cent either sympathized with or acquiesced in guerrilla activity. Among his three defined functions of command – algebraical, biological and psychological – the last embraced the motivation of both guerrilla and population and, also, the undermining of the morale of one's opponent.

People's war

It is possible that Lawrence had some influence on another theorist in the first half of the twentieth century, whose own theories marked the real transition to modern revolutionary guerrilla warfare – Mao Tse-tung (1893–1976). Initially, Maoist guerrilla warfare in China in the 1930s was still as much a weapon of the weak against the strong as it had always been, but, for Mao, it had also become a framework for a protracted social and political revolution. However, it should be noted that the theories were only evolved gradually amid considerable internal debate among the hierarchy of the Chinese communist party and arose through the utter failure of the Leninist model of urban insurrection to win power in a predominantly rural peasant society. The peasantry was essentially conservative and parochial in outlook, and thus the concept of a 'protracted war' was as necessary in order to mobilize popular support for the revolution as it was in terms of creating an effective army from the disordered elements who had survived the 'Long March' to the sanctuary of the Shensi and other mountainous regions in 1934–35.

It is also important to emphasize that the creation of a regular conventional army was always the ultimate aim and that guerrilla warfare itself was a means to survive and to win the time deemed essential to effect the revolutionary process as a whole. 'Time' would be won by trading 'space' but this did not imply a passive defence and would enable the communists to build 'will', namely a determination among both the guerrillas and the population upon whom the guerrillas were entirely dependent. The process would also take place in the context of three 'phases' of revolutionary war. Different authors have given these phases differing names, but the essential concept remains the same, although it must be appreciated that, in practice, the phases were less distinct than in theory and could merge into each other. Temporary defeat might also compel the revolutionary forces to revert to a less developed phase of revolutionary war and, in any case, there was no precise timetable for the application of each phase.

The first phase, essentially a pre-revolutionary one, has been variously described as that of 'strategic defensive' or even 'conspiracy'. The aim was to expand party organization and to establish an infrastructure for the further development of the revolution. Cadres would be infiltrated into key positions and party workers recruited and trained to generate support for the revolutionary movement and to build up a momentum. Preparation would be both covert and lengthy, although limited force might be applied to intimidate and coerce the population before being directed more precisely at the institutions of the opposing authority in order to create a climate of dissent, civil disobedience and economic unrest. Popular support would be increased, opponents neutralized or eliminated, and the authorities discredited.

The careful political preparation of the first phase would give way at the appropriate time to the second phase of 'strategic stalemate' or 'equilibrium', in which there was deemed to be sufficient popular support, sympathy or acquiescence to allow the expansion of terrorism into guerrilla warfare. Bases would be established, the tempo of recruitment increased and regular units trained for future employment. Minor guerrilla actions would become widespread and a pattern would emerge in which revolutionary domination of a particular locality would result in the establishment of a revolutionary adminis-tration. This competition in government would demonstrate that the revolutionary movement was capable of providing an alternative and better administration than that of the existing authorities, who would be further weakened and disheartened.

Finally, in the third phase of 'strategic offensive' or 'decision', the balance would have clearly swung in favour of the revolutionary movement and the struggle would have assumed the characteristics of a people's war. Mobile warfare would now commence with the regular units being introduced in a near conventional conflict, although retaining some of the characteristics of guerrillas. The final phase would only occur after very careful deliberation and might not actually be required at all if the earlier phases had been successful.[9]

The marked feature of Maoist thought was thus its political nature, the decisive elements being not purely military factors but political and psychological. There would be complete political control throughout and carefully co-ordinated political, economic, psychological and military measures to win popular sympathy. Yet, it allowed even the most primitive of societies to adopt a militant political stance and a form of military and political resistance that could prevail against a vastly superior enemy and, as such, it was a formula widely copied after the success of the Chinese communists in 1949. In Indo-China, for example, the works of both the principal Vietnamese theorists of revolutionary war, Truong Chinh (1909–) and Vo Nguyen Giap (1912–), were heavily based on Mao, although both tended to put greater stress on the mobilization of international opinion in support of the revolution. Like Mao, Truong Chinh stressed the total mobilization of the masses at all levels in a prolonged struggle. He envisaged the struggle as one of opposing 'strengths' with, for exam-ple, Vietnamese political and motivational strengths prevailing over French military and technological strengths in the first Indo-Chinese war between the Viet Minh and the French between 1946 and 1954. Both Truong Chinh and Giap restyled Mao's three phases, with Truong Chinh referring to them as those of 'contention', 'equilibrium' and 'general counter-offensive'. Giap placed less emphasis on mass support and more on the role of conventional military operations, being a notable exponent of the 'bloody blow' to break the opponent's will. Consequently, in practice, Giap sought to achieve a short cut in the protracted struggle by moving too early into the third phase in his war against the French in the Red River delta in 1950–51 and against the United States forces and their South Vietnamese allies in the Tet offensive of 1968. On both occasions, Giap suffered heavy military defeat, although this did not prevent his ultimate victory.[10]

Maoist principles were also applied by communist or other guerrilla movements in such states as Malaya (1948–60), the Philippines (1946–54), Algeria (1954–62), Angola (1962–74), Rhodesia (1972–80) and the Dhofar region of Oman (1965–75). In Africa, in particular, the Maoist influence was clear in the case of Amilcar Cabral, who led the *Partido Africano da Independência de Guiné e Cabo Verde* (PAIGC) movement against the Portuguese authorities in Portuguese Guinea (now Guinea-Bissau) between 1956 and his assassination in 1973, and in the case of Robert Mugabe, who emerged as the leader of the Zimbabwe African National Union (ZANU) in Rhodesia in 1974.[11] Another African exponent of guerrilla warfare, although with no actual experience of it, was the first post-independence head of state in Ghana, Kwame Nkrumah, whose work on the subject was published in 1968, two years after his overthrow in a military coup. Nkrumah's book stresses the importance of Maoist-style liberated zones, although in the context of a pan-African struggle against neo-colonialism to be waged by a pan-African guerrilla army.[12] Further afield, the Indonesian nationalist, Abdul Harris Nasution (1918–), produced his book on guerrilla warfare largely independently of Maoist thought in 1953, but it still bears striking similarities in terms of its exposition of people's war and the ultimate aim of creating a conventional army.[13]

From Guevara to terrorism

Application of Maoist theory did not automatically produce victories for the insurgents. Since the 1930s there had been many political, ideological and technological changes. Not the least important of these was the global growth in urbanization. A concept based on rural action was thus increasingly less relevant even in many parts of the Third World. A clear example of the changes that would be forced upon the modern guerrilla was the failure of the so-called 'foco' theory of guerrilla warfare, which was developed in Latin America in the early 1960s as an alternative model for rural revolution by the Frenchman, Regis Debray (1941–), and the Argentinian, Ernesto 'Che' Guevara (1928–67). It showed that a theory formulated by an individual in a particular situation was not necessarily easily translated into an entirely different situation elsewhere. Foco was based upon the success of a relatively small group of revolutionaries – initially just 81 strong and soon reduced to 22 effectives – in toppling the Batista regime in Cuba between 1956 and 1959. But, to a great extent, Fidel Castro's victory against Batista was fortuitous. Batista's regime was hopelessly corrupt, unpopular and inefficient, the Cuban army contriving to lose a war in which it appears to have suffered only 200 dead in three years. Moreover, Batista also lost the support of the United States through his lamentable human rights record.

From this success against a regime ripe for defeat, Debray and Guevara evolved a model for revolution, which they believed could be reproduced as a matter of course throughout Latin America if not the Third World as a whole. In contrast to Mao, who stressed the organization of parallel political and military structures and the primacy of the political, Debray and Guevara argued that the guerrillas themselves were a revolutionary fusion of political and military authority. Instead of developing a comprehensive infrastructure through a prolonged period of political preparation, they assumed that objective conditions favourable to revolution already existed through a minimum level of discontent with the authorities. By military action alone, an elite group, introduced into a suitable location and utilizing its mobility, would provide a 'foco' or focus for the revolution. Progressively larger numbers of sympathizers would attach themselves to the foco as the guerrillas' decisive action exposed the corrupt and brutal nature of the authorities, forced into over-reaction against the population as a whole in its frustration when unable to detect or eliminate the guerrillas. Thus, the guerrillas would prove a catalyst of revolutionary dissolution and the regime would crumble. The action would be based firmly on the countryside and, although there was some recognition that urban action could assist in taking pressure off the guerrillas, it was conveniently forgotten just how much support Castro had derived from urban-based groups such as the '26 July Movement' on Cuba. Indeed, Debray made a positive virtue out of keeping the guerrillas distinct from the population.[14]

Foco proved attractive through its reduced emphasis on lengthy preparation, but it was a manifest failure in Colombia (1961), Guatemala and Ecuador (1962) and Peru (1963). The greatest failure of all was that of Guevara himself, in Bolivia in 1966 and 1967. Bolivia had actually enjoyed a measure of land reform in the 1950s, sufficient to deprive any foco of even that minimum level of discontent required by Guevara and Debray. The terrain was not like that on Cuba and militated against the hard-hitting mobile operations that guerrilla warfare demanded. Moreover, Guevara's band of 27 men and women of assorted nationalities, none of whom spoke the language of the local Indians of the Nancahuazú region where the foco was launched, were regarded as little more than aliens by the indigenous population. The Bolivian communist party did not find Guevara's emphasis on military control of the revolution congenial and there was no attempt to mobilize the radical tin mining community. Having spent much of its time lost in the jungle between November 1966 and October 1967, the guerrilla foco was trapped and eliminated by Bolivian Rangers, trained by the United States, which had invested heavily in building up counter-insurgency expertise in Latin American armies and police forces after Castro's rise to power.

The discrediting of foco was partly responsible for the development in Latin America of the theory and practice of urban guerrilla warfare. Although Castro was moved to describe urban areas as the 'graveyard of revolutionaries', the recognition that the great majority of the Latin American population simply no longer lived in the countryside favoured a reassessment by later theorists. By 1967, at least 50 per cent of the population of every state in the sub-continent with the exception of Peru was urbanized, and in some states, such as Uruguay and Argentina, more than 70 per cent of the population inhabited urban areas. With high unemployment, high inflation and the concentration of a large proportion of a relatively young population in urban slums and shanties, the widespread sense of deprivation appeared ready for exploitation. Moreover, urban terror had been attempted in other guerrilla campaigns such as that of EOKA against the British authorities on Cyprus between 1955 and 1959, the *Front de Libération Nationale* (FLN) against the French in Algeria between 1954 and 1962, and the *Fuerzas Armadas de Liberación Nacional* (FALN) in Venezuela between 1962 and 1965.

As a conservative nationalist, the military leader of EOKA, George Grivas (1898–1974), had written an account of his campaign[15] as a kind of primer for Western governments faced with communist insurgency. His use of terror, however, by letter and parcel bomb, ambush and execution squad, and the emphasis both on small unit action and on youthful participation were ideally suited for imitation by later urban guerrillas. Like Guevara, Grivas believed that independent military action by guerrillas alone could succeed without the necessity of forging a Maoist conventional army; but, unlike Guevara, he did not neglect either careful preparation before the opening of his campaign or cultivation of popular support. Although the disastrous outcome of urban action for guerrilla movements in Algeria and Venezuela should have served warning of its inherent dangers, urban guerrilla warfare gained considerable popularity. Youth itself was becoming widely politicized and radicalized in the Western world through disillusionment with the US involvement in Vietnam and the rise of the 'New Left', the drugs cult and black radicalism in the United States. Other alternatives to violence also appeared unlikely to succeed in view of US intervention in the Dominican Republic (1965) and its involvement in the overthrow of Salvador Allende's radical socialist government in Chile (1973).

While the idealized, ennobling and morally cleansing form of revolutionary violence preached by radical authors such as Herbert Marcuse and Franz Fanon contributed to the frighteningly blinkered psyche of many of the emerging urban guerrilla and terrorist groups, the theory of urban guerrilla warfare itself found expression in the writing of new theorists. One was the Spaniard, Abraham Guillen (1912–), who influenced the Tupamaros group in Uruguay.[16] Another was the Brazilian communist, Carlos Marighela (1911–69).[17] Not unlike Guevara and Debray, Marighela rejected the need for painstaking preparation of the population for revolution. The urban guerrillas would also be a small elite band of highly dedicated and self-sacrificing individuals, whose 'armed propaganda' would create a revolutionary situation by undermining the government and security forces and alienating the population from the authorities by forcing government over-reaction. Eventual rural action was not necessarily ruled out, but the cities would be the principal battleground, with the media representing the vital component for the successful promotion of guerrilla action. That action would be designed to be spectacular and aimed not just at the establishment but also at foreign multinationals, with a subsidiary intention of weakening the economy by forcing foreign capital out of the country.

Marighela himself attempted to paralyse Brazil by concentrating attacks in the three main cities of Rio de Janeiro, Sao Paulo and Belo Horizonte before his death in a gun battle with police in 1969. His *Minimanual* (1969) was a mine of information for the potential urban guerrilla in terms of the minutiae of assaults, ambushes, street fighting, kidnapping, sabotage and other tactics. But it was largely devoid of any wider political strategy and, like many other urban guerrilla groups that emerged in the late 1960s and early 1970s, Marighela's *Asçâo Libertadora Nacional* (ALN) movement soon degenerated into unbridled violence regardless of the apparent likelihood of popular support. As a result, a degree of popular welcome was afforded at least to the initial stages of the kind of counter-terrorist policies adopted in many Latin American states in the face of the challenge of urban guerrilla warfare. In the process, democracy was sacrificed, but institutionalized counter-terror by the state ensured that few, if any, of the urban guerrillas survived to exploit the situation they had brought about.

Numerous urban guerrilla groups in Latin America cultivated links with each other and this was very much a feature, of course, of those groups that also emerged in the 1960s and 1970s, which tended to be described as international terrorists. Like guerrilla warfare, terrorism was not new and could be detected in the distant past. The zealot sect of the *sicarii* active in Palestine in the first century AD and the muslim *Assassins* sect of the eleventh to thirteenth centuries were clearly highly organized terrorist groups. Mention has already been made of Johannes Most, but nineteenth century Russian anarchists such as Bakunin also advocated terrorist violence perpetuated by secret revolutionary cells. Terrorism was not central to either Leninist or Maoist thought and it was also rejected by Guevara. However, Debray and the influential Spaniard, Alberto Bayo, who had trained Castro and his followers for their campaign in Cuba,[18] had evinced a belief in the use of terror tactics. As already remarked, it was also an integral part of the urban guerrilla action advocated by Marighela and his imitators.

Indeed, in many respects, the distinction made between the urban guerrilla and the terrorist appeared one of terminology only, since the methods and the ideology were often strikingly similar. Nevertheless, international terrorism went beyond urban guerrilla warfare in its recognition of the way in which urbanization and technological change, especially in terms of the advances in communications and transport, had made the international community as a whole more vulnerable to the application of extreme violence for political ends. Those ends, like those of guerrillas, have been varied and complex. Indeed, the failure of the United Nations to agree a commonly acceptable definition of international terrorism is an indication of the difficulties in differentiating between domestic and international terror. Clearly, too, many terrorist groups have elevated indiscriminate violence to a strategy in itself, without any obvious wider political aim. The situation is further complicated by the existence of state-sponsored terrorism associated with countries such as Iran, North Korea, Syria and Libya. In fact, it may be more profitable to use the term terrorism to define the nature of the act, which is invariably effected without any humanitarian restraint, rather than to describe either the practitioners or their particular cause.

The response: counter-insurgency

Insurgency in its various forms and international terrorism have posed serious threats to many Western governments. The experience of most major armies since 1945 bears testimony to this in that few have fought conventional wars but virtually all have waged campaigns against guerrillas and terrorists. In the case of the United Kingdom, for example, British servicemen have been on active service somewhere in the world in every year since the end of the Second World War except in 1968. Yet the British army has been involved in only three conventional conflicts – the Korean War (1950–53), the Suez affair (1956) and the Falklands War (1982). The remaining years have seen conflicts waged against insurgents. Much the same is true for the French and United States armies and even the Soviet army. Not unexpectedly, therefore, most armed forces have developed theories variously described as counter-guerrilla warfare, counter-revolutionary warfare or, most frequently, as counter-insurgency.

Although modern counter-insurgency theory naturally evolved as a direct response to the new forms of insurgency experienced after 1945, its roots lie in the nineteenth century, the stage being provided by the expanding colonial empires. Most modern armies enjoyed relatively easy victories over native opponents, and both this and the preoccupation with conventional roles ensured that little coherent doctrine emerged. The British experience, with the exception of the

Irish campaign of 1919–21, was largely confined to what was described as 'Imperial policing' and this gave little understanding of the emergence of the political dimension to guerrilla warfare. The only armed forces that appear to have taken counter-insurgency doctrine seriously before 1945 were the United States Marine Corps (USMC) and the French army. The French envisaged a slow expansion of French administration hand in hand with a military presence, with pacification engulfing the population like an oil slick, or *tache d'huile*. While *tache d'huile* survived to be applied to the French campaign in Indo-China between 1946 and 1954, the USMC doctrine was forgotten with the involvement of the Corps in major amphibious operations during the Second World War (see pp. 26–31, 38–9).

With the possible exception of the French, therefore, most Western armed forces were unprepared for the kind of insurgency that emerged after 1945 and *tache d'huile* proved of little value against Maoist-style tactics. The first requirement appeared to be an adequate understanding of such tactics, and it can be noted that the work of theorists on counter-insurgency, such as Sir Robert Thompson, Brigadier (later General Sir) Frank Kitson, John S. Pustay and John J. McCuen devoted much of their own works to a description of Maoist insurgency, before suggesting an appropriate response.[19] McCuen, in particular, developed a theory of 'counter-revolution' that precisely mirrored what he saw as four phases in Maoist revolutionary warfare: subversion, terrorism, guerrilla warfare, and mobile warfare. Similarly, McCuen identified five strategic principles equally applicable to the revolutionary and the counter-revolutionary forces: preserving oneself and annihilating the enemy, establishing strategic bases, mobilizing the masses, seeking outside support, and unifying the effort.[20] In the United States, the US Army and other branches of the armed forces bought out the entire first edition of Robert Taber's description of communist guerrilla warfare, *The War of the Flea*, while emerging theorists of new French doctrines of *guerre révolutionnaire*, such as Charles Lacheroy and Roger Trinquier, also consciously imbibed communist ideology in order to comprehend and defeat it.[21]

Much of the doctrine that emerged, therefore, was based on early Maoist insurgency as experienced by the British in Malaya, the United States in the Philippines and the French in Indo-China. The most influential experience was that of Malaya, upon which Robert Thompson based his 'five principles' of counter-insurgency.[22] Of these, four were essentially political in nature and, thus, a reflection of the acceptance of insurgency as requiring an adequate political and military response on the part of the security forces. Thompson believed that the first requirement was that the government should have a clear political aim to defeat insurgency. Secondly, the government and the security forces should always act within the law. Thirdly, there should be an overall plan in which the responsibilities of all agencies involved in counter-insurgency should be defined and all sections of the administration, military and police properly co-ordinated. Fourthly, priority should be given to the defeat of political subversion rather than to that of the guerrillas in the field and, lastly, the government should ensure that its own base areas were secure before mounting military campaigns. In operational terms, Thompson envisaged four stages of 'clearing' an area of insurgent activity, 'holding' it for the government, 'winning' its inhabitants, then moving on to another area.

The pattern that emerged in British counter-insurgency was one of unity and co-ordination of effort at all levels, with the emphasis firmly upon the political aspects as the authorities engaged in a competition in government with the insurgents. The contribution of the military would be in the context of civil political control and the primacy of the police, while there would be a retention of the rule of law and the application of minimum force and minimum numbers. The pattern was not always universally successful or applicable, Kitson in particular providing a critique of some aspects of Thompson's traditional approach in terms of the role of the army vis-à-vis the police.[23] Nevertheless, it has been more consistently successful than most other counter-insurgency doctrines, primarily owing to the pragmatic and flexible way in which it has been applied. The same was hardly true of *guerre révolutionnaire*.

Guerre révolutionnaire resulted from the catalyst of the French defeat in Indo-China, theorists such as Lacheroy and Trinquier making the assumption that the defeat was due both to a global communist conspiracy and also to the efforts of dedicated revolutionaries who utilized a new cocktail of military and psychological methods. One of the new French theorists, Georges Bonnet, simplified this to an equation of 'partisan (guerrilla) warfare + psychological warfare = revolutionary warfare.'[24] Having identified the phases of Maoist insurgency, the French theorists assembled a counter-revolutionary doctrine, which was aimed at the vulnerability they detected in the initial stages of the insurgency. It was envisaged that the insurgent would be isolated from the population through such methods as resettlement and the erection of physical barriers to infiltration, accompanied by military action against insurgents in the field and a determined psychological warfare campaign. It required, too, an ideological strength of purpose equal to that of the insurgent and an absolute commitment by the authorities to the support of the army in its campaign. The kind of pacification advocated by Galliéni and Lyautey had also had political implications, since the latter had suggested that the army might be required to regenerate French society itself, and, of course, the combination of political and military action was well established in *tache d'huile*. However, *guerre révolutionnaire* posted a far greater challenge to the French political authorities through the army's implied involvement in the political sphere through psychological action. Many of those who developed *guerre révolutionnaire* were thus not only involved in allegations of brutal interrogation techniques employed by the French army in Algeria but also implicated in opposition to de Gaulle's policy of quitting the country, culminating in the attempted army coup in Algiers in April 1961.[25] Indeed, some French officers went on to found their own terrorist group, *Organisation d'Armée Secrète* (OAS), which plotted de Gaulle's assassination.

The counter-insurgency doctrines of other armed forces since 1945 have not been codified to the same extent, but the kind of principles outlined by Thompson and McCuen have remained central to the continuing debate on the most appropriate response to insurgency. One such debate is current in the United States following the reassessment of the defeat suffered in Vietnam, although, in many respects, it appears to be echoing that of the late 1950s and early 1960s.[26] Equally, Western governments have been exercised by the need to combat international terrorism. Since the institutionalized counter-terror of Latin American states is unacceptable to liberal democracies, solutions have been pursued in terms of special legislation, improved co-operation between international police and intelligence agencies, and the deployment of special forces.[27] However, it is clear that further developments are required, not least in terms of a greater willingness to allow extradition of terrorists to countries where they are wanted for offences.

The problem of modern terrorism, like that of insurgency in general, is thus likely to persist, for these forms of limited conflict will almost certainly remain the most common in a nuclear world.

Notes: Chapter 8

1 P. Janke, *Guerrilla and Terrorist Organisations: A World Directory and Bibliography* (Brighton: Harvester, 1983).
2 Lt Col. Grandmaison, *La petite guerre ou traité de service des troupes legères en campagne* (Paris, 1756); M. de Jeney, *Le Partisan, ou l'art de faire la petite guerre avec succès, selon le génie de nos jours* (The Hague, 1759).
3 A. Emmerich, *The Partisan in War* (London, 1789); J. von Ewald, *Abhandlung von dem Deist der leichten Truppen* (Schleswig, 1796).
4 C. von Decker, *Der kleine Krieg im Geiste der neueren Kriegsführung* (Berlin, 1821); Le Mière de Corvey, *Des partisans et des corps irréguliers* (Paris, 1823); W. Chrzanowski, *O wojnie partysanckiej* (Paris, 1835); K. B. Stolzman, *Partyzanka ezyli wojna dla ludow powstajacych najwlasciwsza* (Paris, 1844).
5 K. von Clausewitz, *On War*, Book VI (Defence), Chapter XXVI (Arming the Nation), reproduced in R. A. Leonard (ed.), *A Short Guide to Clausewitz on War* (London: Weidenfeld and Nicolson, 1967), pp. 223–8.
6 Carlo Bianco di St Jorioz, *Della guerra nazionale d'insurrezione applicata all'Italia* (1830); J. Most, *Revolutionäre Kriegswissenschaft* (New York, 1884).
7 C. Townshend, *The British Campaign in Ireland, 1919–21* (Oxford: Oxford University Press, 1975); T. Bowden, *The Breakdown of Public Security* (London: Sage, 1977).
8 T. E. Lawrence, *Revolt in the Desert* (London: Cape, 1927); T. E. Lawrence, *Seven Pillars of Wisdom* (London: Cape, 1935).
9 S. B. Griffith (ed.), *Mao Tse-tung on Guerrilla War* (New York: Anchor Press, 1978); Mao Tse-tung, *Selected Military Writings* (Peking: Foreign Language Press, 1967).
10 Truong Chinh, *Primer for Revolt* (New York: Praeger, 1963); Vo Nguyen Giap, *People's War, People's Army* (New York: Praeger, 1962).
11 A. Cabral, *Revolution in Guinea* (New York: Monthly Review Press, 1969); J. McCulloch, *In the Twilight of the Revolution: The Political Theory of Amilcar Cabral* (London: Routledge and Kegan Paul, 1983); R. Mugabe, *Our War of Liberation* (Gweru, Zimbabwe: Mambo Press, 1983).
12 K. Nkrumah, *Handbook of Revolutionary Warfare* (London: Panaf, 1968).
13 A. H. Nasution, *Fundamentals of Guerrilla Warfare* (London: Pall Mall Press, 1965).
14 R. Debray, *Strategy for Revolution* (Harmondsworth: Penguin, 1973); R. Debray, *Che's Guerrilla War* (Harmondsworth: Penguin, 1975); R. Debray, *The Revolution on Trial* (Harmondsworth: Penguin, 1978); E. Guevara, *Bolivian Diary* (London: Cape, 1968); E. Guevara, *Guerrilla Warfare* (Harmondsworth: Penguin, 1969); E. Guevara, *Reminiscences of the Cuban Revolutionary War* (London: Allen & Unwin, 1968); E.

Guevara, *Episodes of the Revolutionary War* (New York: International, 1968); D. James (ed.), *The Complete Bolivian Diaries of Che Guevara and Other Captured Documents* (London: Stein & Day, 1968).
15   G. Grivas, *Guerrilla Warfare* (London: Longman, 1964); C. Foley (ed.), *The Memoirs of General Grivas* (London: Longman, 1964).
16   D. C. Hughes, *The Philosophy of the Urban Guerrilla: The Revolutionary Writings of Abraham Guillen* (New York: William Morrow, 1973).
17   C. Marighela, *For the Liberation of Brazil* (Harmondsworth: Penguin, 1971); R. Moss, *Urban Guerilla Warfare,* Adelphi Paper No 79 (London: IISS, 1971).
18   Alberto Bayo Giroud, 'One hundred and fifty questions to a guerrilla' in J. Mallin (ed.), *Terror and Urban Guerrillas* (Coral Gables: University of Miami Press, 1971); pp. 117–62.
19   J. S. Pustay, *Counterinsurgency Warfare* (New York: Free Press, 1965).
20   J. J. McCuen, *The Art of Counter-revolutionary War* (London: Faber & Faber, 1966).
21   R. Taber, *The War of the Flea* (London: Paladin, 1970), p. 12; R. Trinquier, *Modern Warfare* (London: Pall Mall Press, 1964).
22   Sir Robert Thompson, *Defeating Communist Insurgency* (London: Chatto & Windus, 1966); Sir Robert Thompson, *Revolutionary War in World Strategy, 1945–1969* (London: Secker & Warburg, 1970).
23   F. Kitson, *Low Intensity Operations* (London: Faber & Faber, 1971).
24   G. Bonnet, *Les guerres insurrectionnelles et révolutionnaires* (Paris: Payot, 1958), quoted in P. Paret, *French Revolutionary Warfare from Indochina to Algeria* (London: Pall Mall Press, 1964).
25   M. Bigeard, *Contre guerrilla* (Algiers: Plon, 1957); Paret, *French Revolutionary Warfare,* op. cit.
26   D. S. Blaufarb, *The Counterinsurgency Era* (New York: Free Press, 1977).
27   Y. Alexander, M. A. Brown, and A. S. Nonen (eds), *Control of Terrorism: International Documents* (New York: Crane Russak, 1979); N. Gal-Or, *International Co-operation to Suppress Terrorism* (London: Croom Helm, 1985); N. C. Livingstone and T. E. Arnold, *Fighting Back* (Lexington, Mass.: Lexington Books, 1986); B. Netanyahu (ed.), *Terrorism* (London: Weidenfeld and Nicolson, 1986); S. Segaller, *Invisible Armies* (London: Michael Joseph, 1986).

Further reading: Chapter 8

Beckett, Ian, and Pimlott, John (eds), *Armed Forces and Modern Counter-insurgency* (London: Croom Helm; and New York: St Martin's Press, 1985).
Beckett, Ian (ed.) *The Roots of Counter-Insurgency* (Poole: Blandford, 1988).
Griffith, S. B. (ed.) *Mao Tse-tung on Guerrilla Warfare* (New York: Anchor Press, 1978).
Guevara, Ernesto, *Guerrilla Warfare* (Harmondsworth: Penguin, 1969).
Kitson, Frank, *Low Intensity Operations* (London: Faber & Faber, 1971).

Laqueur, Walter, *Guerrilla: A Historical and Critical Study* (London: Weidenfeld & Nicolson, 1977).
Laqueur, Walter, *Terrorism* (London: Weidenfeld & Nicolson, 1977).
Marighela, Carlos, *For the Liberation of Brazil* (Harmondsworth: Penguin, 1971).
Pimlott, John (ed.), *Guerrilla Warfare* (London: Bison, 1985).
Taber, R., *The War of the Flea* (London: Paladin, 1970).
Wilkinson, Paul, *Terrorism and the Liberal State*, 2nd edn. (London: Macmillan, 1986).

9

The Battlefield Since 1945

JOHN PAY

The nuclear dimension

Perhaps the most important change in the battlefield since 1945 has been the impact of nuclear weapons, threatening the survival of millions and raising questions about whether war is still a usable means of achieving political ends. The ability of these weapons to destroy large numbers of men and material in a very short time has shaped not only the strategy developed to deter war but also the tactics of war. The threat of nuclear destruction – with perhaps 140 million American, 100 million Soviet and 40 million British lives at risk – has rightly attracted the attention of national leaders. The stakes of war are now national survival in a quite literal sense. In this situation, faced with the choice between assuming that a potential nuclear- armed aggressor would never resort to such an attack and assuming that there is a small possibility that he might, there has been an unusual degree of consensus among leaders of states as diverse as the Soviet Union, the USA, China, Great Britain and France that prudence dictates the route of caution and requires some insurance against nuclear attack. As conventional forces offer no protection from a nuclear attacker, the statesmen have concluded that the only answer to the possibility of nuclear destruction is to build a nuclear force to deter any potential attacker by threatening a nuclear response to any nuclear aggression. The nuclear insurance policy has become the central feature of and first priority of these states' defence policy, on the basis that manning the conventional walls of the castle is rather pointless if the castle itself has been vaporized by nuclear attack beforehand.

This insurance has proved expensive. Great Britain has been un- usually fortunate in being able to buy nuclear delivery systems from the United States since 1960, with the benefits of reduced costs this has brought. Even so, provision of a replacement for the Polaris system, in the form of the Trident submarine launched ballistic missile, is estimated to take up to 6 per cent of the defence budget. In France, where nuclear weapons take 20 per cent of the defence budget, and in the United States and the Soviet Union, where the figure is around 15 per cent, the effect has been far greater. If and when the battlefield moves to space, with the deployment of strategic defence systems, the impact on conventional forces seems likely to become even more marked. The greatest threat to US conventional forces in particular may lie not from Soviet conventional weapons but in the logic of the budgetary battlefield, where vital strategic systems seem more necessary than conventional forces designed to protect overseas interests.

The problem of nuclear weapons, however, goes beyond the mere fact that nuclear weapons and defences against them cost money that might otherwise be spent on conventional forces. Nuclear weapons have also to some extent assumed the role of conventional forces. The development of tactical nuclear weapons has meant that any army commander facing a nuclear power has had to calculate that his conventional forces might cease to exist within minutes. This is a very real threat, and one that has proved impossible to remove when it is recognized that nuclear weapons offer tremendous advantages to any army that has them if it has to fight another that does not possess them. It is also one area where arms control cannot easily remove the threat, because the very nature of tactical nuclear weapons – small, innumerable, easily concealed and designed to be fired from conventional or highly mobile delivery systems or dropped from aircraft – means that disarmament in the tactical nuclear field is even more difficult than the abolition of strategic nuclear forces. Just as in the strategic field, rather than hope that an opponent does not have or will not use tactical nuclear weapons on the battlefield, all of the nuclear powers have to date chosen to deter the opposing force from using its weapons by providing their own forces with a retaliatory capability.

But, if the prime role of nuclear weapons is to deter nuclear attack, this has not stopped such weapons from acquiring other missions. The very destructiveness of nuclear weapons has led some to conclude that the threat to use tactical nuclear weapons, and the risk that the war would expand until it involved strategic nuclear attacks against the opposing state's cities, are themselves enough to deter an opponent from attacking. Such a war would be so clearly against everyone's interest that no one would willingly start it. Given that no national leader can ever be certain that his conventional forces will stop an attack and that an enemy might otherwise be prepared to gamble that he would only suffer losses to his army if a conventional attack failed, nuclear weapons have been seen in some quarters to offer a better guarantee against war than any massive investment in conventional forces. With one nuclear weapon currently costing half as much as one tank, using the threat of nuclear weapons to deter conventional war has also emerged as a cheaper option. On the wider budgetary battlefield, with defence competing against the growing demands of social security, health and education budgets, a cheap option has obvious attractions. Nuclear weapons have thus raised a series of question marks over conventional forces. In some cases, such as Israel, nuclear weapons have become a final insurance against conventional defeat – providing a capability to destroy the attacker if he wins the conventional battle. This serves to make attackers think twice about their objectives before attacking. Elsewhere, the use of nuclear weapons – the threat of escalation – is still relied upon to provide the major deterrent to attack.

Nuclear weapons have brought other changes. Certain military operations are less conceivable in a nuclear context. Launching a major, strategically crucial, amphibious assault like the D-Day landings of 1944 would be particularly foolish against a nuclear-armed enemy who had concluded that the stakes were such that the landing should be opposed by nuclear means. Tactical deployments have also changed. All armed forces now have to be dispersed to try and reduce the effect if the enemy decides at some stage to switch from conventional to nuclear operations. This is a point often neglected by critics of nuclear weapons, who do not make allowance for difficulties facing a conventional defence if the enemy did not have to disperse his attacking force as he does at present under the nuclear shadow. Nor are the effects of nuclear weapons limited to armies. Airforces have found their air defence role challenged by critics who point out that shooting down 90 per cent of attackers is not very useful if the survivors carry nuclear weapons. Finite numbers of airfields are also very inviting targets for nuclear attack. Navies have also had problems. If war is to be nuclear – perhaps with only a short conventional phase – there will be no protracted maritime wars to fight. If only one nuclear-tipped missile penetrates the defence, what use is that defence? In the nuclear age all conventional forces have had to learn to face difficult questions such as these.

These questions are not unanswerable. The major limitation on nuclear weapons has been that their use is so potentially dangerous that it is unlikely that any leader would use them against an opponent who also had nuclear weapons. Although the threat of nuclear war should deter all attacks, it just might not. A state that relied totally on nuclear weapons could well find itself attacked conventionally by a nuclear-armed opponent, who had gambled that it would never use its nuclear forces. It would then face the options of surrendering or initiating the use of nuclear weapons – a potentially suicidal course of action. Few states relish being placed in this situation, and so the result has been that all of the major powers continue to see some role for conventional forces. Nuclear weapons are relied upon to deter nuclear attack and to threaten nuclear escalation, but conventional forces have also retained some role in defending against, or at least delaying, conventional attacks. The relative role of conventional and nuclear forces differs between states, with the Soviet Union building up large forces of both kinds, NATO tending to rely more on the threat of nuclear escalation and China depending on her massive manpower to deter conventional or nuclear attack. Recent trends, however, show NATO becoming more interested in a credible conventional capability, China more interested in nuclear and modern conventional forces, and the Soviet Union adding to its existing conventional capability by building up its capacity to fight a conventional war for longer than NATO. If anything, there seems to be a growing consensus among the major powers that more conventional capability is needed. Though nuclear weapons are still considered vital to deter nuclear attack, their limitations are increasingly appreciated and the theoretical (but not always the financial) threat to conventional forces from nuclear weapons is declining.

The conventional battlefield

Problems for conventional forces in the United States, the Soviet Union, the rest of NATO and the Warsaw Pact and for some of the Middle Eastern states, however, do not only arise from the nuclear shadow. Conventional warfare itself has contradictions and poses unanswerable questions. Some of these are apparent if we examine the fortunes of NATO conventional forces and how technology has developed since 1945.[1] Until 1966, although conventional forces existed, they were seen as a tripwire for nuclear weapons – a force designed to confirm that NATO was being attacked before NATO retaliated with nuclear weapons. After 1966, the idea of responding to any conventional attack with conventional forces won some support in the new 'Flexible Response' strategy but little was done to build up conventional forces, not least because of US involvement in Vietnam. After 1975, with the US Army interested in the conventional defence of Europe, new equipment becoming available and the Soviet Union showing interest in a quick conventional victory in Europe, conventional defence emerged as a high priority for the alliance. However, the consensus on how many conventional forces to provide remains somewhat fragile, with some states slower than others to meet NATO's goal of providing 30 days of warfighting capability. The ability to fight a long war still does not feature in NATO planning. As General Rogers, when NATO's Supreme Allied Commander Europe, pointed out:

> If ACE (Allied Command Europe) were attacked conventionally NATO political authorities would face fairly quickly the decision to authorise the release of nuclear weapons. This situation results primarily from a lack of sustainability with trained manpower, ammunition, and war reserve material.[2]

The aim of NATO conventional forces is to gain time to negotiate, to stop the Warsaw Pact from winning so quickly that NATO is defeated before its leaders have time to react or, at best, to deny Soviet leaders the certainty of a quick low-cost conventional victory. Fighting a protracted conventional war and providing a capability to 'win' conventionally are not agreed goals.

This does not only reflect the attractions of defence 'on the cheap' through nuclear reliance. Different geographic perspectives tend to produce different attitudes to conventional deterrence. Any war in Europe would see West Germany as the major battlefield, and German leaders have tended to prefer to rely on the deterrent effect of nuclear weapons rather than to prepare for protracted conventional war that could well produce nuclear effects in German cities and villages. Thirty per cent of the West German population live within 100 kilometres of the Inner German Border and would quickly be at risk in any Soviet offensive. Although the spread of housing into the countryside, with suburbs of major and minor German towns merging one into another, does offer considerable benefits for the defender, it does, however, make even starker the dilemma that the Third World War would be fought in the yards, houses, basements, gardens and streets normally occupied by German civilians.[3] Nor, necessarily, do new conventional weapons offer an escape from this problem. Although some accurate new weapons – guided bombs and shells and precision-guided anti-tank weapons, for example – may make war safer for civilians, others such as cluster-bombs, submunition dispensing shells and multiple rocket launchers are designed to gain their effect by spreading their explosive effect over a wider area. Large Soviet stocks of chemical weapons, estimated at 300,000–400,000 tons, also pose a potent threat to civilians if the Soviets are not deterred from their use by a NATO capability to respond in kind or with nuclear weapons. Even without chemical weapons, any war would almost certainly prove uniquely destructive. US sources credit the Soviet Union with an ammunition stockpile of 13,000,000 tons – considerably more than was expended in the Second World War.[4] Although the equation is slightly misleading, this is equivalent to 1000 Hiroshimas – to which would have to be added the smaller, but noticeable, effect of NATO using its own ammunition in its own defence.

Large-scale conventional war would not merely resemble the First or Second World War; it could be far, far worse. Since 1945, the armed forces of the NATO and Warsaw Pact powers, and to some extent those of Israel and her opponents in the Middle East, have become more mechanized, more sophisticated and more expensive. Armed forces have been designed to secure quick success and to deny such success to the enemy. Fielding obsolete equipment has seemed an inadequate response against potential enemies who have chosen to deploy new technology. After a certain point the old adage that a good old one will beat a new one does not apply. Old equipment may prove suicidally inadequate against an enemy who can fire at longer range, who is protected by better armour or electronic systems, or whose aircraft are more manoeuverable or better armed. The result has been a constant process by which new equipment is developed to match new arms developed by possible foes. This has been paralleled by a series of changes in strategies concerning how these forces might be used, as the Warsaw Pact and Arab states have changed their doctrine in a seemingly continuing effort to find some way of overwhelming NATO or Israeli defences.

This competition has proved expensive. Modern US tanks cost £1.5m to £2m each, fighter aircraft £45m, destroyers £500m and air-to-air missiles £600,000 each.[5] With such high unit costs, it is not surprising that it has proved extremely difficult to maintain numbers of aircraft, tanks and ships. Budgets, moreover, have not only had to procure new equipment, but have also had to maintain and operate it. Tanks that can cross terrain three times as fast as those they replace tend to burn twice as much fuel in doing so. High technology equipment also tends to require highly trained men to operate and maintain it. Gone are the days when mass armies could be pulled off the streets and rapidly trained to use the technology of war. Gone also are the possibilities of producing vast numbers of planes and tanks once the war has begun. Even with full mobilization, there is just not the capability to replace weapons stocks that may have been accumulated during the last 30 years in the limited time that might be available.

The effects of this continuing increase in the cost of conventional weapons can be over-stressed. The armies of the Warsaw Pact and NATO have both acquired increasing equipment stockpiles as time has gone on, by the simple expedient of retaining equipment replaced in front line units. Service lives of equipment have generally been stretched to maintain numbers, with 20-year lives for aircraft, 25–30 years for tanks and 20–35 years for warships becoming standard, and with US aircraft carriers seemingly destined for active lives of 45–50 years. It is also the case that much modern equipment is easier to maintain, and sometimes even to use, than that which it replaces. However, numbers of modern tanks, ships, aircraft and helicopters are becoming increasingly finite and stocks of ammunition are limited.

This assumes greater significance when set against the other principal feature of modern conventional weapons – the fact that they are very effective. Most high technology weapons have predicted probabilities of kill in the 80–90 per cent range – they should destroy 80–90 per cent of the targets at which they are fired. Given the cost of such weapons, and the lack of any need to kill the enemy forces more than once, they are likely to be procured in limited numbers. All of which tends to produce a situation where sustained conventional war becomes less and less probable. If the weapons work even half as well as planned, they have the capability to destroy the enemy in days rather than weeks. If they do not work, there will be no more weapons to fight the war, because they have not been procured beforehand. Modern conventional war, using all that modern technology can offer, thus seems likely to be nasty, brutish and short: if the weapons work. Like the First World War, assuming there are no early breakthroughs, the Third World War seems likely to have a rapid, intense, initial phase followed by a return to static warfare, which would in all probability rival 1914–18 for horror. Alternatively, if high technology does not work, the war might rapidly degenerate into a stalemate, where small stocks of munitions are used up and large numbers of useless platforms remain. The reality of modern conventional war in the 1980s is probably that no one can be certain that it can be fought for any length of time. Conventional forces, threatened since 1945 by nuclear weapons, may face an equal or greater challenge owing to their very capability to destroy each other.

Land warfare

These problems affect all three services. Armies since 1945 have seen a continuous increase in the capability and cost of the equipment available to them. In 1945, the standard Western tank – the Sherman – weighed 31.5 tonnes, was powered by a 500 hp engine and carried a 76 mm gun. By 1986, a standard tank, the US M1 AE, weighed 54 tonnes, had a 1500 hp engine and a 120 mm gun. In 1945, a standard gun, the British 25 pounder, could fire a 22 lb shell 7.5 miles; by 1986, a standard artillery piece such as the US M109 A3 could fire a 96 lb shell 14.9 miles. The M1 tank has the ability to move across country at 30–35 mph and has sophisticated computerized infra-red and laser targeting equipment, designed to give a high probability of hitting the target with the first shot, at long range, at night, if necessary while on the move, and with the capability to swiftly engage another target. The M109, unlike most artillery in the Second World War, is itself mobile and is targeted by a variety of computerized sensors. It fires a range of ammunition – from rocket-assisted long-range rounds to anti-tank mine dispensing rounds – which would vastly surprise Second World War gunners.

Even the infantry has marched a long way since the Second World War. Because the battlefield has become increasingly fluid and lethal with the increase in the capability of tanks and guns, the infantry has itself taken to tracks. Most NATO and Warsaw Pact armies are now equipped with a range of heavily armoured infantry fighting vehicles and armoured personnel carriers. The infantry has also become more heavily armed; current US mechanized battalions operate more than 120 major anti-tank weapons compared with the eight carried by a similar unit in the 1950s. Even lighter weapons have proliferated with more (and more capable) machine guns, assault rifles, light anti-tank weapons and grenade launchers.[6]

The modern army, in fact, bears little resemblance to the army of 1940, 1950 or 1960. In 1940, Hitler had 2500 tanks against 3200 French and British. Of his army's 150 divisions, 138 depended on their feet or horses for their mobility.[7] In 1986, the Warsaw Pact was estimated to have 94 divisions available to attack on NATO's Central Front in Germany out of a total of more than 260 divisions worldwide. All of these units were armoured or mechanized, with the exception of three airborne divisions which each possess 300 infantry fighting vehicles. This force would total 29,260 tanks and 32,200 other armoured vehicles. To this would have to be added NATO's 9000 tanks and 17,000 armoured vehicles.[8] No such mechanized war has ever been fought in history.

Nor do superlative numbers end here. Munitions consumption in any future major European war is likely to prove exceptional. British experience in the Falklands, where some guns fired 400 rounds per day, contrasts markedly with Second World War averages of 25 rounds per gun per day.[9] Nor does there seem to be any escape from the problem of high kill rates. The US Army currently plans to buy 48,000 Hellfire anti-tank missiles, which would allow the 600 or so planned AH 64 helicopters 80 missiles each. This would permit each helicopter to fly five sorties carrying a full load of 16 missiles. Each helicopter could fly 5–10 sorties per day. Given that each attack helicopter might destroy 20 tanks before it was itself destroyed, simple mathematics suggests that after very few days of combat there might well be very few helicopters, even fewer missiles and fewer Soviet tanks left on the battlefield. Similar sums can be done with most precision guided missiles.[10] They suggest that, if modern equipment works with anything like predicted efficiency, conventional war on land would be extremely difficult to sustain.

The air war

What is true of ground forces also seems true of air forces. Since 1945 air forces have decreased in size but vastly increased in capability and complexity. The US airforce, which in 1945 had 22,393 bombers and 18,770 fighters, by 1986 had only 1786 frontline fighters and 372 bombers with few reserves to replace losses. Between 1940 and 1945, the US produced 139,000 combat aircraft to sustain its operations. In 1986, the US Navy, Marines and Airforce between them ordered only 399 combat aircraft.[11] With the complexity of modern airframes, avionics and engines there is little potential to increase these production rates in an emergency – although recent moves to simplify specifications of smaller items like bombs, torpedoes and missiles might allow industry to produce some of these for a diminishing number of irreplaceable aircraft to use in combat.

Air warfare has gained enormously in complexity since 1945. Today's fighter aircraft live in hardened aircraft shelters – individual concrete and steel hangars designed to protect the aircraft from all but a direct hit with a very large bomb. The airfield itself may be defended by dedicated air defence units and its runways will be repaired by engineers assigned to fill in any craters produced by enemy attack. Once it does take off, the aircraft will be operating in an environment where it is threatened by ground-or air-launched missiles with ranges from 2–100 miles. Pilots now train to penetrate to their targets at low level, using the contours of the ground to shield them from enemy radars. Aircraft now commonly carry electronic counter-measures designed to confuse the radar guidance systems of attacking aircraft and missiles, usually backed up with dispensers that release flares and chaff (strips of metal foil) to divert and confuse the homing heads of infra-red and radar guided missiles. Meanwhile, the aircraft themselves have become more and more manoeuvrable. Engines have become more efficient and powerful, and avionics and radars have become increasingly capable. Gone are the days when Second World War night bomber crews rarely succeeded in getting within five miles of the target. Modern navigation systems, supported by night-vision equipment that allows aircrews to see in the dark, have brought dramatic improvements in the ability of aircraft to find and destroy their targets in any weather, at night, and with accuracies measured in metres rather than miles.

Aircraft weapons have also improved, and concepts of how war should be fought have changed. Modern munitions offer far higher capabilities to destroy targets with fewer aircraft sorties. Since the early 1970s this has been particularly marked. In the later stages of the Vietnam war laser-guided bombs destroyed with one bomb targets that hundreds of previous attacks had left standing. RAF estimates suggest that twelve Tornado strike aircraft could be as effective as 566 Second World War Lancaster bombers.[12] By the late 1970s, the introduction of new avionics systems even allowed similar accuracy with old, unguided, 'dumb' bombs. This all allows targets to be attacked by fewer aircraft, which in turn means that more targets can be attacked at once and that each attack force is less likely to be detected. The development of sophisticated cluster-bombs, specialist mine-dispensing and anti-runway munitions has added considerably to the potential ability of airpower to destroy opposing ground and air forces. The growing role of tanker aircraft to refuel combat aircraft en route to their targets also offers new options for states to bring explosive influence to bear even on distant problems. The US raid on Libya in 1986 and Israeli raids on Iraq and Tunisia earlier in the 1980s are perhaps harbingers of things to be bombed. The recent decision to assign a conventional role to nearly all of the US Strategic Air Command's bombers witnesses a rising potential that may prove more attractive than using lighter, locally based units.[13]

Air combat has also come into its own again. After playing a vital role in Korea, where United Nations air forces won air superiority by shooting down the opposing air force, there was a trend in the 1960s to see air combat as an obsolete form of warfare. The Israeli success in 1967 in destroying the vast majority of Arab airpower on the ground in a pre-emptive first strike raised further questions about how airpower could best be deployed against opposing airpower. Current thinking, drawing on later Israeli and US experience, sees a major role for the air combat fighter, which relies on avionics, manoeuvrability and pilot skill as well as its guns and medium-and short-range missiles to shoot down the enemy's airforce, at the same time as specialized interdiction aircraft try to disrupt and destroy his airbases. The two missions are in fact complementary – fighters that cannot take off cannot join the air-battle and fighters that are shot down cannot defend their own, or attack enemy, airfields.

This air war is likely to be extremely complex and one increasingly influenced by electronic techniques. Survival today depends on electronic warning devices, a range of electronic and other counter-measures and the skill of the crew. Air defences rely increasingly on airborne warning and control aircraft – flying radar stations with their own fighter controllers. Attack aircraft rely on a range of tactical and strategic reconnaissance systems to locate their targets. Indeed, some recent experience suggests that this electronic combat may bring unpleasant surprises. Israel in 1973 lost 40 aircraft to Soviet supplied surface-to-air missiles whose capabilities were not fully appreciated. In 1982 the Israeli airforce destroyed 19 missile batteries and 82 Syrian aircraft for the loss of only one plane.[14] Whose equipment and tactics would work on the day is perhaps the key question of modern air warfare.

Another unknowable is how long war in the air could last. Experience in Vietnam, the Middle East, the Indo-Pakistan wars and off the Falklands suggests that, although losses may be acceptable per mission, large numbers of aircraft are likely to be lost in a relatively short period of time. Current planning sees airforces flying at very intensive rates for perhaps a week in any major war, with 2–5 missions a day. This is vastly greater than the tempo of Vietnam or the Second World War. After such a week of operations some pilots would be left (as most airforces have more pilots than planes), but it is questionable how many of the pilots would have aircraft that were flyable. Like land war, air war is hostage to the iron logic of short-division sums. Stocks of modern bombs and air-to-air missiles are limited. The USAF estimates that it has only five and a half reloads of air-to-air missiles for its aircombat fighters, with far fewer available for its strike aircraft for their own self-defence. Overall stockpiles are more than adequate, however, to destroy the proportion of the Soviet Airforce that US planners estimate the US Airforce will have to deal with. Similarly, although there are 'more than enough' munitions to meet the USAF's current objective of being able to fight for 60 days, stockpiles of modern munitions are far more finite. USAF munitions procurement plans in 1986 included (among other items) 150,000 modern cluster bombs and 60,000 Maverick guided missiles. But even such seemingly high totals would soon be consumed by 3000 or so aircraft flying at intensive rates.[15] With each of these weapons projected to have the ability to kill 25–80 per cent of the targets they were aimed at, the impact of using them in anything like the available numbers seems devastatingly obvious.

War at sea

Naval warfare has taken a similar course.[16] Navies have become more and more involved with strategic missions – with the Soviet Navy in particular giving nuclear warfare and nuclear weapons first priority. But, after disappearing from service after 1953 (with only the USS *New Jersey* returning to duty off Vietnam), the battleship seems to have found new favour in the last quarter of the century. The US Navy's revival of four battleships needs to be seen in terms of a more general interest in using naval power to influence events ashore by gunfire diplomacy. It also provides an interesting example of how technology can be used to keep ships in service for 20–50 years, a policy that seems to be dictated by rising costs and decreasing orders. The current battleship, with cruise missiles, anti-ship missiles, remotely piloted vehicles for finding targets and with new longer-ranged guided shells a future prospect, has far more in common with her modern counterpart – the Soviet *Kirov* class battle-cruisers – than she does with her sisters of the Second World War. Indeed, naval warfare since 1945 has been characterized by an ever-increasing rush of new technology, with guns, missiles, sonars, electronic warfare systems, propulsion systems and computerized command and control systems continually improving against a tactical background where there have been no clear breakthroughs. The battle against the submarine still remains difficult and for most navies gets more so. The anti-ship missile can be mastered, but the questions remain about who is prepared to pay for defences to do so and how many incoming missiles can be stopped. The large aircraft carrier remains the only means of taking adequate numbers of capable long-range aircraft to sea to defend the fleet and, in the strike role, can carry far more intelligent target acquisition systems (not least the aircraft's pilot and navigator) out to longer ranges than any missile. Naval warfare is getting more and more complex, with everything from satellites to submarines involved. The threat to navies from each other is growing, and the threat to large navies from small ones with capable guided-missile attack craft, mines and shore-based missile-armed aircraft is particularly notable. So, with 8000-ton destroyers and submarines becoming standard in the Soviet and US navies, is the cost of any major naval capability.

Navies also have suffered from the dilemma of the short war. Naval warfare is itself likely to be a protracted affair. It is easier to hide in miles of ocean in inclement weather than it is to hide an attack by 29,000 tanks down the roads of the Central Front. Submarines, and indeed surface ships, have also been designed to hide themselves at sea and put considerable effort into doing this. Nevertheless, there are problems with the idea of a protracted conventional war at sea. If the land and air war ends in weeks, the mission of navies in resupplying that war looks suspect. If the naval war itself is fought offensively, with the emphasis on drawing the enemy into battle and destroying his shore bases, naval war itself may be quickly over. Attrition in such a war would be high. Nor are navies much better prepared to fight a long war than are the other services. The US Navy, like the other US services, has as its objective under the US 1986–90 defence programme only the ability to fight a 60-day war. There are no replacement ships. Torpedo stocks are insufficient to provide a reload for each US submarine when it has fired off its magazine of torpedoes. Missile stocks, although increasing, were inadequate in 1985 to fill the magazines of each ship in the US fleet even once. Surface-to-air missile launchers in the fleet could theoretically fire their complete missile stocks in five minutes.[17] This would, if the missiles work, be enough to destroy the vast majority of attacking aircraft and missiles. It does not, however, lead us to assume that war at sea could last much longer than the ground and air war.

The conventional dilemma

In fact, there is reason to assume that, if anything, this analysis understates the problems of fighting a protracted conventional war. Complex war requires complex training, which reduces the utility of reservists. This is a problem for the Soviets, who risk losing the advantages of surprise by taking time to mobilize all of their reserve formations, and for the United States, whose reservists would take months in training before they could be deployed as combat divisions. The complex nature of warfare has also produced massive demands for specialized personnel, with seemingly absurd consequences. The US Army in Europe, for example, in 1985 had roughly 205,000 men. Of these 19,000 were signals personnel. There were only 17,661 infantry specialists to man the trenches and the total of combat troops of all types was only 58,335.[18] With so few troops actually available for frontline combat in a modern army and with those in the frontline likely to die most quickly, the idea of a long campaign seems ever more improbable. Indeed, it is doubtful if mere men could function for long on the modern battlefield. Not only is that battlefield lethal, but it also threatens to be continuous. The introduction of night-vision equipment today brings with it the possibility of 24-hour warfare and means that the question of how long men can fight without sleep will be an important factor in deciding such a war. Another will be how long they can operate when wearing protective clothing against chemical weapons. If chemical weapons are used, estimates suggest that there will be a 50 per cent reduction in the ability to fight and that within a few hours most troops will be incapacitated. No one has yet fought an air or land war in a situation where a chemical attack has occurred or where constant precautions have to be taken in case it occurs at any instant.[19] Nor has war occurred in circumstances where communications, command, control and logistics are so vital and where so much capability exists to disrupt them in the form of electronic counter-measures, strike aircraft and special forces.

There seems no relief from this predicament. Some writers have suggested a return to less sophisticated equipment, greater numbers of lightly armed militia-type units and a more mobile, offensive style of warfare. There are problems with all of these approaches. Mobile warfare actually needs superior equipment and well-trained men to overcome enemy numbers and firepower. Less sophisticated equipment may be useful if additional numbers offset loss of capability. Most proposals to buy greater numbers of unsophisticated fighter aircraft armed only with short-range weapons would, however, prove suicidal in actual combat against an enemy with smaller numbers of sophisticated long-range missile-armed aircraft. Similarly, an airforce that gave up its 'offensive' capability to attack its opponent's bases would find itself hopelessly outmatched in a real war. At sea, also, many proponents of greater numbers of smaller ships seem to miss the basic point that ships are built to provide capabilities rather than numbers of hulls. There is no logic in the argument which claims that one large ship cannot survive concerted attack but implies that two less capable ships could. Actually, the result of building large numbers of incapable units is likely to be that the enemy is faced with a still manageable number of eminently manageable targets.

Equally with land forces, much is written about the prospects of infantry armed with anti-tank missiles costing £1000 each destroying tanks costing £1,000,000. Unfortunately, reality is not like this. The trend is for anti-tank weapons to get larger and heavier as tank armour improves. The shoulder-fired anti-tank weapon, which had some success in the Arab-Israeli war of 1973, is considerably less effective against modern armour properly employed. The size of today's anti-tank weapons and the need for them to be mobile to concentrate enough firepower against an enemy's thrust means that they are carried around the battlefield mounted on, or carried in, expensive armoured fighting vehicles and helicopters, which cost as much if not more than the tank they might destroy. Large numbers of lightly armed infantry are likely to find themselves immobile, unprotected from artillery fire, in the wrong place and in inadequate numbers to stall an attacker who has more firepower, greater mobility and the initiative. Even if their weapons do work, it is debatable whether the anti-tank missile (which actually costs rather more now than £1000) is a better buy than a modern anti-tank shell for one's own tank, which also costs £1000, or the shell for an aircraft anti-tank cannon, which only costs £18. Obviously there is a balance between reducing the complexity of warfare and matching threats, but the task of finding that balance is not made any easier if it is sidetracked by simplistic arguments or writers who confuse the failure to provide enough resources with the different question of how resources can be used most effectively. Simple answers to the problem of high technology warfare seem destined to be simply wrong answers.

Trends, in fact, point elsewhere. Since the early 1970s a great deal has been written about the coming of the electronic battlefield. As is often the case, the rhetoric arrived well before the reality, but by 1988 the reality also seems imminent, as new intelligence, command and control and weapons systems begin to come into service or begin to find their way into procurement plans for the early 1990s. These weapons use many of the advances of the revolution in microelectronics that has occurred since the mid-1970s, which provide far greater capabilities than are offered by current systems. Although some ideas, like the use of unmanned sensors to track enemy forces, were tried in Vietnam, and Arab and Israeli forces have deployed some modern weapons in their wars of 1973 and 1982, we do not have any experience of a war that used weapons comparable to those now projected for the 1990s and beyond. New technology is designed to find the enemy, to follow his movements and to engage and destroy his forces at long range using 'smart' weapons that can each seek out and destroy their own target. Attrition is likely to be far greater, perhaps by factors of 3–10, in any war using such weapons. Unit costs of such weapons will be high. Manoeuvring and concentration on the battlefield will be suicidally dangerous. War will become even nastier, even more brutish and even more short than at present.

This prospect increasingly beckons. War in the air and war at sea threaten to get ever more complex as technology advances and detection devices increase in capability. In the air and at sea, however, there is an active race going on between those trying to detect aircraft, ships and submarines and those trying to make them less visible to eyes, ears, radar and sonar by employing a variety of counter-measures, stealth and quietening techniques. The possibility of not being 'seen' may actually be increasing, particularly with the next generation of stealth aircraft and quiet submarines. On land, however, hiding thousands of armoured vehicles is likely to prove more difficult – not least because attacking forces must concentrate and move at speed in the open if they are ever going to go anywhere. Generals may well find their forces tracked at long distance by satellite or aircraft mounted radars and attacked at long range by missiles carrying terminally guided munitions and aircraft carrying cluster-bombs with similarly deadly weapons. The air above their heads will be filled with unfriendly, unseen drones reporting their every move and crashing destructively on to their own radar and radio sets, shells homing in on radio transmissions or dispensing yet more smart munitions on their forces, and stand-off bombs en route to take out key bridges, storage sites, command posts and airfields. Night and all-weather equipment for aircraft will alone change the face of war, as the 4–5-hour flying day available in Europe in winter expands to 20 hours.

War thus threatens to become ever more difficult to fight and to predict. The question needs to be asked whether defence budgets can grow fast enough to meet the escalating costs of this new technology. Doubts will probably increase about whether any war's outcome is predictable, given the great number of technical and human uncertainties involved and whether any modern war could be sustained for more than a few days or weeks. Nor will leaders find much help from recent history, as they look for answers. Partly because of the fear of nuclear weapons and partly because of the unpredictability of conventional warfare, even on the few occasions when war between the Western and Communist blocs in Europe seemed possible (as in the Berlin crises of 1948, 1958 and 1961) it was studiously avoided as a political option. None of the major European armies has fought a mechanized war since 1945; nor indeed have the Soviet or US armies.

The historical experience 1945–87

One of the main features of the modern, mechanized battlefield is that it represents unknown territory for most armies. Apart from the victims of the Soviet army, their own governments and terrorists, the vast majority of the millions who have died in conflicts since 1945 (and we should not forget that there have been millions) have died outside Europe. The European powers' only experience of war has come in efforts first to maintain their former empires overseas; then to manage decolonization and give assistance to those former colonies that request it. They have seen action in states as varied as India, Vietnam, Kenya, Malaya, Cyprus, Aden, Djibouti, Zaire, Chad and the Falklands. All of these tasks called for lighter forces than those maintained on the Central Front in Germany. Even here, however, real questions were raised about the ability to sustain operations at a distance from home. There has also been a tendency for opponents either to prove so elusive that large forces are required to seek and destroy them (e.g. British involvement in Malaya) or for the opposition to use modern technology in limited numbers to spring unpleasant surprises on what was, on the face of things, the more modern and sophisticated force: this was the French experience in Indo-China at the hands of Vietnamese artillery and British experience off the Falklands in 1982 at the hands of Argentine Exocet anti-ship missiles.

Similar experiences have befallen both superpowers. The United States in Korea found itself matching technology against the massive numbers of simply armed 'volunteers' committed by communist China. In Vietnam, US forces fought a relatively high technology war with massive firepower against an enemy making full use of skilful guerrilla tactics and hiding in vast areas of difficult terrain. Firepower proved a two-edged sword, as it destroyed the country US forces were pledged to protect. Partly because of the way US forces were recruited, led, organized and trained, and partly because far more troops would have been needed, US forces never provided an adequate level of security that could have allowed the South to develop politically and economically to the point where it could have stood alone. Fighting an opponent who believed that US willpower was weaker than his own, and unable to stop infiltration into the South by invading North Vietnam because of the fear that this would provoke a wider war with China, there was a very strong logic that this was a war that the US army could not conclude and that US public opinion would not sustain.

The Soviets also seem to have learnt the limitations of modern military forces the hard way in Afghanistan. Here, unlike the relatively easy policing operations in Hungary and Czechoslovakia, the Soviet army has found itself engaged against determined guerrilla fighters, who exploit the size and terrain of their country against the foreign invader. Though Soviet leaders have avoided some of the mistakes of Vietnam, they seem no more likely to succeed than did the United States. Indeed, with high technology weapons, such as shoulder-held surface-to-air missiles, becoming available to the Afghan guerrillas, the Soviet Union may find itself in a similar situation to US and South Vietnamese forces in Vietnam, where their technological superiority was blunted by the combination of low and high technology available to the opponent.

Although there still remains a role for (and at some times a strong temptation to use) military power, both superpowers seem likely to face continuing difficulties when actually deploying their forces to secure foreign policy goals other than those that deter attack on their major allies. High technology equipment is often heavy and difficult to deploy and support. The export of great numbers of sophisticated weapons has left few defenceless targets. For the USA particularly, the ever-present television camera has threatened to bring the inevitable horror of war into the voters' homes, raising real questions about whether US public opinion could find any war worth such suffering. There seems now a tendency for political leaders to seek short, sharp, surgical applications of force to meet their goals, which was the case with US action in Grenada in 1983 and against Libya in 1986. This may become more common as the precision-guided munitions, new bombers, conventionally armed cruise-missiles and naval forces now planned enter service. It may be that deterrence and punishment alike will increasingly be provided by naval power deployed over the horizon and by home-based, long-range airpower using in-flight-refuelling to reach its targets. Deterrence of the other superpower seems likely to remain the superpower priority, with the occasional raid an additional future feature. Venturing into a major conventional war, against the background that such a war may prove unpredictable, hugely costly and uniquely destructive, and may even lead to nuclear devastation, is unlikely to prove attractive to any major power.

The future

Wars, however, are unlikely to cease. Three escape routes remain from the conundrum that major conventional war, like nuclear war, is becoming too destructive to achieve political ends. All three routes have been used time and time again in the Third World since 1945. The first is that there is always room to hope for success, however forbidding the battlefield actually is. The temptation to fight a short war in the belief that one will win it still seems likely to prove attractive, as it has in the past in the Arab–Israeli and Indo–Pakistan wars and as it did when Argentina invaded the Falklands and Iraq attacked Iran. Even in Europe, the risk remains that, if a balance were not maintained between Warsaw Pact and NATO forces, a quick conventional, or possibly even a quick nuclear, victory would prove irresistible to Soviet leaders in some circumstances. This seems more likely still in disputes such as the Syria–Israel conflict, where the limited geographic area, the nature of the dispute and the likelihood that a long war would be ended by superpower pressure might make a quick military option to regain territory or remove a threat very attractive to either party. Recent history shows that dreams of *Blitzkrieg* success are still alive and attacking in the 1980s.

The second type of war that remains relatively likely consists of clashes in the Third World. Many small states have border, political or tribal disputes and the capability to sustain limited or guerrilla combat for long periods. Even more dangerous is the potential for war between some of the major developing powers. Countries such as China, Vietnam, North and South Korea, India, Pakistan, Iran and Iraq have large armed forces and, in particular, large armies. Unlike the armies of NATO and the Warsaw Pact, these armies are not particularly mechanized. They have many foot or lorry-borne infantry with relatively little armour.[20] With, perhaps, some access to external supplies of ammunition to augment domestic production, all of these armies would have the manpower to fight a traditional infantry war for a protracted period of time. They are, in a sense, obsolete enough to be used and not strong enough to rapidly destroy each other. This seems to be borne out by the experience of the Chinese invasion of Vietnam in 1979 and by the Iran–Iraq war between 1980 and 1987. It might be noted that all of the states with large, predominantly infantry, armies in the list have territorial disputes with other states in the list. There seems to be some danger, therefore, that those most able to fight a protracted conventional war against a similarly armed opponent are also among those most likely to find cause to go to war. Given what has happened in the Iran–Iraq war – and perhaps even if there is a winner in that war – the experience of this war should, however, act as a powerful disincentive to anyone lightly contemplating resorting to force to settle disputes.

The third type of warlike activity that seems, unfortunately, to have a future is the use by individuals, or governments, of terrorist tactics to advance their objectives. The use of terrorism may be a less dangerous activity for governments and poses immense problems for those who are the terrorists' targets. Finding and dealing with terrorists is difficult enough, but it becomes even more so when the terrorists are supported or even controlled by states. With the number of individuals with a dispute apparently growing and technology providing new terrorist capabilities, this threat is likely to take up more and more time and effort. Already there has been a proliferation of specialist units trained to respond to such threats, and it seems likely that such units will be even more active in the future. It may also prove the case that the model of the 1986 US attack on Libya will be repeated, as states retaliate against those they believe to be supporting the terrorists who have attacked them. Future wars may again start with assassinations or with airline passengers being blown out of the air by terrorist bombs.

The battlefield of the future thus offers us many faces, from the high technology killing field where war might prove unsustainable to the tense and secretive world of international terrorism. Since 1945 perhaps 50 million people have died on the world's battlefields. Although many died in vain, the fact that Vietnam is now united, Korea is still divided, Bangladesh is independent and the Falkland Islanders still enjoy independence from Argentina are just four cases which, conversely, show that military force has often proved effective in securing popular and political objectives. In Europe, who can tell what the political and economic fortune of Europeans would have been if the nuclear and conventional balance had not been as it has since 1945? The fact that it may be becoming increasingly difficult

to wage war effectively is hardly any guarantee that future leaders
will not believe they should go to war. While men believe in ideas
and nation's interests conflict, war is likely to continue to prove
an attractive instrument from time to time. Nor, while we examine
the implications of modern technology, should we forget the human
dimension. Wars have never been cost free and to die on the modern
battlefield can be no more pleasant than to die on any other battlefield
before or after 1945. The battlefield fought by intelligent robots may
be on the way in the next century, but it is not with us yet. If anything,
the range of demands on military personnel to act as diplomats,
discreet protectors of society from terrorism and skilled practitioners
of complex modern war, places far more emphasis on the quality of
servicemen than in the past. On every battlefield from Israel in 1948,
to Goose Green in 1982, from the trenches of Basra to the operations
rooms of the Royal Navy at San Carlos, success or failure has relied on
skill and courage as well as on technology. Just as wars have always
started in the minds of men, they are still won or lost by men.

Notes: Chapter 9

1   L. W. Martin, *Before the Day After* (London: Newnes, 1985), pp. 36–42.
2   *Senate Armed Services Committee Hearings FY 1986* (Washington DC:
    USGPO, 1985), pt 3, p. 1370.
3   L. W. Martin, op. cit., p. 42.
4   *Soviet Military Power 1987* (Washington DC: USGPO, 1987), p. 95.
5   *Department Of Defense Annual Report FY 1988* (Washington DC:
    USGPO, 1987).
6   L. W. Martin, op. cit., pp. 66–77.
7   M. Jacobsen *et al.*, *Contingency Plans For War In Western Europe
    1920–1940*, Rand Report R3281-NA (Santa Monica, Calif.: Rand Cor-
    poration, 1985), pp. 107, 187.
8   *Soviet Military Power 1987*, p. 93; *Military Balance 1986–87* (London:
    IISS, 1986), pp. 223–7.
9   W. Fowler and M. Chappell, *Battle For The Falklands – Land Forces*
    (London: Osprey, 1985), p. 28; R. Elberton Smith, *The US Army In
    World War Two – The Army and Economic Mobilization* (Washington
    DC: The Department of the Army, USGPO, 1959), p. 207.
10 *House Armed Services Committee Hearings FY 1986* (Washington DC:
    USGPO, 1985), pt 2, pp. 226–8, 231, 286–7; *Senate Armed Services
    Committee Hearings FY 1985* (Washington DC: USGPO, 1984), pt 3,
    pp. 1289, 1300–2.
11 R. Elberton Smith, op. cit., p. 27; W. F. Craven and J. L. Catered, *The
    Army Airforces in World War II* (Chicago: University of Chicago Press,

1955), Vol. 6, p. 423; *DoD Annual Report FY 1987* (Washington DC: USGPO, 1986).
12 *Statement On The Defence Estimates 1987* (London: HMSO, 1987), p. 47.
13 *Airforce Magazine*, January 1987, pp. 20–4.
14 J. Laffin, *The War Of Desperation* (London: Osprey, 1985), pp. 62–76.
15 *Senate Armed Services Committee Hearings FY 1986*, pt 4, pp. 2004–8.
16 cf. J. Pay, 'New conventional technology – the maritime sphere', in I. Bellany and T. Huxley (eds) *New Conventional Weapons and Western Defence* (London: Frank Cass, 1987).
17 *Senate Armed Services Committee Hearings FY 1986*, pt 4, pp. 1848–50, 1875–6.
18 *Senate Armed Services Committee Hearings FY 1986*, pt 3, p. 1400.
19 ibid., pp. 1453–1560.
20 *Military Balance 1986–87.*

Further reading: Chapter 9

Barnaby, Frank, *The Automated Battlefield* (London: Sidgwick & Jackson, 1986).
Bellamy, Chris, *The Future of Land Warfare* (London: Croom Helm, 1987).
Bertram, Christopher (ed.) *New Conventional Weapons and East–West Security* (London: Macmillan, 1979).
Dinter, Elmar, and Griffith, Paddy, *Not Over By Christmas* (Chichester: Antony Bird Publications, 1983).
Herzog, Chaim, *The Arab-Israeli Wars: War and Peace in the Middle East from the War of Independence to Lebanon* (London: Arms and Armour Press, 1985).
Lewy, Guenther, *America in Vietnam* (New York: Oxford University Press, 1978).
Martin, Laurence, *Before the Day After* (London: Macmillan, 1987).
Mearsheimer, John, *Conventional Deterrence* (Ithaca, NY: Cornell University Press, 1983).
Spiers, Edward M., *Chemical Warfare* (London: Macmillan, 1986).
Watson, Bruce W., and Dunn, Peter M. (eds), *Military Lessons of the Falkland Islands War: Views from the United States* (Boulder, Colo.: Westview Press, 1984).

Further Reading

Baylis, John, Booth, Ken, Garnett, John, and Williams, Phil, *Contemporary Strategy*, 2 vols, 2nd edn (New York: Holmes & Meier, 1987).

Creveld, Martin van, *Supplying War: Logistics from Wallenstein to Patton* (London: Cambridge University Press, 1977).

Creveld, Martin van, *Command in War* (Cambridge, Mass.: Harvard University Press, 1985).

Holmes, Richard, *Acts of War: The Behaviour of Men in Battle* (New York: Free Press, 1986).

Paret, Peter, ed., *Makers of Modern Strategy from Machiavelli to the Nuclear Age* (Oxford: Clarendon Press, 1986).

Posen, Barry, *The Sources of Military Doctrine: France, Britain and Germany between the World Wars* (Ithaca NY: Cornell University Press, 1986).

Strachan, Hew, *European Armies and the Conduct of War* (London: Allen & Unwin, 1983).

Index

Abd el-Krim 30, 40, 44
Abyssinia, see Italy: Abyssinia (Ethiopia)
  War
Air Power 57, 60, 74, 113–37, 224–4
  colonial warfare 43–6
  naval aviation 94, 96, 97, 100, 105
  (see also Aircraft Carrier)
Aircraft Carrier 95, 98–9, 101–2, 225
Amphibious Operations 96, 97, 105–7
Amritsar Massacre 34–5
Anglo-Irish War 35–7, 47
Anti-tank Weapons 72, 221, 227–8
Armoured Warfare, see tank and blitzkrieg
Artillery 43, 54–7, 74, 220–1
Assured Destruction 149, 151, 184
Atomic Bomb, see Nuclear Weapons

Battleship 90, 92–5, 99–102, 225 (see also
  Dreadnought)
Beatty, Admiral Earl 90
Blitzkrieg 67–73, 75
Boer War 24, 33-4, 35, 51
Britain
  colonial warfare 25, 31–7, 44–5, 46
  counter insurgency 207–8
  navel power and arms race 81, 84–94,
    96–8, 100
  nuclear weapons 141, 144, 154–7, 172
  strategic bombing 116–19, 121–35
  World War 1 6, 9–21, 53, 58–9, 63,
    87–93
  World War 2 9–21, 65–6, 68, 71,
    97–8, 100
  see also Boer War and Anglo-Irish War
Bugeaud, Marshal Thomas-Robert 26–7

Calwell, Major Charles 31–4
Castex, Raoul 95
Chemical Weapons 8, 46, 60, 218, 227
China, 199–200

Korean War 167–8, 181
  nuclear strategy 160–1
Vietnam War 179–80
Churchill, Winston S. 46, 91, 127, 155
Corbett, Sir Julian 83–4, 91, 93
Counter-Insurgency (COIN) 206–9
Countervailing Strategy 150–1
Cuba, missile crisis 175
  revolution 202

Debray, Regis 202
Deterrence 140–6
Dogger Bank 89
Douhet, Giulio 119–20, 121, 135
Dreadnought 85 6
Dulles, John Foster 146–7

Eisenhower, Dwight D. 146, 169
Electronic Warfare 228
Ethiopia, see Italy: Abyssinia (Ethiopia)
  War

First World War, see World War 1
Fisher, Admiral J. 85–6
Flexible Response 14, 172, 185, 186, 188
Foco 202–3
France 64–5
  colonial warfare 26–31, 37, 44–5, 47,
    62
  Indo-China 200, 207
  nuclear strategy 157–60
  World War 1 9–21, 52–3, 57
  World War 2 10–21, 66, 68–9, 71
  see also Guerre Revolutionnaire
Fuller, J.F.C. 64, 75

Gallieni, Joseph-Simon 26–8
Gas, see Chemical Weapons
Germany
  colonial warfare 41–3, 47

naval power and arms race 81, 84–6,
    88–93, 96–8, 100
strategic bombing 114–18
World War 1 13–21, 52, 56–64,
    88–93, 114–18
World War 2 13–21, 66–76, 96–8,
    100
Giap, Vo Nguyen 200–1
Graduated Deterrence 155, 172
Grivas, George 203–4
Gorshkov, Admiral Sergei 103–9
Guerre Revolutionnaire 208–9
Guevara, Ernesto "Che" 202–3
Gwynn, Major-General Sir Charles 32,
    34–8

Imperialism 5
Indo-China War, *see* France: Indo-China
Indo-Pakistan War 101
INF (Intermediate Range Nuclear Forces)
    187–8
Ireland, 197 (*see also* Anglo-Irish War)
Italy 47, 61
    Abyssinia (Ethiopia) War 24, 46–7
    navy 96–7

Japan, 9, 96, 98–100, 134–6 (*see also*
    Russo-Japanese War)
Jeune Ecole 81–2, 92
Johnson, Lyndon Baines 178, 182–3
Jutland 90–2

Kahn, Herman 142–3, 172–6, 185
Kaufmann, William 169–70, 183
Kissinger, Henry 149, 169, 170, 182
Korean War 166–9, 171, 175, 177, 230
Kruschev, Nikita 153

Lawrence, T.E., "of Arabia" 198
Lehman, John 108–9
Liddell Hart, B.H. 64–6, 75, 94, 155,
    165, 172
Linebacker I and II 136, 182–3
Lyautey, Hubert 26, 28–31, 36, 38

McNamara, Robert 148–9, 172, 179,
    184–5, 188
Machine Gun 43
Mackinder, Halford 81–2
MAD (Mutual Assured Destruction) *see*
    Assured Destruction
Mahan, Alfred Thayer 80, 82, 93, 98
Mao Tse–Tung 167, 198–201

Marighela, Carlos 204–5.
Maritime Strategy, The, (US) 109
Marwick, Arthur 2–3, 12
Massive Retaliation 147–8, 151, 155,
    169, 172
Mitchell, Billy 94, 120

NATO 145, 148, 167, 174, 184–9,
    217–19, 221
Nixon, Richard Milhous 136, 149,
    182–3
NSC 68 166, 169
Nuclear Weapons 101, 103, 135–6, 140,
    184–8
    neutron bomb 187
    see also INF, and nuclear strategy of
    Britain, China, France, USA and
    USSR

Palestine 45, 48
Passchendaele (Third Ypres) 8, 62
People's War Doctrine 160–1
Philippines, *see* US: colonial warfare
Portugal 40–1, 47

Razzia 26–30
Reagan, Ronald 108, 151
Richmond, Admiral Sir Herbert 95
Riff Rebellion and War 30–1, 40, 46
Risk Theory, *see* Admiral Tirpitz
Rolling Thunder 133, 136, 181–2
Russo-Japanese War 51

Scheer, Admiral 90–2
Schelling, Thomas 172–6, 181, 185
Schlesinger Doctrine 150
Second World War, *see* World War 2
Somme 8, 53, 55–6, 62
Smuts Report 117–18
Spain 39–40, 47
Stalin, Josef 152–3, 167
Strategic Defense Initiative (SDI) 151
Submarine 81, 89, 92–4, 97, 100, 105–6

Tank 64–7, 74, 219, 220
Terrorism, 205–6 (*see also* Urban
    Guerrilla Warfare)
Thompson, Robert 207–8
Tirpitz, Admiral 85
Trenchard, Lord 121–2
Truman, Harry S. 146, 166
Tukhachevsky, Marshal 39, 65, 66, 71
Turner, Admiral Stansfield 108

U-boats, *see* Submarines
Union of Soviet Socialist Republics 26,
    65, 186–7
  colonial warface 39
  Korean War 167
  limited war 176–7
  naval power 97–8, 104–8, 110
  nuclear strategy 148, 152–4, 184
  world war 1 15, 61
  world war 2 70–76, 97–8,
  see also Russo-Japanese War
United States 231
  civil war 51
  colonial warfare 37–9, 45
  guerrilla warfare 207
  naval power 83, 94, 96, 98–100, 108
  nuclear strategy 146–52, 184
  strategic bombing 131–6
  world war 1 13–21
  world war 2 13–21, 73–4, 98–101,
    131–6
  world war 3 166
  see also Vietnam War and Korean War
Urban Guerrilla Warfare 203–5

Vietnam War 133–6, 176–84, 201,
    230

Women in War 15, 17–18
World War 1 7ff., 25, 51ff., 165
  economic changes 12–14
  industrial changes 16
  political changes 12–14
  social changes 14–21
  total war 7ff.
  naval war 88–93
  strategic bombing 114–19, 122
  see also Passchendaele, Somme,
    Jutland
World War 2 7ff., 68–76, 165
  economic changes 12–14
  industrial changes 16
  political changes 12–14
  social changes 14–21
  total war 7ff.
  naval war 96–101
  strategic bombing 123–33,
    134–6
World War 3 166